Policy and practice in multicultural and anti-racist education

Since the 1970s, schools and education authorities in Britain have developed policies on multicultural and anti-racist education. In order to examine the effects of such policies on practices within schools, Peter Foster spent two years observing the staff and students of an inner city, multi-ethnic comprehensive school. On the basis of this lengthy classroom observation, Foster shows:

- how the school developed its multicultural and anti-racist policies
- how teachers interpreted these policies
- how they acted upon them in the classroom

He also explores the impact of within-school processes on the educational opportunities of ethnic minority students and on ethnic relations among students. This fascinating case study of how policies work out in a real school is placed in the wider context of debate about multicultural and anti-racist education, and provides the basis for suggestions in the shaping of future policy.

A source of guidance for people involved in policy and research in this crucial area of education, the book will also be of interest to students of education and sociology.

The Author

Peter Foster has taught in a number of urban, multicultural schools and colleges, and now teaches sociology at Xaverian Sixth Form College, Rusholme, Manchester. From 1985 to 1987 he was Research Fellow at the Centre for Research in Ethnic Relations at the University of Warwick.

Policy and practice in multicultural and anti-racist education

A case study of a multi-ethnic comprehensive school

Peter Foster

London and New York

First published 1990
by Routledge
11 New Fetter Lane, London EC4P 4EE

Simultaneously published in the USA and Canada
by Routledge
a division of Routledge, Chapman and Hall, Inc.
29 West 35th Street, New York, NY 10001

Typeset by LaserScript Ltd, Mitcham, Surrey
Printed and bound in Great Britain by
Biddles Ltd, Guildford and King's Lynn

British Library Cataloguing in Publication Data

Foster, Peter, *1951–*
    Policy and practice in multicultural and anti-racist education: a case study
    of a multi-ethnic comprehensive school.
    1. Great Britain. Multicultural education
    I. Title
    370.11'5
    ISBN 0-415-03848-0
        0-415-03849-9 (pb)

Library of Congress Cataloging in Publication Data
also applied for

Contents

Acknowledgements

The field work and initial writing of this book was conducted between September 1985 and August 1987 whilst I was a Research Fellow at the Centre for Research in Ethnic Relations at the University of Warwick. I was given much encouragement, advice, and support during this period and subsequently by colleagues at the Centre, especially Barry Troyna, Wendy Ball, and John Rex, and by Martyn Hammersley of the Open University. Bob Burgess, Andy Hargreaves, and John Scarth also gave useful help and support during the field work. My thanks are also due to the head, staff, and students of Milltown High School who gave generously of their time and allowed me to observe their everyday practice, despite the fact that this often placed them under considerable extra strain. A number of staff were involved closely in the research, and although, for reasons of confidentiality I cannot name them, I would like to acknowledge their help. Finally I would like to thank my wife, Helena, who has given me considerable moral support and encouragement throughout.

I am grateful also to Manchester Education Authority for allowing me two years leave of absence from my teaching post in order to work on the research.

Preface

In 1981 the ESRC Research Unit on Ethnic Relations, then based at the University of Aston and now the Centre for Research in Ethnic Relations at the University of Warwick, established a research programme entitled 'Education and Ethnicity'. Its aim was to provide 'an account of the demands made on the education system by ethnic minorities and the ways in which the educational system has responded'. The first stage of this research programme concentrated on the development of policies on multicultural education in four Local Education Authorities (LEAs) (Rex, Troyna, and Naguib 1983). The research attempted to observe and reconstruct historically the process of policy making in the area of multicultural education and examine the complex political, ideological, and educational factors which influenced the process. It sought also to examine the role and function of such policy developments and to comment on their efficacy. One of the LEAs studied, in the centre of a large conurbation in the north of England, the research team named Milltown.

The second stage of the research programme aimed to examine the way in which LEA policies were received and implemented in schools, and whether or how they influenced teacher practice at 'the chalk face'. Barry Troyna and Wendy Ball, who conducted the initial work, decided to concentrate their efforts in Milltown LEA (see Troyna and Ball 1985). They first interviewed a sample of the LEA's headteachers, arguing that they would be key figures in the translation of policy into practice and that their responses to LEA policy would thus be of crucial importance. This survey revealed that the LEA's policy had made limited impact. Whilst most heads expressed an awareness of and support for the policy, few had made very much effort to translate it into action. Moreover, the schools that had made attempts were in general those with high proportions of ethnic minority students. This seemed to fly in the face of the LEA's commitment to foster multicultural education in all its schools. They found a similar pattern in their subsequent postal survey of a sample of departmental and faculty heads in the LEA's secondary schools and sixth form colleges. This discrepancy between policy and practice in multicultural education led Troyna and Ball, in an article in the *Times Educational Supplement* (1983), to ask whether multicultural education policies were actually 'worth the paper they're written on' and to question their efficacy as change-agents.

The research which is described here forms part of this second stage of the 'Education and Ethnicity' programme. Following their interview and survey work, the members of the Education Team were interested in examining in more detail how schools and individual teachers responded to LEA policies on multicultural education, and what the effects of these policies actually were at school level. They wanted to find out more about what teachers were doing, rather than what they said they were doing, and so they decided to conduct a number of ethnographic studies in order to observe practice in schools from the inside. This book reports the first of these investigations. In 1984 contact was established with the newly appointed headteacher of a multi-ethnic secondary school in an inner city area of Milltown, which will be referred to here as Milltown High School. After fairly lengthy discussions access was negotiated for a member of the Education Team to work in the school over a two year period (September 1985 to July 1987).

The school was interesting for a number of reasons. First, the headteacher professed a strong commitment to the LEA's policy on multicultural and anti-racist education. Indeed, he had been appointed partly on the basis of his commitment to the philosophy and practice which the LEA wished to encourage in its schools. Second, the school had something of a history of engagement with the issue of multicultural education. In the late 1970s, well before the LEA formulated its policy, a school working party had been formed which spent three years examining the subject and its report espoused a strong commitment to multicultural education. In the early 1980s the school had been one of the first in the LEA to formulate an 'institutional policy on racism', and in its 1985–6 brochure for parents its commitment was made clear:

> Milltown High is a multiracial school. We are developing policies
> to promote equal opportunities and equal esteem for all our
> students, girls and boys, black and white. It is very important to
> help everyone in our school community understand the causes of
> racism and sexism in our society, and the part we can play in
> fighting against them.

Thus Milltown High was a favourable setting in which to investigate what a school committed to multicultural and anti-racist education was doing in practice. The school also represents a 'critical case' in terms of the implementation of LEA policies. If we did not find policy implemented here, where staff professed a commitment, we would be unlikely to find it implemented elsewhere. The school was also interesting quite simply because it is a multi-ethnic school, and as was made woefully apparent by the publication of the Report of the Committee of Inquiry into the Education of Children from Ethnic Minority Groups, the Swann Report (1985), shortly before this research began, very little is actually known about what goes on in such schools. They have remained a neglected area in educational research which seeks to inform policy making.

The research that is described here (a more detailed account of the research is contained in Foster 1989) is, therefore, a case study of one multi-ethnic, inner city comprehensive school in Milltown, and focuses on the interpretation and implementation of policies on multicultural and anti-racist education. It examines the practices and procedures employed in the school and the ways in which the teachers have responded to the fact that the school is multi-ethnic in its intake and is serving a multi-ethnic society.

Chapter one

Introduction: research questions and theoretical issues

In a report submitted to the Swann Committee describing the work of the Education Team at the Centre for Research in Ethnic Relations (Rex, Troyna, and Naguib 1983; see also Rex 1986a and 1986b) John Rex suggested that one way of approaching the study of educational policy and practice, in the area of race and ethnicity,[1] is to consider the extent to which they meet certain key principles to which most of those who operate the educational system would formally subscribe. First, equality of opportunity and second, the preparation of students for a non-racist, multicultural society. Rex went on to formulate a list of criteria against which policy and practice could usefully be examined. In conducting this study I adopted a similar approach. I sought to clarify the principles, as I saw them, of multicultural and anti-racist education and specify their implications for practice. My aim was to identify a model of multicultural and anti-racist education with which the reality of policy and practice at Milltown High School could be compared. This enabled me to establish my main research questions and clarify the values underpinning them. This is the subject of the first part of this chapter. The clarification of these principles also raised several theoretical questions which the work addresses and which I will discuss in the following part of the chapter.

The central principles of multicultural and anti-racist education

In my view there are two principles at the heart of multicultural and anti-racist education. First is equality of opportunity and second is a notion of how we might use education to work towards the realization of a non-racist society. It is around these two themes that I will focus my discussion.

Equal opportunites

The principle of equal opportunities has been at the heart of much educational research, debate, and policy throughout this century (Silver 1973). However, the term is often used in different ways. Here I want to clarify its meaning and examine its importance to multicultural and anti-racist education.

In perhaps its weakest form equal opportunities in the field of education implies the elimination of laws or rules which bar the entry of particular groups or individuals to parts of the education system. In this sense equal opportunities has existed in Britain for some considerable time. However, during the early years of this century there were increasing demands that the principle be extended so that all children no matter what the economic resources of their family should enjoy equal chances of getting a secondary education, that is of going to grammar schools (Tawney 1931). Later, similar demands were made about access to higher education. In this stronger version society affords equal opportunities in education if children are not prevented by the economic situation of their family or by their gender, race, or ethnic group, from entering the component parts of the educational system. This view has emphasized the elimination of practices which limit the access of students from certain groups and has underpinned many of the major educational reforms of this century, such as the 1944 Education Act.

A third, more radical view of equal opportunities emerged in the post-war years. It became evident that students did not enter the educational system with equal resources and support. Many came from backgrounds which were educationally disadvantaged (Davie *et al.* 1972; Wedge and Prosser 1973) and so began the educational race from unequal positions. Thus, even if access to provision within the educational system was made more equal, educational outcomes would still diverge widely. According to this view, as Silver (1973) pointed out, 'equality of opportunity could only have meaning if those who began with unequal chances had unequal support from the educational system'. In other words for equality of opportunity to become a reality it was necessary to compensate those who started at a disadvantage by positively favouring them in the educational system. The aim of equal opportunities became, in Halsey's words, 'not ... the liberal one of equality of access but equality of outcome for the median member of each identifiable non-educationally defined group' (Halsey 1972: 9).

Behind these views is the essentially liberal, meritocratic principle that all individuals should enjoy equal chances of success and that those with similar ability and motivation should be able to achieve similar social positions and rewards. The aim, as Green (1988) points out, is essentially one of 'competitive equality of opportunity' in which individuals compete for desired social positions or opportunities which are allocated fairly to those most competent to perform or use them, and all enjoy an equal chance to prepare for competition. Such a system, it is argued, recognizes the inherent differences in the talents and abilities of individuals, and achieves a fair and just allocation of social positions and rewards. In addition it should ensure that the most talented are allocated to the 'functionally most important positions' (Davis and Moore 1945) which results in maximum efficiency and therefore ultimately benefits all in society.

Of course, this principle has been subject to considerable criticism. Michael Young (1958), in his satire *The Rise of the Meritocracy*, painted a bleak picture of a socially polarized society in which only the most able occupy the top positions in the social hierarchy. Others (see, for example, Schaar 1971) have pointed to the exaggerated inequality and inevitable elitism that they feel would result if the principle were fully applied. In such a society, it is maintained, advantages of genetic endowment would merely replace those of social background, thus substituting one form of injustice for another. It has also been argued that the principle of equal opportunities can in effect buttress an unjust status quo by providing a seemingly just rationale for social inequality (see Bowles and Gintis 1976). These criticisms have led some to argue that social justice requires equality in society rather than equal opportunities. Their aim has become not the achievement of equal social positions for those of equal ability, but the elimination of social hierarchies and inequalities: in short, an egalitarian society (see, for example, Halsey 1978).

In my view multicultural and anti-racist education does not necessarily require a commitment to equality in society (though some might argue that it does), but it certainly involves at least a commitment to work towards the more radical view of equal opportunities in education outlined above. This would be a situation in which all students would enjoy equal chances to maximize their educational potential. It would mean first that we should try to ensure that the education system is free from discriminatory practices which reduce the chances of educational success of certain students; and second that we should endeavour to provide all individuals with roughly similar educational resources across their school and non-school educational careers. This would mean providing additional resources in the educational system for those from educationally disadvantaged backgrounds.

However, there may be limitations on the extent to which equal opportunities in education can be achieved given the present organization of society. Their realization present enormous practical problems. Equalizing opportunities could, as Coleman (1973) pointed out, involve providing all students with the educational resources available to the most privileged, something he regarded as impossible. If not theoretically impossible this would be extremely difficult to do in practice. It would involve assessing the extent to which individuals or groups were educationally disadvantaged and devising schemes to allocate appropriate educational resources to them. The problems of defining and operationalizing the concept of educational disadvantage are enormous. Disadvantage is often defined in socio-economic terms, and indicators such as income level and housing facilities are used. Whilst there clearly are links, a lack of material resources may not always be synonymous with educational disadvantage. Cultural resources may be more important. The idea of cultural disadvantage raises a whole host of questions about which aspects of particular cultures disadvantage, and to what extent, but, perhaps most important, who is to decide on these issues. Further, the notion of cultural disadvantage, as Bernstein (1970) pointed out, can create the misleading and erroneous impression that the cultures of disadvantaged groups are inherently inferior. What form positive provision should take in order to be effective is also problematic. This issue was raised by research conducted in America in the 1960s (Coleman *et al.* 1969) which questioned the extent to which educational provision could actually compensate for disadvantages of social background.

Moreover, some critics have also pointed out that providing equal opportunities in education means that the differential influences of social background should be minimized and this may clash with other important values in society. Taken to its extreme it would involve the enforced removal of children from their families and their education in state-run nurseries and boarding schools (Lloyd-Thomas 1977; Coleman 1974) which clearly runs counter to the belief in the family as the primary agent of socialization and of parental responsibility for the child. Minimizing background differences also conflicts with the idea of cultural pluralism in a culturally diverse society. If cultural differences are to be accepted, or even fostered as some versions of multiculturalism and anti-racism imply, then it would seem to be undesirable to attempt to minimize background differences. This point raises one of the most serious dilemmas within multicultural and anti-racist education. To what extent should the aim be to ensure equal opportunities within an education system based on universalistic cultural forms and to what extent and in what ways should cultural diversity be respected and encouraged? The former requires the emphasis to be on the teaching of the skills, values, and norms of mainstream society and by implication the minimization of the influence of home background. The latter stresses the maintenance and teaching of the cultural forms of the child's home community.[2] In my view the former should have priority in the education system and the role of this system must be to give students as far as is possible equal opportunities in terms of the universalistic values of society. But having said this, the rights of individuals and families to cultural difference should be respected, and this will inevitably place limitations on any programme designed to minimize the influence of social background.

Thus there are problems in achieving equal opportunities in education and we must accept that in practice programmes of positive provision may have to be limited, based on crude and inadequate criteria, and will be unable to identify and reach all those who are educationally disadvantaged. But, as Green (1988) points out, 'there is every reason to pursue a just goal which can (only) partially be fulfilled'.

How do these ideas relate to multicultural and anti-racist education? I have suggested that equal opportunity is an essential aspect of multicultural and anti-racist education. This would specifically require first, eliminating from the educational system any practices which are racist or which indirectly restrict the chances of success of members of a particular racial or ethnic group. It would also involve offering additional resources within the education system in order to compensate children who are educationally disadvantaged by virtue of their membership of a particular racial or ethnic group.

It is important at the outset to clarify what I mean by racism. I intend to adopt a general use of the term which subsumes both belief and practice. I will use it to refer to practices which restrict the chances of success of individuals from a particular racial or ethnic group, *and* which are based on, or legitimized by, some form of belief that this racial or ethnic group is inherently morally, culturally, or intellectually inferior. Such beliefs could obviously be held by any individual in the education system. Teachers might, for example, regard students from a particular racial or ethnic group as inherently less intelligent or less academically able, or might view a particular group's culture or cultural practices generally as inferior.[3] These beliefs could be expressed openly or, of course, they might be kept private and unarticulated, existing only within the individual's personal consciousness. As much social behaviour is non-reflective even here the individual may be only partially aware of their existence.

More important though are the actions that may be based upon such ideas. If such views form the basis for inferior treatment of students from a particular racial or ethnic group then this would clearly be racism. How might this happen? It is possible that differential treatment could occur across the educational system, if, for example, the schools attended by ethnic minority students were allocated poorer resources on the basis of racist beliefs. Within schools as teachers are frequently in the role of evaluating and making decisions about the educational treatment of their students then it is clearly a possibility that teachers subscribing to racist beliefs might treat students from a particular racial or ethnic group less favourably. They might, for example, make overt

5

references to the inferiority of a certain culture in the classroom which might damage the self-esteem and thus the motivation of students belonging to that ethnic group. Teachers might also evaluate such students less highly in the academic status system of the classroom because of characteristics attributed to their racial or ethnic group. This might result in their inferior treatment in the classroom, which could involve giving them less attention than white students, less praise, less physical contact, or indeed, less of any of the personal and material resources that teachers have the power to distribute. When making more formal decisions about the distribution of opportunities within the school, for example about allocation to streams, bands, or sets, and examination entries, teachers could clearly make racist judgements. For example, if students from a certain racial or ethnic group are seen as inherently 'less able' and 'more disruptive' they might be allocated disproportionately to the lower bands or streams or to 'units for difficult pupils', where they are likely to receive inferior treatment. Teachers are also in the position to make decisions about what is included in the school curriculum. Those motivated by racist beliefs would be unlikely to include references to the cultural practices or history of a group they felt was inferior, or they might include derogatory references. This again might disadvantage students from this ethnic group as their educational motivation could be weakened.[4]

Racism might also affect ethnic minority teachers. Racism in the labour market has frequently been identified. It is possible that there are also discriminatory practices in appointments and promotion in the teaching profession.

There may also be practices in the education system which indirectly and unintentionally restrict the chances of success of students from a particular racial or ethnic group.[5] For example in the system as a whole it may be that the schools attended by students from a particular ethnic group are for some reason poorer or less effective than other schools (cf. Plowden Report 1967). Or it might be that such schools teach an inferior curriculum depriving students of access to important knowledge and skills. Such a criticism has been levelled, ironically, at some proponents of multicultural education (by, for example, Stone 1981). It has been suggested that the attempts of multiculturalists and others to foster the cultures of minority groups in the school curriculum serve to deprive the students of such groups of full access to mainstream culture and a curriculum which will permit them to compete on a par with indigenous students. I am not convinced that this is actually the case in schools which practise multicultural education. Such schools have generally attempted to enhance the academic performance of ethnic minority students by including reference to their lives and concerns in the curriculum, and thus, in theory, increasing student self-esteem and motivation. However, if schools over-emphasized minority culture at the expense of mainstream culture then one can see that this might disadvantage ethnic minority students.

Examples of within-school practices that might indirectly disadvantage students from a particular racial or ethnic group might be disciplinary or uniform regulations which make no concessions to cultural or religious customs and which therefore in effect bar a certain ethnic group from entry, curriculum form and content which make no reference to the culture and history of a particular ethnic group in the school, school meals which take no account of the requirements of a different ethnic group, assemblies which pay no attention to the different religions of students attending the school, and communication with families which takes no account of language differences. Methods of assessment and evaluation which are culturally biased or inaccurate[6] and therefore result in unequal opportunities or inappropriate educational treatment would also be examples. Of course it could be argued that much assessment that occurs in working-class schools is 'culturally biased' in that teachers evaluate their students on the basis of their ability to display competence in the cultural forms of the dominant groups in our society (Bourdieu 1974), but my meaning of cultural bias is somewhat narrower than this. In a differentiated society there must inevitably be assessment criteria and these will ultimately derive from certain values and a conception of the qualities required to perform particular social roles or use particular opportunities. Thus some degree of cultural bias in the broad sense implied by Bourdieu is perhaps inevitable. What I mean by the term is when assessment or evaluation procedures include requirements to display qualities, skills, or knowledge which are irrelevant to the position or opportunity being competed for and which a certain racial or ethnic group would not normally have access to. One instance might be a test which assumed knowledge of cultural practices with which members of a particular ethnic group would not be familiar and which was irrelevant to the skills being tested. Another might be when details of culturally different family patterns or practices were used as information in making educational judgements. As evaluation is frequently based on conformity to norms of behaviour another instance of cultural bias might be unnecessary disciplinary rules which effectively made the cultural norms of a particular ethnic group deviant. It is important to emphasize here that I am not advocating assessment and evaluation practices that are biased in favour of ethnic minority students. What I am advocating is that these processes should be based on universalistic criteria which are the same for all students, and that every effort should be made to ensure that such criteria are always relevant and necessary and therefore do not indirectly discriminate against students of a particular ethnic group.

Something else which might indirectly disadvantage might be a lack of specific school policies and practices to deal promptly and effectively with incidents of racism, racial abuse, and violence. As a recent Commission for Racial Equality report (CRE 1988) made clear, if students are not educated in an environment free from racial harassment and violence then they will not enjoy equal opportunites. A lack of knowledge amongst staff of the cultural backgrounds of their students so that they are unable to deal sensitively and effectively with them and their parents would also indirectly disadvantage. Similarly if teachers make no special efforts to communicate or consult with the parents of ethnic minority students then the students may be placed at a disadvantage given the language and cultural differences which frequently exist between minority parents and school.

Again it is also possible that the careers of ethnic minority teachers may be disadvantaged indirectly by practices within the educational system. As with procedures used to assess students it is possible that culturally biased and irrelevant criteria may be established for particular teaching posts, thus lessening minority teachers' chances of appointment and promotion. The methods used to attract applicants may also indirectly disadvantage. If, for example, posts were advertised by word of mouth and only became known to the friends of the existing teachers who of course were disproportionately white (Ranger 1988).

It is important to emphasize that inequality of educational outcome between racial or ethnic groups is not necessarily an indicator of racism or practices which disadvantage racial or ethnic groups within the education system.[7] It does not follow that if students from one ethnic group perform less well than those from another in some particular educational field that one or more of the practices described above is in operation. To establish this would require investigation of the actual processes involved. Inequalities of outcome are the result of many complex factors, some of which will relate to material and cultural disadvantages of home background. It is this aspect of equal opportunities that I want to turn to now.

As well as ensuring that the type of practices mentioned above do not occur equal opportunities would also involve, I have suggested, some element of compensation in the education system for the educational disadvantages suffered by children as a result of their membership of particular racial or ethnic groups. However, the problem with this idea is that it is very difficult to decide whether children from a particular racial or ethnic group are educationally disadvantaged, and if so in what way or to what extent. This makes it very difficult to specify ideally what positive provision for such groups should look like. In fact it is possible at present for LEAs to provide some additional provision through Section 11 of the 1966 Local Government Act to 'meet the needs of Commonwealth immigrants' and their children, but these needs have rarely been clearly assessed or specified.

One might argue that particular racial and ethnic groups are economically disadvantaged (Smith 1977; Rex and Tomlinson 1979; Brown 1984), and therefore less able to provide adequate extra-school educational resources for their children. As a result, their children are likely to be educationally disadvantaged and additional educational resources should be allocated to them. But, whilst particular racial or ethnic groups may suffer higher levels of economic disadvantage as a result of racial discrimination, economic disadvantage is not confined to such groups. Thus it is difficult to see how positive provision specifically to racial or ethnic groups could be justified on this basis. More sensible would be a scheme to allocate positive provision to *all* those suffering from economic disadvantages, in other words positive provision on the basis of socio-economic class rather than racial or ethnic group.

There is perhaps only one clear way in which members of racial and ethnic groups are disadvantaged and therefore where positive provision directed specifically to them is justifiable. This is in the area of language. Commonsense would lead us to conclude that if a child's first and home language is not English, as is the case with many ethnic minority children, then he/she is likely to be at a disadvantage in an educational system in which English is the dominant language.[8] There is a case to be made here for additional provision for such students to enable them to develop English skills comparable to their white peers so that they are able to compete on equal terms. As Rex (Rex, Troyna, and Naguib 1983) pointed out this provision should aim to provide adequately for both first stage, i.e. the introduction to English as a second language, and second stage, i.e. English skills beyond the introductory stage, language instruction. Moreover, such additional provision should not, whilst providing needed language skills, disadvantage in other ways, as sometimes appears to happen when ethnic minority students are placed in special language units where they do not have access to a full school curriculum. Further, the aim should not be the elimination of the child's mother-tongue as this may damage self-esteem, and bi-lingualism is, for most children, a positive asset. Problems do arise, however, with the definition of 'first language other than English'. Clearly children who speak Vietnamese or Urdu as a first language would come under this heading, but do Afro/Caribbean children who speak creole at home? I would suggest that they do and that they may also have language disadvantages and needs (Trudgill 1975; Edwards 1979) which, of course, may be more of the second stage variety. Thus one might argue justifiably for a programme of positive provision to compensate students from particular racial or ethnic groups for language disadvantages, but other positive provision, I would maintain, should at the moment be based on criteria other than racial or ethnic group.

I have argued that one of the central principles of multicultural and anti-racist education is equal opportunities and I have tried to specify the implications of this principle for educational practice in the area of race and ethnicity. My aim has been to develop a model of multicultural and anti-racist education against which I can compare the practices at Milltown High School. One of my basic research questions in examining the implementation of policies on multicultural and anti- racist education therefore was: to what extent did practices within the school resemble the ideal of equal opportunities I have outlined? This involved finding out whether there were racist practices or practices which indirectly disadvantaged members of particular racial or ethnic groups in the school, and whether the school provided additional or compensatory provision for students from particular racial or ethnic groups.

Education for a non-racist society

The second major aspect of multicultural and anti-racist education which I want to discuss is how we might educate students for a non-racist society. There has been considerable debate here between those who advocate a strategy of multicultural education and those who favour anti-racism. My own view represents a synthesis of these two positions.

Multiculturalists aim to eliminate racism by teaching all children about the cultures and histories of ethnic minorities and projecting a more positive image of these groups in the school curriculum. This approach was adopted by the Swann Committee (Committee of Inquiry 1985) which recommended changing the process of socialization in schools so that students would be taught a more accurate view of ethnic minority people and as a result hold informed and, by implication, non-racist, views and opinions.

However, it has been suggested that multicultural education rests on several, rather shaky premises (Bullivant 1981). One is that teachers can actually teach a more accurate version of ethnic minority culture and history than they do at the moment. This they may be able to do, given the time and resources, but some have questioned the ability of largely white indigenous teachers to do this without seriously diluting and misinterpreting ethnic minority culture and history, or they have questioned the extent to which valid conceptions of minority cultures can be transmitted in an already over-crowded school curriculum. Another assumption is that students taught such information will passively consume it and become less prejudiced as a result. This may be the outcome of such teaching and one would hope that it is, but it may also be a possibility that students will selectively interpret the information and use it to support their own racism.

Proponents of multicultural education have also been criticized for implying that racism is merely a product of errors in the socialization process. John Rex (1986a) suggests that there is a tendency to see racism as solely a problem of attitudes and beliefs, and to ignore the social and economic structures which frequently underpin it. Stuart Hall made a similar point in a talk concerning teaching about racism:

> There is a liberal common sense way of approaching the topic
> which fastens on to questions of discriminatory attitudes between
> people from different ethnic populations, prejudicial actions,
> beliefs and opinions, etc. One tendency in teaching is to take these
> immediate surface manifestations of the problem at face value and
> to look at how these prejudices arise through a kind of attitudinal
> or social psychological perspective. There is a second strategy
> which says all of this is mere surface appearance and we must go to
> the structures which generate particular kinds of attitudes. I tend to
> favour the second of these alternatives.
>
> We have to uncover for ourselves, in our own understanding, as
> well as for the students we are teaching, the deep structural factors
> which have a tendency persistently not only to generate racial
> practices and structures but to reproduce them through time; and
> which therefore account for their extraordinarily immovable
> character.
>
> (Hall 1980: 5)

I have some sympathy with these criticisms of multicultural education. Teaching about the variety of human cultures and about the different ethnic minority cultures in Britain is important, but I believe that if education is to be effective in helping to work toward a non-racist society it must go further than this. It should attempt to be more directly anti-racist. What would this involve?

Anti-racist education should first of all ensure that where information about other cultures and ethnic minority groups is included in the school curriculum it does not degenerate into over-simplified caricature. It should also pay attention to the way in which such information is received and interpreted by students. In fact a consideration of this issue and the broader ones of how racist attitudes are formed and influence social relationships, and the mechanisms of interpersonal perception and interaction, are of crucial importance. These issues could be raised in a number of subject areas and at different levels of complexity during a student's educational career – from simple ideas about, for example, how individuals respond to strangers or newcomers in the early years of secondary school[9] to the more abstract sociological notions of human interaction in the later years – and ought to form a major part of a school's programme of social education. They are also likely to arise more informally from interstudent relationships which, unfortunately, can sometimes be fraught with racial animosity and tension. The pastoral care and advice given to students therefore should attempt to foster the values of anti-racism. The aim must be to encourage non-racist attitudes and behaviour by giving students the knowledge, understanding, and skills to be able to critically assess the information they receive, to examine their own responses to such information, and to reflect critically on their own and others' attitudes and social behaviour. It is also important that teachers in their interaction with students, parents, and colleagues set appropriate anti-racist role models for their students.

Whilst not wishing to discount the importance of individual attitudes, it is also important to consider with students the social structural factors which help to create and recreate racism. Thus anti-racist education should also aim to equip students with a critical awareness of the ways in which societies are structured and organized and of the role of ideologies and belief systems. It should raise questions about why societies are organized in the way they are and the justice or morality of such forms of organization. More specifically, it should involve a consideration of the way in which racism figures in Britain and other societies, past and present, and of how racism is transmitted, reproduced, reworked, and can be resisted. Such teaching could not be conducted in an isolated or minor curriculum slot, but ought to become a central part of a comprehensive programme of social and political education.

What form might such a programme take? Its major aim would be to provide students with a broad knowledge of social and political issues and relationships, and the skills and qualities which would enable them to analyse, understand, participate in, and possibly change the society in which they live. Well-developed literacy skills are clearly important, as are oral, listening, research, organizational, and co-operative skills. Also important is the development of commitments to democratic values, such as the importance of free debate and discussion, rational argument, the use of evidence, and respect for the opinions of others. Such aims involve a commitment to a particular curriculum content and pedagogy. A curriculum which contains a strong element of social and political education would include, wherever possible, teaching about social and political issues, one of which would be racism. Obviously such teaching is most likely to be found in the 'Humanities' areas, in subjects like History, Geography, Social Studies, and English, but it could also be incorporated into subjects like the Sciences, through, for example, teaching about the social and political implications of scientific developments, and Mathematics, where, for example, the use and meaning of certain types of statistics could be discussed.

However, as Whitty (1985; see also Gleeson and Whitty 1976) points out, often where social and political education has been taught its aim has been to buttress the status quo by socializing young people into established ways of thinking and proceeding. As a result its content has frequently presented a favourable and uncritical view of current social relationships and organizations. Social and political conflict, inequality, and injustice have often been under-played and society portrayed as a healthy, consensual union. This would not be the form of social and political education that I would advocate. Merely encouraging students to accept and fit in to society as it is at present is unlikely to give them the knowledge or the skills to work toward the creation of a more just, non-racist society.

Students should be encouraged to examine a variety of different viewpoints including those which are critical of the society they live in and which present alternative forms of social organization and suggest ways in which established systems might be changed. Social and political education would require approaching the study of often controversial social and political issues from a variety of perspectives, from the conservative to the radical. It could also involve a strong element of what others (for example Hargreaves 1982) have called 'community studies', so that students could develop their understanding through a study of issues which affect them and their own families. This would also give them the chance to learn about the contemporary experiences and concerns of local ethnic minority groups in the context of those of the wider community.

At time of writing the Conservative government is introducing a national curriculum for all secondary schools which may severely restrict the introduction of social and political education. Indeed, it has been argued that the government's proposals are in part designed to prevent what is perceived as an attempt by anti-racists and others to 'politicize' the school curriculum. There may, however, be space within the framework of the National Curriculum for teachers and others to introduce particular content along the lines that are suggested here.

The type of social and political education I have in mind would also involve a particular form of pedagogy. I would argue that in order to develop the skills mentioned above students need to experience situations in which they are actively involved in discussion and debate, in which they can utilize their own knowledge and experiences (cf. Barnes 1976) and in which they are encouraged to reflect upon their own ideas and attitudes. It would mean employing teaching styles which emphasize collaboration and group discussion rather than didactic transmission and individualistic task performance, and more egalitarian rather than authoritarian teacher-student relationships. Such styles would also encourage tolerance and respect between students which is essential in order to establish a climate of anti-racism in the classroom. This also implies that students be involved as much as possible in the wider school decision-making structure, so that they may experience and learn about the nature of democratic organization at first hand.

Thus anti-racist education in this broader form involves a conception of what and how we want students to learn. This derives from a view of the particular qualities we want students to develop in order that they become non-racist themselves and are equipped to be able to work for a just, non-racist society based on the principles of equal opportunities, non-racism, and democracy. In this sense anti-racist education does have a 'political' aim and basis. It seeks to produce people with certain kinds of knowledge, skills, and attitudes who are committed to a particular kind of society, and it derives from particular 'political' beliefs and values. In fact all decisions about what and how to teach are based on ideas of this kind, although they often remain implicit. This does not mean that anti-racist education should, as some (for example Jeffcoate 1984a and 1984b) have claimed it does, attempt to 'indoctrinate' students by presenting them with a single, narrowly prescriptive political view of the world or of the nature of a non-racist society. Such an aim would contradict the commitment to the type of curriculum and pedagogy outlined above which emphasizes debate and discussion and in fact encourages students to consider a variety of arguments and perspectives. But it does mean that decisions about what and how to teach are based on certain values and beliefs about the nature of a just and good society. It also suggests that these values and beliefs will consciously be fostered and therefore others will be regarded less valid. These values place limits, albeit broad ones in a democratic society, on what can be regarded as legitimate opinion. Thus teachers could not be expected, as Jeffcoate (1984a and 1984b) appears to imply, to accept racist views as valid and legitimate in the classroom in the interests of 'balance' (just as they could not accept anti-democratic views). There is, of course, sometimes a very narrow and difficult line to draw between racist views and legitimate political opinion, and teachers must exercise careful judgement here.

This then is the model of education for a non-racist society that I wish to employ in examining the teaching practices at Milltown High School. One of my main research aims was to discover to what extent the conception of multicultural and anti-racist education held by the teachers at Milltown High matched my own and to assess the extent to which practice of multicultural and anti-racist education in the school resembled the sort of model that I have drawn.

Theoretical issues

The questions I have outlined also relate to issues of more theoretical concern. Of central interest in the sociology of education has been the question of how educational outcomes – i.e. academic attainment, value orientation, and attitudes – are produced, and thus of how the educational system contributes to the reproduction of the basic social characteristics of an industrial capitalist society.

A number of writers have focused on the significance of broader structural or 'macro' factors, seeing these as largely determining the nature and product of the education system. This has been common in Marxist approaches. Bowles and Gintis (1976), for example, argue that, through the 'hidden curriculum' of schooling, students learn the basic attitudes and dispositions which are necessary in capitalist organizations, and that social class is by far the most important determinant of educational qualifications and post-school success. Althusser (1971) claims that schools, through their overt and hidden curriculum, pass on to children from different social backgrounds the 'ideological predispositions', as well as the knowledge and skills, appropriate for their future roles in a capitalist society. Bourdieu (1973), argues that students are assessed in terms of their performance in the cultural forms of the dominant classes who, through their representatives in schools, define what is regarded as worthwhile knowledge, skill, and ability. As the majority of working-class students lack the 'cultural capital' to enable them to conform to these definitions they are likely to be seen as failures.

Many other writers have also stressed the significance of structural factors in explaining differential educational achievement. In Britain a number of empirical studies have emphasized the significance of material inequality (Wedge and Prosser 1973; Wedge and Essen 1982) and social class variation in parental attitudes and values (Jackson and Marsden 1962; Douglas 1964; Plowden Report 1967; Sugarman 1970). The work of Basil Bernstein (1971a) has drawn attention to differences in social class language 'codes' and their effect on educational performance. Raymond Boudon (1974) has argued that social class differences in attitudes and values constitute the 'primary effects' of stratification on educational opportunity. But more important, he maintains, are the 'secondary effects' which involve the different financial and social costs and benefits of continuing and being successful in education to individuals from different social class groups. At each 'branching point' in a student's educational career the cost to a working-class student and their family of continuing in education will tend to outweigh the possible benefits. The reverse is likely to be true of the middle-class student.

However, some writers have suggested that schools themselves may have effects which are independent of these macro-factors; that what goes on within schools and the outcomes of schooling are not simply a product of wider structural forces. Within-school processes may, it seems, mediate the effects of structural factors. It is possible that the significance of such external factors may be reduced (see Lacey 1966), but more often it appears that they accentuate differences between students deriving from external social factors. Within-school processes seem frequently to place greater obstacles in the path of those who enter the educational system already disadvantaged.

In considering within-school processes three main theories have been developed. The first derives partly from the 'cultural' Marxism of Bourdieu (1973) outlined above which played a central role in what came to be known as the 'new sociology of education' (Young 1971). From this viewpoint, of critical importance in schools are the definitions of which particular forms of knowledge, skill, and ability are desirable, and the ways particular individuals come to be seen as more or less successful in terms of these definitions.

Whilst these ideas originate in the main from Marxism they have links with two other, interrelated theories which derive from more interpretivist approaches in sociology. First is the idea of the self-fulfilling prophecy, which was first systematically expounded by Merton (1949), and has subsequently been developed in symbolic interactionist approaches to educational research (see D. Hargreaves 1975 for a review). In education this theory has claimed that a teacher's initial perception of a student influences their expectations of the student's future progress. This expectation may cause them to treat the student in a particular way. This treatment can either directly bring about the predicted progress (or lack of it) or it can influence the student's conception of his/her own ability, which affects motivation, and thus ultimately brings the student's progress into line with the teacher's original expectations.

Most research on this theory has been conducted in America (Rosenthal and Jacobson 1968; Rist 1973; Brophy and Good 1974) whilst in Britain another theory has developed. This theory is mainly associated with the work of David Hargreaves (1967), Colin Lacey (1970), and Stephen Ball (1981) and has concentrated on the link between what has been termed 'differentiation' and 'polarization'. The former term refers to the ways teachers evaluate their students in terms of the dominant value system of the school at the informal classroom level and at the formal school level through the school's system of ability grouping. The latter term describes the student adaptions and sub-cultures that are produced in reaction to differentiation. The theory argues that differentiation, which in schools is generally based on academic achievement and behavioural conformity, tends to result in the polarization of student attitudes. Those students who are successful in terms of the school's academic and behavioural values and are, as a result, given high status, by, for example, being allocated to the top streams, will become positively orientated to school and what it stands for. More especially those who are not successful and are given low status will tend to reject school and its values (Hammersley 1985).

Hargreaves, Lacey, and Ball suggest that such processes tend to amplify the effects of existing class inequalities in educational resources in ways similar to those outlined in the theory of the self-fulfilling prophecy. Once differentiated, students are categorized. They become D-stream or C-band students, for example, and disproportionate numbers of working-class students are allocated to such low status groups. These categories become the basis for the allocation of educational resources, and for teacher expectations and behaviour. Often low status groups receive inferior resources, such as the least experienced teachers, and teachers approach them with low expectations and treat them accordingly, for example by setting them less-demanding work or accepting lower standards. Moreover, once categorized, students tend to take to themselves the attitudes and expectations held by their teachers and signified by their position in the school status system. Thus the D-stream and C-band students tend to think of themselves as failures and their academic motivation is further reduced. As a result low status students, who are more often than not working class, are even less likely to succeed.

These theories appear to demonstrate some of the possible ways that within-school processes can create or amplify educational inequalities. Versions of them, especially the idea of the self-fulfilling prophecy, have been applied recently to the area of race and ethnicity where there has been growing concern about the educational underachievement of students from certain ethnic minority groups, most notably Afro/Caribbean students.[10] In explaining this phenomenon increasing prominence has been given to the role played by processes occurring within individual schools.

It has been suggested that certain teachers have unfavourable views of Afro/Caribbean students and perceive them in a negative light. In the Swann Report, it was suggested that such views could be 'intentional' or 'unintentional', but were more likely to be the latter. The Committee concluded that such views were likely to influence the academic performance of Afro/Caribbean students:

> . . .we find ourselves all the more convinced of the major role
> which the particular expectations and attitudes which many
> teachers have, not only of West Indian pupils, but indeed of pupils

from the whole range of ethnic minority groups, can and do play in the educational experience and perhaps the academic achievement of these pupils...research findings and our own evidence have indicated that the stereotypes that teachers tend to have of West Indian children are often related to a particular and generally negative, expectation of academic performance.

(Committee of Inquiry 1985: 25)

As a consequence of such negative perceptions it is argued that Afro/ Caribbean students are likely to be treated less favourably than their white peers in the classroom, receiving less and poorer physical and human resources, and less-demanding work. They are more likely to be categorized as low status, problem students and allocated to low streams and bands, or to ESN schools or units for disruptive children, where they experience an inferior curriculum and low, inappropriate expectations. They are more likely to be suspended or referred to child guidance units, thus missing vital school time. It is suggested that such differential treatment may in itself create the underachievement of many Afro/Caribbean students. Alternatively it is argued that such treatment affects the academic self-image of students who come to view themselves as 'failures' thus losing motivation, becoming progressively more alienated from the educational system, and hostile to their teachers, and developing polarized anti-school sub-cultures. This in turn leads to underachievement.

A variation on this theory is the notion that curriculum content and school ethos are largely mono-cultural. This implicitly (and sometimes explicitly) denigrates or systematically ignores ethnic minority cultures and achievements, conveying a subtle message of inferiority. As a result many ethnic minority students become alienated from school and their teachers. Again, it is argued, this leads to poor self-image, low motivation, poor teacher-student relationships and thus underachievement. Bhikhu Parekh neatly summarizes both these theories:

Like the white children, some white teachers have grown up on a mono-cultural diet and share their cultural arrogance and insensitivity. Consciously or unconsciously they approach their black pupils with the familiar stereotypes; they expect little of them, tend not to stretch them to their fullest, and fail to provide them with necessary educational and emotional support and encouragement. Not surprisingly many black children tend to underachieve, rarely feel relaxed in school, lack trust in their teachers and go through the school with a cartload of frustrations and resentment. When constantly fed on an ethnocentric curriculum that presents their communities and cultures in a highly biased and unflattering manner, black children can hardly avoid developing a deep sense of inferiority and worthlessness...The black child raised on a mono-cultural diet in an English school experiences profound self-alienation.

(Parekh 1986: 25)

Another idea, less frequently advanced, was put forward by Driver (1979) following his ethnographic study of a multi-ethnic secondary school. He suggested that white teachers lacked cultural competence in their interaction with Afro/Caribbean students. They tended to misinterpret Afro/Caribbean cultural expression in the classroom and found it difficult to deal confidently with these students. As a result, Afro/Caribbean boys especially tended to become alienated from school and underachieve.

It is also possible to apply Bourdieu's ideas to the education of ethnic minority students. It could be argued that definitions of knowledge and ability dominant in schools make little reference to the cultural forms of minority groups, who are, of course, mainly working class, and there is therefore little likelihood that minority students will be able to display the sort of 'cultural capital' that is required in order to be seen as successful. It is not surprising, then, that they are found disproportionately amongst the failures of the educational system.

Unfortunately there is very little empirical evidence at present to allow us to judge the validity of these ideas. In fact there has been very little research work done at all on the ways in which within-school processes affect ethnic minority students. In investigating practices that relate to equal opportunities at Milltown High School I was interested in the extent to which some of the processes outlined above occurred and thus in whether school processes contributed to racial/ethnic inequalities in performance and consequently in life chances. It was not possible to investigate every aspect of these processes, but I was able to examine questions such as: How did teachers' conceptions of knowledge and ability relate to minority cultural forms? How did teachers perceive their students and how did students' race or ethnicity influence these perceptions? How did teachers interpret and respond to cultural variations in student behaviour? How did teachers differentiate their students informally at the classroom level and did this relate to race and ethnicity? Did teachers treat students differently on the basis of race or ethnicity in the classroom? At the more formal level: Did race or ethnicity influence decisions teachers made about students, such as in the allocations to ability bands or sets? Were ethnic minority students disproportionately allocated to low status groups and receive inferior educational treatment as a result? Were anti-school minority group sub-cultures produced? Thus this study provides empirical data on some aspects of within-school processes in a multi-ethnic school which should help us to decide whether such processes do accentuate racial and ethnic inequalities.

The study also relates to an aspect of the 'macro' theories discussed above. Writers such as Bowles and Gintis and Althusser argue that schools for the working class, through their formal and hidden curriculum, produce appropriately socialized workers,[11] trained to fit in with, and accept unquestioningly, an unequal, exploitative and oppressive capitalist system.[12] I have argued elsewhere that one might expect the curriculum of schools performing this function to present:

> A generally uncritical picture of the social world. Established social structures, institutions and modes of behaviour would be shown in a favourable light, functioning efficiently, fairly and for the benefit of all. Social conflict we would expect to be largely ignored or, where presented, shown as occurring and being resolved within the established and legitimate social institutions of liberal, democratic society. Issues of power, inequality, disruptive social conflict and change would be largely ignored.
>
> (Foster 1985: 20)

Moreover, one might anticipate that the pedagogy utilized by teachers would stress the didactic transmission of knowledge, individualized task performance, and extrinsic rewards, and that teacher-student relationships would be largely autocratic, involve close supervision, and emphasize obedience and conformity to teacher-imposed standards and expectations.

However, the form of anti-racist education that I have outlined bears little resemblance to this model of education and would not perform the same function. One of its aims would be to produce students who were able to view their society critically and to challenge established systems and practices if they perceived them to be unjust or unfair. It advocates a curriculum which would encourage students to consider issues of conflict, inequality, social change, and alternative forms of social organization, and a pedagogy based on greater student participation and control and more egalitarian teacher-student relationships. As such it would be a form of education that might ultimately be disruptive rather than supportive of the status quo.

This study tries to assess the extent to which teachers in one school are committed to and can put into practice this form of education. It thus assesses, in a small way, the question of whether education reproduces or challenges the established knowledge and attitudes of a capitalist society.

Research methods

In addressing the questions outlined above I employed ethnographic research methods (see McCall and Simmons 1969; Hammersley and Atkinson 1983; Burgess 1984; Woods 1986). I spent three days a week (usually) in the school for a year. My aim was to actually see school practices from, as far as possible, an insider's viewpoint, and to minimize reactivity, i.e. changing the behaviour of subjects because you are observing them, by spending a long period 'in the field'. For most of the time I adopted a role similar to that adopted by Woods (1979, 1986) which he describes as the 'involved observer'. I 'hung about' the school, observed lessons where teachers were willing to have me, occasionally helping out, but more often watching and noting down the things I saw, sometimes using a small portable tape-recorder. I participated in staffroom life often spending breaks and lunchtimes chatting and listening, and attended most staff meetings and INSET sessions. Whilst at the beginning of the research I attempted to avoid becoming associated with any one group of teachers and sought a general view of the institution by sampling times, places, people, and events, as the research began to focus I developed very close relationships with some staff. A number became key informants providing me with detailed information about past and present events in the school. I also mixed informally when I could with students, especially the older ones, though this was difficult to do regularly because of obvious role and age differences. I also conducted interviews, some structured, others less so, with both staff and students, and examined a large number of school documents.

When I began the research I planned to adopt a more collaborative research model in which teachers were involved more closely in the research process than has often been the case (see Foster and Troyna 1988). Unfortunately my field work took place in the 1985–6 academic year which was marred by teacher industrial action and this was not possible. Thus my research followed a pattern similar to other ethnographic case studies of schools (see, for example, Hargreaves 1967; Lacey 1970; Ball 1981; Burgess 1983).

Chapter two

The social context and social structure of Milltown High School

The local area

Milltown was a local authority at the centre of a large, industrial conurbation in the north of England. Once a prosperous manufacturing centre, the city suffered from many of the familiar economic and social problems of Britain's industrial heartland – a declining industrial base, high unemployment, poor housing, and falling population. The local authority was Labour controlled and its policies of relative high spending in order to protect local jobs and services resulted in conflict with the Conservative controlled central government.

Milltown High School was a small neighbourhood comprehensive school serving two main areas of Milltown which I will call Chesham and Richmond Hill. The local area was perhaps typical of many inner city areas. The population was predominantly working class, and, because of migration out of the area, was declining and often transient. Unemployment was high especially amongst young people (around 50 per cent amongst males under twenty-five). Partly as a result there was serious urban disorder during the summer of 1981, and relationships between young people (especially Afro/Caribbean) and the police were far from harmonious. There was a high proportion of one-parent families – around 40 per cent of children in the area came from one-parent households – and of single, elderly people, and the chronically ill.

Although many people in Richmond Hill lived in privately owned or rented housing, the majority in the area as a whole lived in council accommodation. In Chesham this consisted of a large 1960s estate of multi-storey 'crescents' and deck-access housing which a local inquiry report labelled 'a disaster'. Many of these houses had problems of damp, poor heating, broken lifts and doors, and poor security. However, more recently built, low rise council housing in other parts of the area provided relatively pleasant accommodation for some.

The area had a history of immigration. Irish immigration was common in the last century, and in the 1950s and 1960s migrants from the Caribbean, mainly Jamaica and Barbados, and Africa settled. There were relatively few Asian settlers. Most of Milltown's Asian community lived slightly to the south of the area. Thus a large proportion of the population of Chesham and Richmond Hill was of Afro/Caribbean origin.

Milltown High School – background

The school was purpose-built with the local estate in the late 1960s.[1] Since then its fortunes had followed a similar course. It was originally built for about 1,300 students, but numbers never got much above 1,000. A declining city population and migration out of the area reduced numbers to around 600 by the end of the 1970s. Surplus capacity was a problem in the city as a whole, and in 1982 the LEA re-organized its 'county' secondary schools. Milltown High became a six form (later a five form) entry eleven to sixteen school. Staff numbers were cut and approximately three-quarters of the established teachers were re-deployed out of the school and replaced by teachers from other schools in the city, causing enormous upset and confusion amongst staff and students alike.

Unfortunately, following this re-organization the number of students attending Milltown High continued to fall. In 1982 there were just over 500 students on roll, but by 1986 this had fallen to 363 and there were only fifty-two students in the first year (only one-third the number that might have been expected to come to the school from its feeder primary schools), giving rise to rumours of possible closure or amalgamation. Because of its location and relatively poor exam results the school did not enjoy a good reputation, and continued surplus school places in the city meant parents could send their children to what they considered 'better' schools. One might speculate that the racism of some parents was also influential. Certainly a considerable number of white parents in the catchment area sent their children to other schools, and during my field work a group of white parents at one of the 'feeder' primary schools organized a campaign to have their school 'linked' to another secondary school. But their espoused concerns were with exam results and school discipline, and it is difficult to tell if they were motivated by racism. It is important to note that a significant number of ethnic minority parents also sent their children to other schools.

The school allocation process was, in fact, exploited in different ways by different ethnic and residential groups. Asian and white parents living in the south of the catchment area were more likely to send their children to other schools than the white and Afro/Caribbean parents in the centre and the north. As a result the ethnic make-up of Milltown High became more dominated by Afro/Caribbean students than would have been the case if all the children from the feeder primary schools had come to the school. At Easter 1985, 51.2 per cent of the school's students were of Afro/Caribbean origin, 41.7 per cent were white, and 5.9 per cent of Asian origin; the remaining 1.2 per cent were from a variety of other groups.[2] The vast majority of the students had parents in manual occupations or parents who were unemployed and thus social class backgrounds were fairly uniform.

Despite its low student numbers the school was generously staffed. The LEA had decided that schools faced with falling rolls should be staffed on the basis of the number of teachers required to maintain a viable comprehensive school curriculum and this was estimated at forty staff, giving a staff/student ratio of 1:9 in 1985–6, the envy of many schools in the city. Thus the school was protected by the LEA from the extreme, immediate problems caused by falling rolls.[3] However, at secondary school re-organization the school proved difficult to staff. It had also suffered from several recent changes in headteacher before the present head, David Benyon, was appointed in April 1984.

Before describing the basic organization of the school I should perhaps mention the teachers' industrial action in support of their pay claim which affected the school quite seriously during my field work. Normal school routines were frequently marred by strikes, lack of 'cover' for absent teachers, and teachers' refusal to attend meetings out of school time and run extra-curricular activities. As a result the school was often closed, students had to be sent home if their teacher was absent and no 'supply' teacher could be found, and school meals, to which many students were entitled free, were inadequately supervised. The results were often chaotic. Moreover, many of the activities and events which are central to the 'community life' of a school, that build a sense of loyalty and solidarity, were sadly lacking. This further alienated many students who at the best of times were difficult to motivate. Truancy rates became high and attendance plummeted. The problem of disorder in classrooms and around the school, which was never far from the surface at Milltown High, was also aggravated. Significant from the point of view of multicultural and anti-racist education was the fact that no meetings with parents could be held outside of school hours. Thus the idea of involving parents more closely in their children's education was almost impossible to implement.

School social structure and organization

Teachers and students

As Burgess (1983) notes the division and control of territory within a school gives a clear indication of aspects of its social structure. Indeed, the control of space, its use and access to it, is one of the key aspects of a school's 'hidden curriculum'. As with most schools there were marked differences between staff and students at Milltown High, showing clearly the power differential between them. The bulk of the space in the school was controlled by the teachers. Classrooms, offices, and even communal areas such as corridors and 'house rooms' were seen as 'belonging' to particular teachers or departments. Apart from an adjoining youth centre, the toilets represented the only real area of student control and these were the centre of various, sometimes illicit, activities that characterized their cultural world. However, even they became subject to fairly rigid teacher control as, following an act of vandalism, they were locked and only opened when a teacher was supervising nearby.

The same difference in status and power was evident in the temporal structure of the school. Teachers controlled the distribution and use of time. They decided the 'timetable' which governed the temporal cycle of the school day, week, and year, and the allocation of resources in time. They also decided what activities were appropriate at what time and enforced rules concerning the use of time. Teachers dominated most other areas of school life too. The selection of the knowledge deemed worthy of transmission (the curriculum), was almost completely in their hands, as were decisions about the means of transmitting that knowledge (pedagogy). Teachers also decided on the methods of grouping students which, especially in the upper years, reflected their judgements about students' academic and behavioural status. They decided the criteria on which students were granted varying degrees of status and reward or punishment, and they controlled the allocation of students to different levels of the school and classroom status systems.

In fact, as in most schools, the whole normative structure of the school lay in the hands of the teachers. This was despite the fact that there appeared (in comparison to my own school days as a pupil) to be a much more egalitarian atmosphere in the school and a humanizing of social relationships. Teachers dressed casually with few of the old trappings of status (no gowns or suits), as did the majority of students (there was a school uniform but it was not rigorously enforced), and often the social interactions between teachers and students were relaxed and informal. These, however, were changes mainly in surface features. Basic differences in status and power remained.

There were a few exceptions to this pattern. An innovative scheme called the 'Alternative Curriculum' introduced in 1986 for a small group of fifth year students did attempt to introduce more flexible curriculum patterns based upon 'negotiation' between teacher and student, and teachers in the English and Integrated Curriculum departments also tried to increase student control over curriculum content and work patterns.

What then was the nature of the values underlying the normative structure the teachers had created? Assemblies are useful to look at here as they are often consensual rituals in which the collective values of the school community are expressed and transmitted. At Milltown High, school and year group assemblies were both held once a week. They were generally secular, except for the occasional visit from a local Anglican priest, and rather brief, consisting of a short talk by the head or a senior teacher on a topical or moral issue. Unexpectedly, given the school's multicultural commitment, few assemblies presented aspects of different cultures or religions. The talks that were given mainly emphasized common humanitarian values such as caring and showing respect for others, patience, tolerance, good behaviour, and hard work. As I will explain in chapter 4 anti-racism was also emphasized strongly by the head.

Academically the school was certainly not what Lacey (1974) called a 'pressured academic environment'. Although examination results and working hard academically were regarded as important, they were not given major emphasis by the head or senior staff in assemblies nor, I was told, in discussions with heads of department.[4] The school did not have the characteristic rituals of prize givings and speech days in which past and present academic successes were highlighted. Nor were academically successful students often held up as role models. Students were not streamed or banded, but were taught in mixed ability groups until the end of the third year when some departments introduced setting, and therefore an academic hierarchy to which they could aspire was not made obviously apparent. Moreover, the majority of teachers deliberately played down academic differentiation (see chapter 8), whilst, the head, although he recognized the importance of paper qualifications, was interested in broader educational aims (see chapter 4). In fact what can best be described as a liberal egalitarianism, rather than an academic elitism, characterized the school. Although the head was criticized by some for this lack of academic emphasis, the majority of teachers agreed that to place undue emphasis on a narrow notion of 'achievement' would result in the demotivation of many of the school's students who were not very successful academically. Thus assessment grades were given for 'effort' more than 'achievement', and 'merit marks' for 'good behaviour' more than high standards of academic work. Indeed, as social control was often difficult to maintain at Milltown High (see chapter 9), 'good behaviour' and social responsibility were the more heavily emphasized values. I do not want to give the impression here that the value structure at Milltown High was totally non-academic. It was not. But it *tended* to de-emphasize the academic and stress the importance of other qualities.

Divisions of status and power, the fact that teacher and student interests frequently diverge, and the compulsory nature of schooling, of course mean that much school life is characterized by conflict (see Waller 1932). Given the frequent value difference between working-class students and their middle-class teachers this is perhaps especially true of schools for the urban working class (Grace 1978). Conflict was never far from the surface at Milltown High.

Teacher control of space was freqently challenged and subverted. Classrooms and other forbidden areas were sneaked into, locked doors broken, walls covered in graffiti, windows smashed, and keys stolen. The staffroom door was banged on or flung open, corridors became places for hanging about and socializing, as did classrooms if the time was right and the teacher 'soft'. There were endless small ways in which students sought in their everyday actions to re-define school space as 'theirs', for their purposes (such as 'having a laugh' or 'messing about' [Willis 1977; Woods 1979]) and to suit their interests. In the same way they challenged teacher control and definition of time. Students would frequently arrive late for lessons, or re-define parts of lessons, thus extending their possession of time. 'Wagging it', i.e. truanting, either for the whole school day or for certain lessons, was common, especially amongst the older students. Curriculum and pedagogy could also be re-defined, as when a teacher's serious point of knowledge was converted into a class joke or when a teacher's 'group discussion' became an excuse to discuss the local football team's performance. As Hargreaves (1967) and Lacey (1970) showed students can also re-define teachers' criteria of status by creating alternative status forms rooted in their own sub-cultures. Status here can sometimes be achieved by academic failure rather than success and poor behaviour rather than conformity. This was certainly the case at Milltown High. Although there was no clearly identifiable anti-school group of the type described by Hargreaves, anti-school attitudes were common and students often aspired to norms and values which were in opposition to those sponsored by the teachers.

I do not want to suggest that every moment of the day at Milltown High was fraught with conflict. There were times when relationships between teachers and students were extremely co-operative and friendly. But, here the basic conflictual nature of schooling was more evident than at other schools I am familiar with. As Grace (1978) notes, schools for the urban working class have tended to be sites not just of generational and institutional conflict, but of class conflict. Indeed it has been argued by some (Willis 1977; Weis 1985) that such schools are important sites for the reproduction of a culture of resistance amongst the working class. As I will explain in chapter 9 the 'resistance' of some students had significant consequences for the educational experiences of all the students at Milltown High.

The teachers – departments and schools

Milltown High was again similar to many other secondary schools in that it was divided into subject departments responsible for the different areas of the curriculum. They provided strong sub-cultures (see chapters 6 and 7) within which school norms and teacher roles were interpreted, and enjoyed considerable autonomy to organize their curriculum and pedagogy. The departments differed in status. Although the ethos of Milltown High did not place great emphasis on 'the academic' it was the traditional academic subject departments that had the highest status. The English, Maths, Science, and Humanities (History, Geography, and Religious Education were not taught separately) departments all enjoyed larger numbers of staff, bigger room allocations, more timetable time, and a large share of resources. These subjects were regarded as the 'core' curriculum and therefore all students in every year took them. An area that was growing in status was the new Integrated Curriculum. The core subjects (except Science) in year one, and in year two from September 1986, had been amalgamated to form this department, to the displeasure of some of the established heads of department who saw their status and responsibilities eroded. It had begun to establish its own distinctive subject sub-culture largely based around a 'progressive' or 'developmental' pedagogy characteristic of many primary or middle schools (A. Hargreaves 1986). Students took a number of other subjects in the first three years. All studied PE and Spanish every week, and Art, Music, Drama, and the Craft subjects formed two subject groups studied on a termly rotating basis. These subjects became options at the end of the students' third year. In the fourth and fifth year students had one lesson each week of Social Education which mainly consisted of careers work.

Competition between subject departments for status, and the control of space and resources that went with it, was a common feature of the internal political life of Milltown High School. When status or its associated trappings were threatened or taken away, as when the PE department were told that their subject would become an option in the fourth and fifth year because of the introduction of the 'Alternative Curriculum', they were often fiercely defended.

The other basic unit of organization at Milltown High was the 'pastoral care' system. A 'house' system was abandoned in 1985 in favour of a 'year' system, headed by three 'heads of school' – one in charge of year 5 (upper school), another of years 3 and 4 (middle school), and another of years 1 and 2 (lower school). Each head of school interpreted and defined their roles somewhat differently, one adopting what he described as a more 'formal' approach, another placing an emphasis on 'counselling'. Their views of their role sometimes conflicted with the expectations of ordinary teaching staff who looked to them primarily for support with disciplinary problems. In fact despite much of the rhetoric of 'pastoral care' which implies that such staff are largely concerned with issues of personal care, guidance, and emotional problems, much of the time of the heads of school was spent dealing with matters of social control (cf. Denscombe 1985).

Heads of school were assisted by class tutors and again there were differences in the way they defined their roles. A minority of tutors, especially those in the Integrated Curriculum and English departments, regarded their tutorial responsibilities as extremely important. They would attempt to deal with any problems that a student might have, spend time in counselling individuals, take responsibility for dealing with disciplinary incidents that their students got involved in, and visit students' homes. But others, the majority in fact, had a narrower interpretation, and regarded the subject teaching side of their role as more important. Some, in fact, did little more than mark the registers in the morning and afternoon.

However, pastoral divisions in the school were far less clear and significant in terms of the allocation of space, time, resources, etc. than were the subject divisions. The 'schools' did not form clearly defined geographical units as did the subjects (except the lower school which was developing along these lines with the Integrated Curriculum). Although there were 'year rooms' few staff used them. Moreover, few activities revolved around the 'schools', especially during the industrial action. They did not meet regularly; 'school' meetings were held approximately once a term, whereas members of departments met informally every day. They did not provide teachers with their basic means of executing their job of classroom teaching, their curriculum, pedagogy, and resources. In short, the 'schools' did not provide the basic sub-cultures to which staff at Milltown High could attach and owe their allegiance, whereas the subject departments did. (Although again the Integrated Curriculum/Lower School set up was becoming the exception here.) Thus it was the subject departments that provided the more significant unit of school organization.

Some mention should be made here of the role of 'Section 11' teachers in the school. In addition to its normal staffing complement, Milltown High was entitled to three extra teachers financed from money provided to the LEA under Section 11 of the 1966 Local Government Act. This money is made available so that LEAs can make special provision for students of 'Commonwealth immigrant' origin 'whose language and customs differ from those of the rest of the community'. Before the 1985–6 academic year such teachers at Milltown High were not identifiable individuals. The extra entitlement had merely been used to increase the overall school staffing level. As a previous head of the school said, 'they were 3/40ths of everyone'. However, following a change in Home Office requirements in 1985, Section 11 staff had to be identified and their roles clearly defined. This stipulation filtered down to school level during 1985–6 and a small number of staff had all or part of their timetables hurriedly designated Section 11 time. In September 1986 three teachers on the staff were more carefully selected. They formed a 'Section 11 department' and were given their own base to work from. It was, however, difficult for them to establish quickly a coherent set of working norms and well-defined roles. Although the LEA provided some INSET for them, with similarly designated teachers in other schools, clear guidance as to exactly how they were supposed to work was not forthcoming. They, with the headteacher's assistance, were left to interpret their role within rather broad Home Office guidelines. This was especially difficult as they faced pressure from a number of local Afro/Caribbean community workers who complained about lack of consultation, and from a number of staff who were sceptical about the nature of their task. I will describe the limited moves the three teachers had made by the time I completed my field work in chapter 5.

School management and politics

Milltown High had a fairly traditional staff hierarchy headed by David Benyon, three deputies, and three heads of school/year. These staff did not operate in a strongly directive or supervisory way. There was no formal system of staff appraisal in the school and most teachers were permitted a considerable degree of day-to-day autonomy under the wing of their head of department. An atmosphere of what might be called *laissez-faire* professionalism seemed to be the norm. Departments on the whole operated co-operatively and curriculum and pedagogy were collectively negotiated rather than rigidly defined by the head of department.

Major school decisions were generally taken by the 'senior management team' after consultation and discussion with staff. A variety of meetings, both formal and informal, were held at which staff could raise issues of concern or discuss new developments and thus influence decisions, but, despite David Benyon's commitment to a participatory style, they were not actually involved in taking decisions. It was also the case that issues which did not conform to the senior staff's view of the 'way we are going' were not placed on the agenda of meetings. At one head of department meeting, for example, a teacher proposed that the whole issue of mixed ability grouping be considered by the staff as he felt that it was not working well. This was quickly ruled out by a deputy head who explained that mixed ability grouping was part of the whole philosophy of the school and that therefore only the pros and cons of different methods of mixed ability teaching could be debated. Thus David Benyon and the senior staff were the main decision makers and initiators of school policy, and other staff were able to influence the way policies were implemented. Governors too influenced rather than took decisions. As in most schools, although the head was officially responsible to school governors,[5] *de facto* power remained with the head and senior staff. There had been an attempt to involve students more in school politics by establishing school councils which met regularly. These did give students a marginally greater influence and an experience of elections and formal meetings, but they did not give students a part in the actual decision-making system itself.

The development of LEA and school policies on multicultural and anti-racist education

This chapter will first briefly review the history of Milltown LEA's policy on multicultural and anti-racist education. This review relies heavily on the work conducted during the first stage of the Education Team's research by Barry Troyna. As the LEA was developing its policy Milltown High School was also reviewing its approaches and I have attempted to trace the history of the school's engagement with the issue of multicultural and anti-racist education. I will describe why and how the school developed its policy in the late 1970s and early 1980s and examine how this related to what was happening at the LEA level. Hopefully this will provide a context for my description of school practices in later chapters.

As this was a historical exercise I inevitably had to rely for data on the recollections of staff and others involved and on remaining documentary sources. I interviewed several members of staff who had been in the school since the mid-1970s, one of whom had been a member of the school's working party which had conducted a detailed study and debate on multicultural education in the late 1970s. I also interviewed two ex-members of staff who had participated on the working party, the deputy head who chaired it (and later became the school's head), and the headteacher between 1977 and 1982. I also examined various school brochures, policy publications, and the report of the working party.

Policy development in Milltown LEA

Before the mid-1970s Milltown LEA's policy in relation to the growing number of ethnic minority students in its schools was basically assimilationist. Initiatives were mainly designed to ease integration by encouraging such students to become competent in mainstream British culture. However, a number of LEA officers became unhappy with such an approach. They increasingly came to the view that the problem was not so much the deficiencies of minority youngsters themselves, as racial prejudice and discrimination by the 'host' community. This, they felt, should become their main target. Thus, after consultation with local ethnic minority organizations, individuals, and schools, in 1980 the LEA formulated a policy, entitled 'Education for a Multicultural Society'. This stated that all schools should be responsible for educating students for a culturally plural society. The aim was to foster good race relations and reduce racism by encouraging mutual understanding and respect, and to achieve this by valuing and teaching about ethnic minority cultures in school.

Following the publication of this policy, the LEA adopted a number of strategies to encourage its implementation in local schools. An Inspector for Multicultural Education was appointed, a small 'Ethnic Studies Unit' staffed by four 'support teachers' was established, five out of its forty yearly secondments were reserved for staff wishing to learn about multicultural education, discussions on a multi-faith religious education syllabus were initiated,[1] and moves were made to encourage the recruitment of ethnic minority staff. However, when Troyna and Ball (1985) investigated the implementation of the LEA's policy in 1983–4 they found that its impact on local schools had been limited.

Before my work began there had been further developments in LEA policy and other implementation strategies. The LEA began to move towards a more emphatic commitment to anti-racism. In May 1982 the Chief Education Officer wrote to all headteachers asking them to report to the LEA 'serious instances indicative of racial tension' within schools and colleges, to ensure the swift removal of racist graffiti, and prevent the distribution of racist literature within schools or at school gates. This request was reiterated later in letters and circulars to schools. Early in 1985 a short anti-racist policy statement was published. This emphasized the LEA's commitment to 'confront and eradicate racism and its damaging effects', and its expectations that 'all its employees (will) share this determination...and comply with and actively promote' the values of 'equal rights and opportunities, social justice and mutual respect'. Unfortunately, this short statement did not specify what the LEA meant by 'racism', how it and its 'effects' could be identified, 'confronted and eradicated', or in what ways its employees should 'actively promote' the values specified.

In terms of implementation the LEA began to place a much greater emphasis on its policy in discussions with headteachers, and in its priorities for INSET. In October 1982 the Chief Education Officer wrote to heads requesting that schools produce 'after appropriate consultations with staff (teaching and non-teaching, parents, and governors where appropriate), institutional policies on racism'. This, it was felt, would place the issues firmly on the agenda of local schools. The LEA also re-organized and expanded the Ethnic Studies Unit into a more broadly based Equal Opportunities Ethnic Minorities Team.[2] It also provided heads and school governing bodies with a summary of the Swann Report and asked them to consider and produce policies on English and community language provision for ethnic minority students.

Policy development at Milltown High School

The rise of multicultural education

Since its creation in 1967 Milltown High had always catered for a substantial proportion of ethnic minority students. In the late 1960s and early 1970s the school's response, as with the LEA, was based on the principles of assimilationism. The then head was 'a very strong secondary modern-type head, who was trying to do his damn best for the children, but basically trying to make them British' explained John Burgess, the headteacher from 1977 to 1982. The school provided some EFL teaching for those immigrant children who had recently arrived and who lacked fluency in English, but did little else.

However, in the late 1970s the idea of multicultural education became an important area of debate and focus of innovation within the school. Following the appointment of John Burgess as head in 1977, a working party was established under the chairmanship of Michael James, then a deputy head, to tackle the issue of 'what the school needed by virtue of being a multiracial school' (Michael James). The working party met regularly for nearly three years and in all seventeen teachers from various subject areas and positions of responsibility were involved. The group met fortnightly after school and reviewed academic writing, visited and reported on other schools, spoke to members of community groups, interviewed school heads of department, and finally submitted a report containing an outline of their activities, a rationale for multicultural education, and a large number of policy recommendations.

Before considering the achievements of this group I think it is important to consider some of the reasons for the emergence of multicultural education on the school agenda at this time. Young and Connolly (1981), in their study of the development of local authority policies, argued that a key role was played by what they called 'policy entrepreneurs' who were 'the prime movers for change'. However, Troyna (1984) maintained that it is important to put the actions of such individuals in their social and political context in order to fully understand why change of the sort advocated was seen as necessary. In the area of LEA policy making Troyna and Williams (1986) identified a combination of national and local factors which provided the context for the consideration of multicultural education as a policy option (see also Rex, Troyna, and Naguib 1983). These included concerns over the threat to social cohesion from alienated black youth, the 'underachievement' of Afro/Caribbean students and their disproportionate allocation to ESN schools, and the development of supplementary schools. Troyna and Williams argued that policies were largely 'reactive', not deriving from 'pedagogical foresight but... impelled by broader and more immediate political and social considerations'.

At the school level I feel it is important to consider both the role of key 'policy entrepreneurs' and the social context in which they were working. The mid-1970s at Milltown High was a time of relatively rapid staff turnover. Several new young staff, trained in the 'radical' educational and social climate of the late 1960s and early 1970s came to the school. They were attracted by the prospect of working in a new, purpose-built comprehensive school which appeared to offer scope for the development of their educational ideals and their own career advancement. Amongst them were teachers committed to a political philosophy of social change who chose to work in the inner city and working-class comprehensives because they saw it as part of this wider commitment. They were advocates of a liberal/radical educational ideology which stressed change, curriculum development and integration, and a progressive pedagogy (see Grace 1978). They were keen to become involved in discussions about change and in a review of the school's practices, many of which they perceived as 'irrelevant' and 'outmoded'. In fact, they represented an increasingly dominant educational ideology, which developed in the 1960s, in which curriculum and pedagogic review was seen as the way to create a more just and efficient educational system and society.

Whilst some of these teachers had already begun to be influential in the school, the opportunity to become more so came with the arrival of a new headteacher to his first headship in 1977. He believed that to create a 'good' school it was essential for teachers to examine their curriculum to ensure its 'relevance' to the students they taught, and for all practices within the school to be placed under scrutiny and regular review. He initiated a number of working groups to consider a wide range of topics – pastoral care, community education, and staff appraisal were just three. He was also aware of the developing national debate about multicultural education. He realized, he said, that, 'here was a tremendous opportunity to do something and for some very odd reason no-one was doing anything about it'. Michael James as deputy head was also beginning to think along the same lines. He was concerned that Milltown High did 'absolutely nothing' in response to the fact that it was a multi-ethnic school. Moreover, he had a deep and strong concern about the growing problem of racism. Thus the ideas and activities of these teachers, or 'policy entrepreneurs', were very influential in raising the topic of multicultural education in the school in the mid-1970s.

But we also need to consider the context in which these teachers were working. At the school level in many areas young working-class students (especially, though not exclusively, Afro/Caribbean) were posing an increasing threat to order. They were increasingly alienated, less willing to accept their schooling, less willing to defer to the traditional authority of their teachers, and less willing to co-operate with institutional practices (see, for example, Willis 1977). In some schools the resistance of working-class youth provoked a crisis of social control and teachers complained of the 'breakdown of discipline and authority' (see Cox and Boyson 1975). In 1974 Dhondy wrote about what he termed the 'Black Explosion in Schools' and described the rejection of the school system by mounting numbers of young Afro/Caribbean students.

Similar problems were emerging in Milltown secondary schools, notably those in the inner city. As one local teacher put it, 'in some schools it was like sitting on a powder keg. It was just a matter of keeping the lid on.' One local school hit the headlines when a substantial number of Afro/Caribbean students 'rioted', smashing windows and furniture in the school. Whilst Milltown High appears to have avoided such sensational incidents, its teachers faced increasing everyday problems of student resistance, disruption, and truancy. As a result there was what Michael James, who joined the school in 1975 as a deputy, described as:

> A very considerable tension in the school between the black pupils and quite a number of the staff . . . I remember feeling there's quite a lot of simmering tension here, antagonism, and dislike . . . which manifested itself mainly in terms of the older black kids being very highly in evidence in all the disciplinary activities of the school. It seemed to me to be almost constantly the black kids who were up in front of the deputies and the head and other senior teachers as well, digging their toes in against authority.

Some teachers at the time apparently responded with demands to return to more autocratic forms of school discipline and more strictly enforced standards. Others, such as those mentioned above, and the new head, seeing the roots of student alienation and disruption in an irrelevant curriculum, outmoded pedagogy, and inappropriate teacher/student relationships, saw the solution more in terms of school reform, curriculum development, more sensitive methods of handling students, and more informal teacher/student relationships. All this gave added impetus to the consideration of multicultural education as a strategy for reform.

Another important factor was the growing concern nationally and locally about the attainment of Afro/Caribbean students documented by a number of research reports in the 1970s (see Tomlinson 1983 for a review). In 1971 Bernard Coard published his influential pamphlet 'How the West Indian Child is Made Educationally Sub-Normal in the British School System' (which was read by several of the Milltown High staff) in which he argued that the negative portrayal of Afro/Caribbean culture in the school and the negative attitudes of teachers combined to produce a poor self-concept and low self-expectations amongst many Afro/Caribbean children. Locally, a small, but vocal, number of Afro/Caribbean parents were beginning to express their concern about the poor progress of their own children in Milltown schools. This prompted Michael James to conduct his own internal survey of exam results and allocation of different ethnic groups to ability bands in 1977–8 in which he found there was 'in English, Mathematics and Science . . . a clear tendency for West Indian pupils to be placed in lower ability sets and to achieve poorer examination grades than White British pupils' (from the appendix to the working party report). Thus a concern with attainment provided another reason for the consideration of multicultural education.

In the late 1970s a number of local Afro/Caribbean community members were also beginning to ask specific questions about what the school was doing to reflect the backgrounds and cultures of its minority students and this provided a further impetus.

It has been argued that the development of multicultural education was merely a response by the state and the state's representatives in schools to the problems of social order and control which were being presented by black youth (Carby 1982, Mullard 1984). But this argument is too simple. Moves to multicultural education were the result of a number of factors. At Milltown High the problem of growing student disaffection and rebellion was significant, but also important were the ideas of new, 'radical' teachers committed to school reform, curriculum development, and more progressive pedagogy, which they saw as part of broader movement for social change. These teachers were genuinely concerned about the attaiment of their students and their consequent life chances and with the problem of racism in society. Their actions also have to be seen in the context of wider national debate and local pressures. These factors combined placed multicultural education on the school agenda in 1977.

Multicultural education 1977–82

What changes occurred at Milltown High as a result of the school's consideration of multicultural education? This is a difficult question to answer with any certainty as I inevitably had to rely on the retrospective accounts of teachers who were in the school at the time, and the evidence contained in the working party report. Retrospective accounts are inevitably clouded by the passage of time and therefore more open to forms of bias. The working party report was something of a public relations document, circulated to LEA representatives and other schools, and therefore presented a particular view of the school.

However, an examination of this data seems to show that certain changes did occur. First, the teachers on the school working party formulated a definition of multicultural education which provided a basis and rationale for school policy and was a clear move away from an assimilationist philosophy. They proposed that: 'Multicultural education is a whole curriculum which also involves an attitude to life. It aims to promote a positive self image and respect for the attitudes and values of others. Such an education will improve academic attainment.' They agreed with statements from the Bullock Report (DES 1975):

> Attainment is related to language, but especially to cultural identity and cultural knowledge.
> No child should be expected to live as though school and home represent two totally separate and different cultures which have to be kept apart. The curriculum should reflect the many elements of that child's life lived outside the school. Too many multi-racial schools ignore the fact that the community they serve has altered radically over the last 10 years or so.

The teachers maintained that low attainment amongst ethnic minority students derived from poor self-image and lack of cultural identity. Their solution was to bring home culture and school culture more closely into line, thereby enhancing the cultural identity of the minority child and consequently his/her attainment and subsequent life chances.

The teachers also argued that the aim of multicultural education was to prepare all students for life in a multicultural society and 'actively foster good relations, on the basis of mutual respect for different cultures in Britain'. This was to be achieved by the permeation of the school curriculum with information about 'the wide variety of social and ethnic groups' that made up 'contemporary Britain' and the 'global village', and the fostering of values such as 'respect for others' and 'tolerance'.

How were these ideas received and executed by the staff in the school at the time? From the data I gathered it does not appear that the idea of multicultural education was seriously challenged ideologically, at least publicly. Whilst there was some opposition from staff who adopted an 'assimilationist' perspective and from one teacher who took a more 'radical' anti-racist stance, both were rather muted and liberal multiculturalism was accepted fairly uncritically as a basis for school policy by the majority of staff.

The working party conducted its own research on the implementation of multicultural education. Members interviewed each head of department in the school about 'what their department was doing in recognition of the fact that the children they teach come to the school from a great variety of cultural backgrounds'. In their answers several teachers made reference to the aims of promoting 'respect', 'tolerance', 'sensitivity towards others', and 'understanding' of different cultural and ethnic groups, and a positive ethnic 'identity', self-image, and pride in 'blackness'. Most pointed to the fact that their departments were approaching these issues through a reform of their curriculum content. The English department claimed to be buying 'a good deal of literature by and about people from the ethnic minorities', and had begun a course entitled 'Language, Accent, Dialect and Communication'. The Remedial department claimed to have 'destroyed several sets of unacceptable texts and...restructured its booklist'. The Geography department said that they had introduced the 'study of population movements, racial patterns in urban and rural areas, and Third World Studies', the History department themes such as 'the emergent nations of Africa and civil rights issues in the USA and South Africa', and the RE department a multi-faith curriculum. The Languages department had established Spanish as the first language because of 'its cultural significance in parts of the West Indies' and aimed to ensure that 'the cultural values and life styles of the Spaniards and the French are understood whilst the language is being taught'. The Science department had bought work cards that 'illustrate naturally the fact of the multicultural society' and hoped to demonstrate the scientific 'achievements' of different world societies. The Art department said that they encouraged students 'to reflect their view of the local environment' in their work and that inevitably some student work represented 'the black idea', and the Home Economics department said they encouraged the use of 'alternative recipes in order to include as many cultures as possible'.

Clearly most of the departments in the school had considered the issue of multicultural education and had made some efforts to change their curriculum content. For some little reform was felt necessary as their existing approach was believed to be synonymous already with multiculturalism (e.g. the Languages and Music departments). But few departments seemed to have considered the broader implications of multicultural education for things like pedagogy, teacher/student interaction, student grouping, school decision making, etc., beyond a generalized commitment to 'tolerance' and 'respect' in relationships with students.

The working party did present a large number of specific policy recommendations (fifty-nine in all). These included proposals that teachers examine their own attitudes on race and teaching in a multi-ethnic school, increase their awareness of racism and the cultural backgrounds of their students, write multicultural aims into their syllabuses and review curriculum content, and pressure examination boards to adopt multicultural syllabuses. The group also proposed the improvement of school/community/parent links, the development of multi-faith assemblies, and the establishment of more extra-curricular activities 'to allow pupils to express their cultural interests', and called for greater support from the LEA. Clearly they hoped staff would move towards a consideration of the wider implications of multicultural education.

It is difficult to establish whether they did. Certainly several of the staff I interviewed pointed to what they felt were positive changes which had occurred in the school. They claimed that there had been a great improvement in school/community relations and explained that the school had become a base for an annual Afro/Caribbean community event called 'Roots'. A number of cultural extra-curricular activities had also been established. They also pointed to an improvement in the knowledge of and respect shown by staff for the cultures and backgrounds of the children, and therefore in teacher/student relationships. Thus many staff seemed to have moved beyond curriculum reform.

A move to anti-racism?

In the years following the working party report there was little incentive to develop policy further. Milltown's secondary schools were re-organized in 1982 and most teachers were looking anxiously to the future. Moreover, the LEA published its own policy statement in 1980 which contained a commitment to multicultural education and this affirmed and legitimized the approach taken at Milltown High. However, in October 1982 Michael James, the new head, received a letter from the LEA requesting that the school produce, after 'appropriate consultations', an 'institutional policy on racism'.

Michael James responded by asking his new staff early in 1983 if interested teachers would write down ideas they might have for the content of such a policy statement. Eight teachers did. On the basis of these ideas, and his own knowledge of the field, Michael James wrote a school policy statement, briefly discussed it with his senior staff and then took it to his newly formed governing body.[3] They accepted the policy with little discussion and the statement was placed in the staff file. 'Consultation' was therefore limited. There was apparently little staff discussion about the policy or its implications for practice. In fact most staff seemed either indifferent or believed that the statement affirmed their present practice.

Nor was there much discussion about how the policy should be implemented. Michael James, in fact, left the school at the end of 1983, and the question of implementation had to await the arrival of a new head, David Benyon, in April 1984. He modified the policy statement slightly with the help of two governors, but accepted the bulk of its content. In September 1984 he initiated a working party on multicultural and anti-racist education to make 'interim reports, including recommendations for action', by Easter 1985. The working party, however, met only two or three times before the teachers' industrial action forced it to abandon its activities. The question of implementation had remained relatively unexplored when I began my field work in September 1985.

But the school had formulated a policy on anti-racist education. This move was influenced indirectly by moves towards anti-racism nationally and by pressure from local community workers and teachers involved in anti-racist work, but the policy was largely the product of the LEA's request. Without this it is doubtful that it would have been a priority at the time. Few staff felt that it was an issue of burning importance, struggling as they were in the months following re-organization to cope with a new and often difficult school environment. Moreover, 'race relations' within the school were apparently fairly harmonious. It is perhaps understandable that few teachers were interested in becoming involved in the process of policy formulation.

What of the policy itself? How did it differ from the school's previous commitment to multicultural education? There certainly appears to have been a shift in the goals of the policy. Whereas in the past the central concern was the 'promotion of a positive self-image' which would thereby enhance academic attainment, now 'racism' and its elimination had become far more central. The document quotes a statement made by Michael James in November 1981:

Some of us have been made painfully aware of the racism which pollutes the air we breath as surely as does the nicotene the dedicated smoker is forced to inhale. We need to realise its habituation within each one of us. We also need to appreciate that it will multiply through our inactivity.

The policy maintains that:

Racism is a human condition which, with immense political and economic power, is built into the institutions of British Society. Racism springs partly from ignorance, and is fed by the media. Whether personal or institutional, whether intentional or unintentional, the racism in Britain today has to be judged by the individual actions and group practices it produces and has to be countered urgently. Education has a vital role to play in this.

Moreover, it is argued that:

Much British education perpetuates racism and can even be accused of preparing pupils to accept future racism by its own practices (e.g. reliance on culture biased test materials, streaming, etc.). Schools must understand the nature and effects of racism, must examine their institutional practices and must confront, and equip themselves to overcome the racism of all who are associated with the institution.

The policy goes on to provide a number of general prescriptions for action to 'counter racism' and promote a 'dynamic multicultural education'. These include commitments that the school should:

1) consult parents, research workers and community groups...(to)...develop a comprehensive training programme to combat racism.
2) be aware of sex, class and race issues in the pupils' communities.
3) teach what racism, prejudice and discrimination are. The whole curriculum should reflect the school's multicultural and anti-racist policy.
4) promote strategies for combatting racism and evaluate the effectiveness of those strategies.
5) keep all aspects of the curriculum, both overt and hidden, under regular review, and make modifications when necessary.

In addition it makes a number of more specific prescriptions including staff racism awareness training, studies of attempts to change racist attitudes in other schools, the purchase of multicultural and anti-racist resources, an examination of the schools grouping and disciplinary procedures for imbalance, positive images in wall displays, the creation of a course to counter racist presentation in the media, and the serious treatment of racist abuse or assault, and a number of others.

However, the policy, in some respects, remains a rather vague and ill-defined statement. Many of its proposals are general rather than specific and their implications for practice in the school are unclear. The policy contains no definition of racism or of concepts such as 'institutional' and 'unintentional' racism and little specification of the forms racism might take in education. Thus it is not clear exactly what, in education or society, the school aims to eliminate or counter.

Whilst it is argued that education 'perpetuates' and legitimates racism, the statement gives only brief mention of the practices and procedures that are involved. Further, the policy does not explain how teachers might identify and combat such practices. For example, in the item on student grouping, the policy does not tell teachers what might constitute an 'imbalance' in 'setting, banding and disciplinary procedures', or what teachers should do if they find one. Teachers are also asked to 'make modifications' to the 'overt and hidden curriculum ... when necessary', but no guidance is given on when this might be necessary or what modifications might be appropriate.

The policy is also unclear about the form education for non-racism should take in the school. A commitment is made to 'develop a comprehensive programme to combat racism' and to teach 'what racism, prejudice and discrimination are', but the policy does not specify in what area of the school curriculum this teaching should occur, what methods could be used or what difficulties might be anticipated and how they might be overcome. It is not made clear how the 'whole curriculum' should 'reflect the school's multicultural and anti-racist policy'. Again, although the policy hints at a community education aspect, it does not specify how teachers should become 'aware of sex, class and race issues in the pupils' communities' or what they might do when they have become aware.

Finally, the policy says very little about implementation. It contains no timetable for or programme to assess implementation. In fact few clear demands are made of any specified individual in terms of policy implementation. All this, as we shall see, resulted in a rather *ad hoc* approach to multicultural and anti-racist education in the school.

Thus the school had made a significant move in developing a policy on anti-racist education. But the resulting statement was, like the LEA statements, rather vague and offered teachers little concrete guidance on how to carry out the principles of multiculturalism and anti-racism in the school. One might speculate that this lack of specificity was one reason why the policy statement was accepted by staff without controversy.

Conclusion

In this chapter I have tried to reconstruct the way in which teachers at Milltown High have in the past approached the issues of multiculturalism and anti-racism. Their school policy appears to have travelled a similar road to LEA policy, moving from assimilationism, to a consideration of multicultural education, towards a notion of anti-racism. The move to multiculturalism was impelled by similar factors to those influential at LEA level – the arrival in the school of a number of 'policy entrepreneurs' committed to change, the threat to social order presented by Afro/Caribbean youth, the concern with the attainment of Afro/Caribbean students, and the pressure of a vocal minority of parents and community representatives. School policy was also influenced by LEA policy development. However, it would be wrong to see this as a one-way process. In fact 'pioneering' schools like Milltown High, which had put these issues on the agenda, influenced the LEA to move in the same direction. In one sense LEA policy did not initiate change, but merely legitimated changes which were occurring at school level.

Teachers' responses to the school's commitment to multicultural education in the late 1970s and early 1980s appeared mainly to be centred around reform of the formal curriculum. This, it was hoped, would increase the motivation, self-esteem, and therefore achievement of ethnic minority youngsters, and reduce prejudice and hostility amongst others.

Following the LEA secondary re-organization the school began a move towards a stronger commitment to anti-racism, but this was motivated more by the need to comply with LEA requests for a policy statement rather than by burning concerns about racism in the school. Discussion of this change in approach was restricted to a small number of teachers, despite a request from the LEA that the school involve a wider group. The school policy itself emphatically states a commitment to work towards the eradication of racism, but in several respects it is a vague and ill-defined statement which does not specify clearly the implications of anti-racism for school practice.

Chapter four

The headteacher, the school, and multicultural and anti-racist education

Headteachers are not all powerful, but they do have a considerable influence over the organization and ethos of their schools, and, as Troyna and Ball (1983) argue, their attitude and approach is crucial in the translation of policies on multicultural and anti-racist education into practice at the chalk face. In this chapter I want to examine the views of David Benyon, the newly appointed headteacher of Milltown High School, on multicultural and anti-racist education, and describe how they influenced his practice. His views were closely related to his broader educational philosophy and to the changes he was encouraging in the school generally, and so I will place them in this context.

The headteacher and the school

David Benyon was committed to what Stephen Ball (1981) described as an 'egalitarian model' of the comprehensive school. He believed strongly in the principle of equal opportunities and argued that schools should not concentrate their efforts on an academic elite, but develop the abilities of all students. He was opposed to the allocation of students to groups on the basis of ability and emphasized his concern about the labelling, demotivation, and unequal treatment which occurred when this practice was adopted. He favoured more equal relationships between adults and young people. Indeed, it is perhaps significant that he always referred to the children in the school as 'students', a more adult and equal status being implied. He said that he wanted Milltown High to become 'a more relationships-based school' and he hoped staff would adopt a strategy of 'talking things through and discussion' in response to disciplinary problems rather than use formal punishments. He conceded that exam results were important, but he stressed the importance of personal and social development because, 'if you go hell for leather for academic success then there are all kinds of people, kids and staff, who are left by the wayside feeling pretty miserable'. A notion of 'learning rather than teaching' was central to his idea of good educational practice. He favoured the development of skills through 'resource-based learning', the teacher as a facilitator of learning, the integration of subject areas, and student involvement in their learning through discussion and activity, and he believed that such an education could be a force for social change by helping to produce socially and politically aware young people. He was also committed to community education. He felt not only that the school should be available for use by the local community, but also that the school curriculum should reflect community concerns and interests, that education should provide students with the skills to be able to participate in community life, and that people in the community should be consulted about the development of the school.

In terms of his role as headteacher he was attracted by the idea of a head playing an equal role with staff in a democratic system of participatory management as described by John Watts at Countesthorpe College (Watts 1977). Although he felt that this was not completely applicable to Milltown High he did emphasize consultation and discussion with staff, arguing that it was important to involve them as much as possible in the running of the school and the changes that were being introduced. With staff he adopted an egalitarian and informal style and saw himself as 'first among equals', stressing that he and the staff were a team which shared a collective responsibility for the smooth running of the school.

David Benyon aimed to develop Milltown High along these 'progressive' and egalitarian lines and by the time I began my field work he had initiated a number of reforms. First, the system of dividing students into ability bands was abandoned in favour of mixed-ability grouping. Second, in the first year (and later the second year) the teaching of English, Maths, Humanities, Drama, and Social Education was combined to form an Integrated Curriculum taught by one teacher to each class. David Benyon also encouraged third year teachers to meet together to co-ordinate the curriculum content of the main subject areas. A third change was the move from a house system of pastoral care to one based on years and 'schools'. This was related to the creation of the Integrated Curriculum in years one and two and aimed to bring together pastoral and academic systems in these years at least. A fourth reform was the introduction of school councils elected by the students to discuss issues of concern to them. These groups were based on the pastoral 'schools' and met regularly in school time.

During my field work the school also became involved in the LEA's Alternative Curriculum Strategies (ACS) scheme, the LEA's response to the government's 'Lower Attaining Pupils Programme' (see DES 1986). However, David Benyon was concerned that ACS schemes which had been set up in other schools in the city were divisive, merely representing 'sink groups or ROSLA groups' under a new name, and were primarily a means of selecting out groups of troublesome or less-able students. This went very much against his commitment to reducing selection and providing equal opportunities, and so he insisted that Milltown High's scheme attempt to involve all students and search for more motivating curriculum and teaching methods for all.[1]

A less specific, but potentially more wide-ranging change that David Benyon tried to introduce was the development of Milltown High as a 'Community Centred School' involving community education of the type outlined above. However, progress here was rather limited. Milltown High was not the automatic choice of school for many parents in the area. There was already a wealth of local community education provision in the area, and local community education workers were hostile to any moves to impinge on their 'territory'. The LEA, whilst supporting the idea, had no clear policy on what 'Community Centred Schools' ought to look like in practice and thus offered little support. The severe disruption caused by the teachers' industrial action also placed a great strain on school/community relations and meant few consultation meetings could be held.

But despite this David Benyon had under often quite difficult circumstances succeeded in introducing a number of significant changes to the organizational structure of Milltown High. In order to push through these changes he put off any radical democratization of the school's decision-making process because he felt that the changes he wanted could not be achieved with such a system. He chose to abandon (temporarily at least) one reform to use his power to achieve others which he regarded as fundamental. He also used his power over staff appointments and promotions to reinforce changes. During my field work he was able to appoint nine new teachers and to promote, internally, three existing teachers, most of whom were, in David Benyon's words: 'the sorts of people who are most likely to bring about the sorts of changes that we want'. He also devoted a considerable amount of time to INSET and explaining his ideas to teachers, and this role in the 'professional development' of his colleagues he regarded as a central aspect of headship.

However, there were significant constraints on David Benyon's power to achieve the changes he desired. In most secondary schools individual teachers and subject departments enjoy considerable autonomy to decide curriculum and pedagogy. Headteachers may influence, but they cannot control. At Milltown High many teachers felt that David Benyon's ideas on good classroom practice were impractical and did not implement them. Moreover, falling school rolls, the poor academic ability and often behaviour of students, the teachers' industrial action, and declining staff morale all made progressive intiatives difficult to put into practice. In addition David Benyon felt there was an absence of 'a culture of change' in the school, in which reviewing practices and continually up-dating curriculum was the norm. Although there was little ideological opposition to the organizational changes he initiated, some staff were concerned about the disruption of school routine and the effect on classroom control and discipline. In fact many felt that school discipline should be the main priority, rather than the implementation of an innovative educational philosophy, and favoured stabilty rather than change.

As a result David Benyon had to accept that the development of some of the practices he wanted to see was limited. He also held back from some changes, such as expanding the role of class tutors and extending the Integrated Curriculum. He was forced to adopt a more pragmatic approach and to modify his views to fit the reality of Milltown High. This involved, 'being much more authoritarian to both staff and students' than ideally he wanted to be, and operating in a less democratic, more traditional style.[2]

It is in this context that we must view David Benyon's ideas on multicultural and anti-racist education.

The headteacher's approach to multicultural and anti-racist education

On several occasions in staff meetings and in written documents David Benyon made it clear that he wanted to see the school do its utmost to implement LEA and school policies on multicultural and anti-racist education. However, as I have noted already, these policy statements did not provide detailed guidelines for practice. David Benyon agreed. He complained about the lack of specific guidance from the LEA and their rather *laissez-faire* approach to policy implementation. He also suggested that this lack of specificity was a feature of much of the debate surrounding multiculturalism and anti-racism and that many academics too had failed to translate general principles into guidelines for practice at the chalk face. In short, David Benyon felt that the school was very much on its own in attempting to translate policy into practice.

How then did he interpret policies on multicultural and anti-racist education?[3] He saw them generally as part of a commitment to equal rights and equal opportunities or, as he said, 'fair chances for all'. He was concerned that all students no matter what their sex, ethnic group, or social background should receive equal chances to realize their full potential, and that school practices or organization should not inhibit their chances. This influenced strongly his ideas about how the school should be organized. He thought that in a streamed or banded school there might be a tendency for Afro/Caribbean children to be misplaced in lower streams or bands, and thereby suffer inferior treatment and restricted opportunities. This view was influential in his decision to abandon the banding system that existed in the school when he arrived and to go for mixed-ability grouping wherever possible. He explained:

My experience and research indicates that streaming tends to work against working-class and black students . . . and for reasons other than ability children tend to get placed in lower bands or streams . . . I was struck in my first term here taking over a second year Humanities group and people in it like Winston Jones who said 'Am I getting moved up?' and he said quite explicitly, 'By ability I should be in the top band . . . and I know it's because I talk back to teachers . . . and I won't do as I'm told for the sake of it I want to know why'. Now the particular way in which he would ask why would be interpreted by a lot of teachers as being aggressive, whereas he would probably see it within his own cultural mores as being merely assertive and not aggressive . . . Now you always use a bundle of criteria for determining streams so that is one reason that I wanted us to go mixed ability as far as we could . . . because it avoids situations where you are actually discriminating and choosing . . . The more streamed you are, the more rigid you are in that kind of procedure the more likely you are to end up doing things which are racist.

Another reform which David Benyon encouraged, and which derived from the same basic ideas, was the change in the 'Remedial Department' from a department which took students out of mainstream classes and placed them full time in the equivalent of a bottom stream, to one which offered extra support to individual students as far as possible within ordinary classes. The department was renamed 'Learning Support'. This change was of course in line with moves nationally to educate children with 'special needs' alongside 'ordinary' children. Thus David Benyon saw a major aspect of a policy on racism as ensuring that the school organization provided equal access to curricula and resources, and avoided formal status differentiation which might involve unfair discrimination.

He also believed the school should ensure that ethnic minority students enjoyed a 'parity of esteem' with white students. This, he suggested, should come through personal relationships between teachers and students and through the school curriculum. He therefore expected all staff to be 'sensitive to race and gender issues' by which he meant:

To be aware of the gross issues like do I ask more questions of boys than girls or white children than black children, and more sensitive issues than that, like the question of the way students treat each other and who sits where and things like that. If an issue did come up, like a student called another a name, I would hope that every teacher would feel equally confident to lead a discussion on what had just happened.

He also expected staff to ensure that texts and visual resources were 'non-racist and non-sexist', and, where possible, incorporate information about the different cultural groups that made up the school into the curriculum they taught so that there would be, in his words:

A parity of esteem so that the black students feel valued and the white students feel there are things in other cultures that they can value . . . so that other cultures' religions and traditions are understood and valued . . . So it's getting everyone to understand each other . . . and ideally to value and esteem each other.

The aim was to create better understanding and greater tolerance of different cultures and thus reduce racism and improve race and ethnic relations. However, David Benyon believed that this by itself was not enough. He felt a commitment to anti-racism should involve more. He explained:

I've described my idea of multicultural education, but that's rather passive. You know, within our island of this little school we can get everyone who comes here to value each other and do everything we can to help everyone to understand what it means to be Vietnamese or Afro-Caribbean or whatever and to understand and appreciate each other, but you haven't actually tried to do anything about the wide world outside, the world that students actually come from or the wider whole global perspective.

For him anti-racism involved teaching about 'great world issues' such as peace and conflict, inequality, human rights, and race relations, and about issues of concern in the local community. He felt that the school had an important role 'in equipping students with the knowledge and skills necessary for effective community participation'. In short, he viewed anti-racist education as part of a broadly based community and political education. When teaching about such issues he hoped that staff would adopt teaching styles based upon open debate and discussion. He explained:

I've been involved in the teaching of the nuclear issue and although I have very strongly held views I think it is very important to present both views if they are areas of current political controversy . . . and I suppose that if you were teaching about the National Front I think it would be right to actually present 'Well this is what they say' . . . for example, 'black people have taken all the jobs or all the houses', and then look at the figures and say, 'Do the figures justify it?' and if they don't ask, 'Where do feelings like that come from?' . . . which would leave open the possibility that some students would end up feeling 'Yeah, well they're right aren't they'. Appalling though that would be I think if it's education then the way you do it has to leave open that possibility.

And when teaching about South Africa he felt that it was important to present the Afrikaaner view. Not to do so could, he said, 'legitimately be described as indoctrination'. Education was about giving students the opportunity to debate both sides of an issue, think things through and to put themselves in the position of trying to understand the points of view of other people before making up their own minds. The teacher's role was to facilitate this process.

This then was David Benyon's view of multicultural and anti-racist education. However, during my interviews he did point out what he felt were some of the difficulties of putting these ideas into practice and the limitations of what multicultural and anti-racist education could achieve. First, he suggested that racist practices in schools were difficult to identify and thus it was difficult to know if students were being given equal opportunities. For example, in terms of suspensions he speculated:

If the number of black students who are suspended is pro rata double the number of white students, then that is a prima-facie case of racism . . . or there's a case to be examined. If you examined each of those individual cases of suspension you would find that at some point in the history of each of those cases the head of year or deputy head made a decision and what you've got to look at is . . . are there ways in which they behaved in those cases which are different from the way they would have behaved had those students been white? . . . It would come down to a detailed examination of the way particular people behave in each case, and that's very difficult to do.

Second, he felt that it was difficult for schools to provide equal opportunities. Although he thought, on the basis of his experience, that direct teacher racism was rare, he believed that 'there are ways in which schools act to reproduce the basic social relations of society and production' because teachers and schools based their judgements of students on the basis of white, middle-class norms of language and behaviour which inevitably place black and working-class students at a disadvantage. However, he found it difficult to see how such disadvantage could be avoided in a society in which standard English and 'middle-class culture' was the norm. Teachers were faced with a difficult dilemma of valuing the languages and cultures of the students whilst giving them the maximum chance of success in mainstream society. Thus he thought that the school had to make it clear to parents and local people that:

> In terms of conventional achievement, exams and all the rest of it, if students from Crick Park estate are going to have an equal chance with students from Daneford (a middle-class area of the city) they have got to succeed in terms of certain things which are taken as standard and desirable in our society and that includes language. They've got to be good at writing and reading and speaking standard English, and that's not a value judgement on whatever else they may speak . . . So perhaps if all teachers, students and parents were clear that that was something schools were doing, not because teachers were middle class and boring and can't work it out for themselves, but because, look we've got to give you an equal chance of achievement.

David Benyon also thought that schools were limited in the influence they had on the attainment of many students. The achievement of equal opportunities in schools would not by itself rectify the underachievement of many Afro/Caribbean students. There were other factors involved: 'The pressures that students perceive in terms of unemployment, racism in their own lives, their own perceptions of their own chances, their own sense of identity apart from school, are all important.' He suggested that for many Afro/Caribbean students in the area there was a strong 'counter culture' which gave them 'an alternative validation of worth' and meant that some rejected school, saying 'I don't need what school can give me because I've got my own thing going for me!'. So:

> Between these two pressures . . . on the one hand unemployment and racism, and on the other the strength of their own culture and the sense of identity that can give them . . . it may be that the school can do little . . . In some cases the school may have a very marginal influence. So just because some students end up doing worse than their potential doesn't necessarily implicate the school. It might well do but not necessarily.

A further point David Benyon made was that, although he believed that schools should do all in their power to educate against racism, they could not be expected to solve the problem of racial inequality in society:

> Every institution, schools especially in terms of education, should do their very best to combat racism and to fight against racism and

should make sure that their employment practices are scrupulously fair and so on . . . But you can also go on to say that schools are not the cause of the problem and therefore schools cannot be expected to be the solution to the problem . . . Undoubtedly British society is racist, both in the personal experiences of individual black people and it's sexist in the experience of individual women, and in all sorts of intangible ways that you can't put your finger on, in terms of say Halsey's definition of equal opportunities, you know that you do not have proportionately equal numbers of black people or women in the House of Commons or in the Crown Court or wherever and therefore society is racist and sexist.

Moreover, there was also the problem of class inequality with which he felt racial inequality was closely entangled:

Basically I see it as an economic problem and therefore as a class problem not as a race problem . . . in other words most black people in this country are working class and face all the problems that working-class people do in getting fair shares or fair chances and black people have an additional disadvantage, but basically the problems that black people face are not different from the problems most working-class people face.

David Benyon's views on multicultural and anti-racist education very much influenced his ideas on good practice within the school, the type of school organization he developed, and his own day-to-day practice. It is to some examples of his practice that I will now turn.

The headteacher and the practice of multicultural and anti-racist education

Headteachers have a key role in staff appointments. David Benyon thought that the methods he used to appoint new staff would be effective in identifying and sifting out job applicants who might subscribe to racist views. In every job advertisement it was made clear that the school was multi-ethnic, that the existing staff were developing multicultural and anti-racist work, and that this would be given a fairly high priority in the school. Here is one example, an advertisement which appeared for the head of the English department which became vacant towards the end of my field work.

Required for January 1987 to lead the English Department, which is a successful, highly regarded department, and has pioneered anti-racist and anti-sexist teaching strategies. A developing aspect of the role is liaison with the Integrated Curriculum in years one

53

and two. Experience of resource-based learning is important. *Milltown High is a mixed multiracial inner city school. All staff appointed are expected to support and contribute to the development of equal opportunities, anti-racist and community policies*

In the further particulars that were sent to prospective applicants David Benyon wrote the following paragraph:

Milltown High has been closely involved in multicultural and anti-racist education for a number of years . . . More recently we have taken major initiatives in equal opportunities and anti-sexist work . . . We are looking at ways in which all departments can contribute to these whole school policies.

The head argued that such advertisements would put off conscious racists and also those who did not feel that they could handle these sorts of issues. In job interviews he thought that applicants who were of racist disposition would have other views and opinions on educational issues which would reveal themselves. As David Benyon said, 'I would be surprised if someone who had thought through something like resource-based learning and of fairly radical educational views would be racist' – and these were the sort of teachers that he was looking for. Moreover, generally specific questions were asked about a candidate's views on school or departmental policy on multicultural or anti-racist education. In these ways, he maintained, the school managed to appoint staff who were committed to multiculturalism and anti-racism.

David Benyon also tried to ensure equal opportunities in appointments. The local authority developed a code of practice on job recruitment and promotion which was circulated to schools in May 1986. It recommended first analysing a job vacancy to ascertain what was required, and then examining the extent to which ethnic minority people, women, and the disabled were employed in the particular type of work involved, and what might explain any imbalances. Second, it suggested drawing up a 'Job Description' and a 'Person Specification' stating clearly the qualifications and qualities required for the job and ensuring that these were not unnecessarily restrictive. Finally it recommended paying attention to the make up of selection panels so that the potential biases of predominately male, white, and able-bodied panels could be avoided.

Prior to this David Benyon adopted a similar approach.[4] He looked at job descriptions to make sure that what was being asked for did not discriminate against particular groups. He wanted to appoint the 'best' staff to the school and so he considered carefully what qualifications, experience, and qualities were actually required for particular posts. In this he avoided an over-reliance on academic qualifications and length of service and argued that energy, enthusiasm, and commitment were more important. He was prepared to take into account possible background disadvantages which particular candidates, especially those who were from an ethnic minority or female, might have faced during their careers, and to make his judgements on the basis of what contribution he felt the candidate was likely to make to the school. If the candidate was from an ethnic minority this was regarded as an asset, given the small numbers of such staff in the school, but not one of overwhelming importance. Over the two years of his headship the number of ethnic minority teaching and administrative staff had increased from two to six.

An example of his approach was when Susan Parker was appointed internally to the position of deputy head. This was a rather controversial appointment as several other applicants had more experience in senior positions than she did. David Benyon's view was that as a woman she had not achieved the seniority commensurate with her talents. On the basis of 'her energy and ideas' and 'commitment to the school' he felt she was the best candidate for the post and he was influential in securing her appointment. Another example was when an Afro/Caribbean woman was appointed to the non-teaching staff. Several white applicants had excellent academic qualifications, but, after considering carefully the skills required for the job, David Benyon concluded that such qualifications were unnecessary. He felt that the experience, even though it had not been in a school, and the qualities which the Afro/Caribbean woman had, equipped her well for the particular post. In addition, he felt that had she been white and middle class she would probably have been able to achieve academic qualifications comparable to the other candidates, and that, given the nature of Milltown High and the ethnic imbalance amongst the staff, it was a significant opportunity to appoint an ethnic minority staff member.

Another major aspect of a head's role is to set the 'tone' of the school, in other words to make clear to both staff and students the basic norms of behaviour in the school. In his study of Bishop McGregor School, Burgess (1983) showed how the headteacher made clear to staff and students how he wanted them to work and behave. David Benyon fulfilled a similar role, and on the issue of racism his views were made clear to both staff and students. The school's policy on racism was contained in the staff file which was given to all staff at the beginning of each academic year. This made clear that racism was completely unacceptable amongst staff and students. Furthermore the policy stated that:

> Instances of racist or sexist verbal abuse and comment are not to be
> ignored or trivialised, but must be dealt with by appropriate staff as

speedily as possible and in the most positive/educative manner. If the matter is judged to be serious or recurrent it should be reported to the headteacher.

In several assemblies during my field work David Benyon made specific mention of racism. As all staff were expected to attend school assembly the remarks he made can be seen as directed to all members of the school community. Following the first assembly of the 1985–6 school year I recorded the following field notes.

David Benyon began his address by welcoming everyone back after the holidays and welcoming the new first years to their new school. He said that he wanted to talk about what school was for and what was expected of students. He said some people say that they just came to school to get exam results and that yes, exam results were important. He stressed that students could do as well at Milltown High as anywhere. But, he explained, school was not just a matter of getting good exam results. He hoped that the students would learn social skills such as confidence in dealing with other people, and he hoped they would learn personal and family skills, which, he said, were especially important for boys to learn as traditionally schools had only taught those things to girls. He also hoped that they would learn communication skills so that they would be able to cope in the outside world and also if they thought it necessary to be able to do something about the world that they lived in, for example by organizing petitions and campaigns. Finally, he explained that he thought it was important that students build up their knowledge of the world and referred to the current situation in Southern Africa and the recent troubles in Handsworth as being worthy of study.

David Benyon then went on to talk about some of the expectations that he had of students. He said they should work hard, do their best, and behave reasonably, meaning that they should treat others in the way they would like to be treated by them. He went on to remind the students of some of the school rules. He also said that serious disciplinary offences such as physical assaults on staff and bullying would be dealt with by suspension or exclusion. In the category of serious offences he included racism and he said that any abuse of a racist nature whether it involved black students or white students would be treated very seriously. He was, he said, especially concerned with racism directed against Asian students, between black students, and from students to staff. He also made it clear that he was concerned with sexism. Finally he explained some of the problems that he thought would occur during the year because of the teachers' industrial action and that he hoped everyone would respond to them sensibly and maturely, and he introduced new staff and explained to students that he expected them to be treated with respect and for students to help them out where they could and not to take advantage of them.

The value of anti-racism at Milltown High was also emphasized by the quite harsh punishment of any student who used racist remarks or abuse. During my field work a number of students were suspended or sent home because of such incidents. This seemed to shock some of them as they regarded such abuse as a normal part of peer group banter. However, David Benyon maintained that it was important to communicate that 'it's a legitimate issue and that certain types of language and behaviour are totally unacceptable'. Another example of this was the way David Benyon dealt with an incident involving some graffiti written about an Afro/Caribbean member of staff. When it was discovered he spent a lot of time interviewing all the children that could have been responsible. In fact the culprit was not discovered, but the fact that it was investigated seriously communicated a clear message to students.

David Benyon also used assemblies to directly transmit knowledge about issues that he felt were important and to make clear his own values and beliefs. During the year South Africa was much in the news and this was the topic for one assembly that David Benyon took which I recorded in my field notes.

David Benyon explained to the students that he wanted to talk to them today about South Africa as there was a special campaign being organized this week. He explained that it was a rich country, but that it was mostly white people who were rich. It was also a country that claimed to be a democracy but it was peculiar because only white people could vote, whereas in Britain everybody could vote. Another reason why South Africa was special, he explained, was that there were laws affecting people – affecting where they could go and where they could live and work – which depended on the colour of a person's skin. Black and white people were very unequal. Black people only owned 13 per cent of the country whereas white people owned 87 per cent of the country. This was an incredibly unfair situation. So, David Benyon asked, what could we in this country do about it? He said, the government could refuse to buy from or sell to South Africa and some big organizations like the Co-op were doing just that. He then told the students about a strike of shop workers in Ireland. A group of women who worked in a shop on the checkouts decided not to pass South African goods. They were sacked, but went on strike and

picketed in support of their view that the shop should not sell South
African goods. The effect of their action has been that many more
shops have stopped selling South African goods. As individuals,
David Benyon went on, we could stop buying things like South
African fruit, Outspan oranges for example. This was only a small
thing but it started people talking. He asked the students to think
about it and said perhaps they could do something however small.
David Benyon then left the hall and the students were dismissed by
Susan Parker, the deputy head.

Another example of the way David Benyon's running of the school was
influenced by anti-racism was the way he handled the issue of police
involvement in the school, a topic which came to the forefront of his
attention during 1985. The powers and accountability of the police were
the subject of intense debate both locally and nationally at this time.
Moreover, relationships between many local people and the police had
been strained since the disturbances in 1981, and some teachers and
community workers were increasingly concerned about the racial
attitudes of local police officers. During David Benyon's headship a
number of incidents had occurred in the school which necessitated
decisions about police involvement. First, two boys smashed a number
of windows. Police were involved, but the school was criticized by local
community members for the methods used and this served to highlight
the sensitivity of school/police contact. Later two students were
assaulted on the school premises and others were involved in a street
fight with students from another school. This raised the question of
whether the school should immediately call the police in such cases or
whether liaison with local community workers might be more
appropriate. A number of staff also raised questions about the
educational role of the police and the aims and nature of school/police
liaison. David Benyon felt that such issues required discussion and
resolution, and he wanted to involve a broad group in this process. So he
decided to set up a school/community/LEA working party and
circulated a letter to staff, governors, the LEA, the local police
monitoring unit, and various parents groups, community
representatives, and councillors outlining his ideas. The letter included
the following statement:

Involvement of the police in the life of the school is an issue which
needs sensitive handling in any school. This is particularly true in
an area like Chesham and Richmond Hill, where many people feel
the police to be part of the problem not part of the solution to their
problem.

A working group, consisting of about twenty members from all the groups circulated (a small number of fifth year students also took part), was subsequently formed and, at the time of writing, had held a number of meetings. Thus David Benyon, with the support of his staff, had entered into a process of consultation on an issue of school policy related closely to the issue of anti-racism. The way this issue was handled must be seen as an example of the way in which he put school policy into practice.

There were a number of other ways in which David Benyon tried to put his ideas about multicultural and anti-racist education into practice. First, in his own dealings with children he always tried to be scrupulously fair. He was always willing to listen and receive the points of view of students, to hear their complaints and concerns. In disciplinary situations students were always given the opportunity to present their perspective, and David Benyon tried to visit the meetings of the school councils as often as he could, not to dominate or set the agenda for the meetings (cf. Hunter 1979), but to hear students' opinions and to answer their questions. He also adopted a self-reflective stance towards his own practice – 'I do try to think carefully about my own preconceptions and how they might affect the way I deal with students', he said. He also supported the activities of other members of staff who wanted to develop their work on multicultural and anti-racist lines or to run special events which might make a contribution in this area. For example, he made it clear in various policy documents that whole school policies such as multicultural and anti-racist education were a priority in the development of the school, he encouraged staff to attend INSET sessions, book and resources displays, and meetings of local anti-racist groups, and he welcomed and provided time for various special events which staff organized such as an Asian Festival in the Autumn term of 1985 and an anti-apartheid week in the Summer term of 1986.

When planning the allocation of school capitation in the summer of 1986 he decided to retain 10 per cent of the allowances that went to each of the main departments. The departments were allowed to have the money on condition that they spent it on materials or activities which contributed to the development of whole school policies. This was not, however, an action that was greeted with much enthusiasm by the heads of department concerned. One likened it to the Conservative government's attempt to exercise greater control over local authorities by rate capping, others objected because they already felt that they were using their resources in this way and were being unduly penalized and asked to do unnecessary extra administrative work. However, David Benyon's action was an indication of the fact that he considered such policies to be of importance.

David Benyon did, however, concede that there were several constraints on his efforts to implement policy on multicultural and anti-racist education. These were similar to those that limited his efforts to reform school organization. He emphasized the problem of time especially in a year disrupted by teacher industrial action. He explained that, because of pressing matters which arose from the day-to-day running of the school, the review of the school's policy had not become a priority and a system to monitor the implementation of policy or to assess its efficacy had not been developed.

Despite this he felt that school policy had been effective in many ways. There were some staff who were doing a lot and the policy had helped to 'shape their consciousness about what needed to be done'. And he said:

> As far as I can gather the idea of parity of esteem does seem a reality . . . It's ever so hard to judge, but I do think that on the whole black students feel that they are equal members of the school community and the school cares for them as much as it does for white students.

But he emphasized that this assessment was largely based upon intuition and conceded 'that's not good enough. We ought to be making time to assess our progress at least once a year.'

Conclusion

To summarize, in this chapter I have tried to show how David Benyon interpreted multicultural and anti-racist education, how this related to his wider ideas about how the school should be organized, and how he attempted to put his interpretations into practice. He was committed to multicultural and anti-racist education as part of a wider approach to education which might be loosely labelled 'egalitarian' and 'progressive' (see Troyna 1985). He saw it as a whole school reform which had implications for school structure and organization, teacher/student relations, school/community relations, and the curriculum. It meant commitment to equal opportunities in the school, a 'parity of esteem' for black and white students, and teaching about social and political issues of local, national, and world importance. It was also part of his wider commitment to the development of a child-centred pedagogy, a breaking down of traditional subject barriers, a lessening of differentiation within the school, more egalitarian teacher/pupil relationships, and a more consultative style of school management.

David Benyon's commitment to multicultural and anti-racist education was shown in his practice in several ways. First, he attempted to ensure that the teachers he appointed were not racist and supported the school's policy. It would have been difficult for a teacher who did not express support for the policy to secure a position at the school. Second, he tried to make sure that the appointment procedures at Milltown High were free from racial or cultural bias so that ethnic minority applicants would receive equal opportunities and appointment on merit. He also did not accept the traditional notion that seniority, qualifications, and experience were necessarily the best indicators of merit. Ideas, enthusiasm, energy, and commitment to his sort of educational philosophy counted highly. He took a flexible and adventurous view, and was prepared to take into account that an ethnic minority or a female candidate may have in the past suffered disadvantages which meant that they were less likely to have a high standard of formal qualifications, seniority, and experience. He also argued that, all other things being equal, being from an ethnic minority would be a positive attribute for a person seeking appointment to the school.

David Benyon had also made non-racism a clear norm of behaviour in the school. Judging from my interviews with students and my own observations around the school this communication was clearly received by the staff and the majority of students. He also used his position to teach more specifically about race-related issues in assemblies, and had begun to make moves toward involving parents and members of the local community more fully in the development of school policy by initiating a working party on police involvement in the school.

Chapter five

Teacher response to school and LEA policies on multicultural and anti-racist education

This chapter will examine how teachers at Milltown High interpreted and responded to school and LEA policies on multicultural and anti-racist education. In researching this question I took the view that any study of educational innovation must centre on the perceptions of practitioners at the chalk face, as clearly they determine the reality of that innovation. I was interested in how individual teachers and groups (e.g. subject departments) responded to the basic idea of LEA and school policy, how they interpreted the content of such policies, and how their views and interpretations influenced their practice and their departmental and pastoral arrangements. I conducted semi-structured interviews with thirty-two of the teachers to explore these questions. Most of the interviews were tape-recorded and lasted between half an hour and one hour.

Teachers' general attitudes to policies on multicultural and anti-racist education

Whilst some teachers confessed an ignorance of specific policy details, nearly all said they were in favour of the basic commitment of LEA and school policies to multiculturalism and anti-racism. Most argued that British society was multicultural and the school should reflect this fact.

Only one teacher was opposed to this. A Craft teacher, his view was very much in the assimilationist mould. He explained that he was in sympathy with Ray Honeyford, and was opposed to ethnic minority groups 'dictating what should be taught in schools'. He believed that ethnic minorities should 'adjust to the British way of life' and schools should not orientate their teaching to minority cultures. He felt multicultural and anti-racist policies were being given a priority in the LEA and schools at the expense of 'things like discipline and behaviour'.

A number of teachers sympathized with this last point. Although they basically supported the principle of multicultural and anti-racist education, they argued that such policies were given too high a priority. They said that Milltown High faced far more pressing and urgent problems, such as a 'breakdown in school discipline', 'ineffective management', and 'the introduction of things like GCSE, the Alternative Curriculum, and the Integrated Curriculum'. A small number of others spoke of their concern at what they saw as the possible 'intrusion' of the LEA into areas that should be reserved for 'the professional judgement of teachers' especially if policy statements prescribed what should be taught or how it should be taught. Some were also concerned that the LEA was making policy statements without any real appreciation of the difficult working situation in many schools. One teacher argued that schools were being expected to solve problems (i.e. racism and racial inequality) which originated in the social structure of British society and which were beyond the power of schools to deal with.

Other teachers complained that the content of policy statements was too vague and what was needed was more precise guidance from the LEA and senior school staff about what they should actually be doing to implement the policies. Some of the more committed teachers were concerned about the lack of time and thought given by the LEA to the problems of implementation, arguing that unless more in-service training and time for discussion were given the policies would remain largely 'tokens' and ignored by most staff. Despite these concerns the majority of staff I interviewed had positive attitudes to policies on multicultural and anti-racist education.

Interpretations of multicultural and anti-racist education

A large majority of teachers regarded the aim of multicultural and anti-racist education as the promotion of 'tolerance' of and 'respect' for cultural differences, better race relations and 'a more harmonious society'. They were in favour of the teaching about a variety of 'cultures' in school, especially those that made up the school's catchment area, and attempting to promote an awareness of and positive attitudes to cultural differences. Most accepted that it was part of their responsibility to challenge racist attitudes amongst the students when they were displayed, although some explained that this could sometimes be difficult in the hurly-burly of classroom interaction. Several also maintained that it was important that the school take account of and be sensitive towards the ethnic backgrounds of the students. The following comments were typical of their views:

> For me multicultural education should be nation-wide. It should involve studying all cultures and learning about all races . . . To

63

achieve understanding between groups, and between nations. (Science teacher)

You have to meet the needs of the pupils you have got and if they come from a variety of cultural backgrounds then you must take on board as much information as you can get from your students and help them acquire the confidence to achieve and if that means you have to do a certain amount of research and finding out what things you don't know about their cultural background then that's your responsibility as a teacher. (Learning Support teacher)

It's all about understanding, tolerance, understanding other peoples' viewpoints and feelings . . . It helps us run a more harmonious, more peaceful school . . . and hopefully this will rub off outside. (Deputy head)

Anti-racist education means dealing with attitudes around the school. Like when the kids say things to each other . . . It's building up the right attitudes in the kids and respecting each other, just having equal respect for people with different cultures. (Domestic Science teacher)

Racism goes on between all races. There's always one group of people jealous of another and that's what I find wrong . . . .I would like to work to combat that. To promote harmony between all people and nations. (Science teacher)

Whilst in favour of including information about different cultures in the school curriculum some of these teachers were sceptical of directly teaching about racism. A head of year who taught mainly social education, for example, argued that: 'the anti-racist thing can be a bit overdone', and that students could become bored. He also felt that too much teaching about racism could cause them to see differences and conflicts in their relationships with white peers and teachers where none existed before. He did not think that teaching about racism was very effective but argued that:

Living it rather than teaching it has a far better and a more long-lasting effect. If you can rub shoulders with kids from other ethnic groups then you're far more likely to think of that particular child in the future as you knew them as you were growing up . . . and I think that will have a far bigger influence on you, than some teacher sitting and chatting about it or whatever.

A minority of teachers, mainly in the English and Integrated Curriculum departments, but including the head of the Science department, had rather different views. Whilst accepting many of the fundamental principles of multicultural education – respect for and valuing of student cultures, education about different cultures, the promotion of tolerance and respect in social relationships – they distanced themselves from what they saw as 'the steel bands, saris, and samosas' approach, which 'smacks of tokenism' (Integrated Curriculum teacher) and 'reeks of people being patronizing and doing good' (Learning Support teacher). For them multicultural and anti-racist education had more 'radical' objectives. They favoured directly teaching about and against racism and saw this as part of a political education, through which students could come to a greater understanding of the social and political world and acquire the knowledge and skills to possibly change that world. It thus involved developing the social and political content of the curriculum they taught and teaching styles which emphasized political discussion and debate. A few of these teachers put forward the view that multicultural and anti-racist education also had implications for the relationship between parents and school. They were in favour of a much 'closer' relationship between parents and the school, and a broader role for class tutors in liaising with parents. I will describe the views of some of these teachers in more detail in the next chapter on the English department, but the following quotations illustrate some of their ideas:

> We need to say to ourselves what are our aims through multicultural education. Is it just to let people know of other cultures and then so what. What about if they know and they still behave and act in an oppressive way . . . With anti-racist education we need to consider the fact that we are a racist society and actually begin to say that in a classroom context. Rather than to say let's get to know each other better. I obviously appreciate that getting to know different cultures is of paramount importance, but if it doesn't actually lead anywhere . . . You're not actually challenging the racism. Now that's very difficult to do, but you begin by saying we are racist and you move on from that statement. (Integrated Curriculum teacher)

> Anti-racist education is making them aware of the racist attitudes that they have and society has, and the way society is actually geared and how it works. (Drama teacher)

> I think anti-racism is basically a political movement which I endorse. It should raise questions about power and wealth, and how they are distributed, as well as about race . . . I do think that schools have to take up the anti-racist thing a bit sharper . . . It seems that societies that are racist are particularly evil, and societies do have a tendency to drift towards that much more often than you would think. (Science teacher)

Most of the teachers I interviewed agreed that multicultural and anti-racist education involved a commitment to eliminate or avoid racism in education and thus ensure that students from all ethnic groups enjoyed equal opportunities. However, they tended to point to different manifestations of 'racism' and so there were differences and uncertainties about what was to be eliminated or avoided. Bias in curriculum content and teaching materials was mentioned most frequently. The curriculum of many schools, they felt, still did not reflect the fact that Britain was a multi-ethnic society. This meant that ethnic minority students were disadvantaged because 'the curriculum does not relate to their backgrounds and recognize the validity of their cultures' (Science teacher), and in all-white schools nothing was done to familiarize students with ethnic minority cultural forms and therefore to 'change attitudes'. Several teachers broadened this view, and explained that they felt that often ethnic minority cultures were ignored or deprecated by the 'normal' working of schools. An English teacher explained that in the past at Milltown High, 'you used to have black girls with beads in their hair put out of lessons, and everything was negative. They were told that they must not talk in "pidgin" English', and she thought this still happened in some schools. About a third of the teachers I interviewed argued that there could be teachers in schools who held racist views and that this would inevitably influence their work with ethnic minority students. Two teachers described other multi-ethnic schools that they had worked in where a minority of teachers voiced derogatory views about ethnic minorities. A small number of staff believed that all white teachers were inevitably racist as a result of their 'mono-cultural' upbringing and education. They argued that teachers could be 'unconsciously racist', perhaps thereby inadvertently favouring or forming closer relationships with white students.

A few teachers argued that broader institutional practices and the workings of the educational system were racist. An English teacher believed that the unequal outcomes of the educational system were a clear indication of this, even though she conceded that part of the explanation lay outside the educational system itself. Another English teacher suggested that institutions that were dominated and run by white people in a society which was multi-ethnic were racist, as ethnic minority people were denied access to power over important decisions which affected the lives of their children, and also that students were deprived of ethnic minority role models. A Humanities teacher pointed out that assessments made in education were largely based on 'white, middle-class values' which he thought disadvantaged ethnic minority students. A Science teacher argued that Afro/Caribbean students were often less conformist than white and that this meant teachers were more likely to judge them unfavourably. A head of school/year, thought the education system as a whole disadvantaged ethnic minority youngsters as he felt they received inferior educational provision because the inner city schools they attended were less effective.

Thus many of the teachers at Milltown High recognized the possiblity of racism in some form in education, although there was a diversity of view on its form. In terms of combatting racism nearly all the teachers I talked to felt that bias in curriculum content had been eliminated at Milltown High. Most also thought that teacher attitudes to and relationships with students were non-racist. Some felt that the school's policy commitment had been significant here in increasing their awareness of and helping them to guard against the possibility of racism. Several teachers explained how they monitored their own practice and made particular efforts to be fair and equal in their relationships with students. However, others said that non-racism was fundamental to their central values as teachers anyway. It was, they claimed, synonymous with good professional practice which hinged around the values of individualism and universalism, and involved treating students as individuals, avoiding racial or ethnic stereotyping, and assessing students on 'merit'. As such, policy developments had not precipitated any review or change in their practice.

There was some disagreement here about whether staff should adopt a policy of 'treating all students the same'. Those who advocated this view emphasized a non-racist, 'colour blind' approach in which common standards applied to all. Others opposed this and argued that teachers should be aware of individual and cultural differences and make positive efforts to value the cultures of ethnic minority students. On further probing it appeared that the two views had much common ground. Both aimed for a sensitive handling of teacher/student relationships based upon non-racist expectations and standards. Often those who advocated the latter view taught in curriculum areas, such as English and Humanities, where positive efforts could fairly easily be made to incorporate ethnic minority perspectives. Those who put forward the former view generally taught subjects like Maths, Science, and Craft where it was less easy to do so. The disagreement did, however, engender some confusion.

Those teachers who pointed to forms of racism in broader institutional practices and the education system as a whole were less confident about combatting them. They were uncertain about the implications of these forms of racism for their practice as individual teachers. They saw many of them as bound up with the basic workings of the education system and inequalities in society and as such beyond their influence.

A small number of the teachers I interviewed had rather different views on combatting racism in education. They felt that the existence of racism in the educational system was much exaggerated and were resentful at the implication contained in policy statements that they or their practices were or might be racist and in need of review and change. They viewed this aspect of LEA and school policies with some cynicism and hostility as a result. They were sceptical about the existence of racist attitudes amongst teachers and questioned the idea that 'hidden' or 'unconscious racism' was a significant factor in relationships with ethnic minority students. They also did not accept that any of the normal workings of the school might operate to the disadvantage of ethnic minority students. In fact they were sceptical of policies which they saw as premised on the existence of racism in school practices, but which failed to specify the nature of that racism.

To summarize, most teachers at Milltown High had favourable attitudes to multicultural and anti-racist education. They agreed that the school should attempt to promote tolerance and harmony in a multicultural society by transmitting knowledge about a variety of cultures in the school curriculum and checking the racial attitudes of students. Some teachers went further and saw multicultural and anti-racist education as part of a broader commitment to political education. Most teachers also accepted a commitment to combat racism in education, but held a variety of views about what this meant and what could be achieved. A minority of teachers thought this commitment unnecessary as they believed there was little evidence of racism in education. This disagreement is perhaps unsurprising given the complexity of this issue and the ill-defined nature of policy statements.

The practice of multicultural and anti-racist education

LEA and school policies gave teachers little specific guidance as to how to incorporate multicultural and anti-racist education into their individual and departmental practices. Teachers at Milltown High were largely left to make their own decisions. What then did they feel they did which represented a 'multicultural' or 'anti-racist' approach? The next two chapters, which consist of case studies of the English and the Humanities departments, will address this question in more detail. I will confine myself here to a more general account of teachers' practice. Most teachers responded to this question by first maintaining that they operated in a non-racist way in the classroom. In terms of specific multicultural and anti-racist curriculum and teaching practice they very much varied according to subject.

Teachers in the Maths, CDT, and Business Studies/Typing departments said that they did very little that could be construed as 'multicultural or anti-racist' beyond checking the text books and materials they used were free from any racist content. They argued that because their subjects were essentially concerned with 'culture-free' skills and concepts then there was little they could do. Their conceptions of their subjects ruled out 'teaching about other cultures' or 'debating social issues'. However, the head of the Maths department did describe how he sometimes taught about Islamic tessellations, and a project he was doing with one group of students which involved using a computer data base containing information on inequality between the developed and developing world. 'Depending on your definition', he said, 'you could say I'm doing anti-racist maths, but I must admit that I'm interested in the statistics and the mathematical skills that are coming out of it primarily.'

The majority of the teachers in the Science department also said they did little in practice that represented multicultural or anti-racist education, beyond 'colouring in faces on worksheets black', for broadly similar reasons. But the head of Science was very interested in the whole area. He explained how he had hoped to develop the Science curriculum around the study of social and historical themes with the emphasis on the view that science is 'non-elitist' and scientific knowledge is the product of many different cultures. He was attempting to modify the 'subject paradigm' (Ball and Lacey 1980) of Science toward an approach which concentrated on the social aspects of the subject. He had made a start and had written a third year, half-term course unit which was called 'The Seeds of History'. He hoped this provided teaching materials which were 'non-elitist, multi-cultural, anti-racist, anti-sexist, and environmentally conscious'. It consisted of a series of lessons and experiments based on some of the major scientific discoveries – farming, pottery, and metal smelting – which it is suggested probably were made by ordinary people in what we now call the Third World.

The head of the Art department was sceptical about some multicultural and anti-racist approaches in his subject. Hargreaves (1983) has observed that most Art teachers concentrate on the practical teaching of skills and visual awareness, rather than transmitting knowledge about the history of art or its relationship with culture. This was very much the view of the Art teachers at Milltown High. The head of Art explained that he had not got the time or resources to teach the history of Art or comparative Art, and anyway he did not really see Art education in these terms. He believed Art shoud be taught as 'a way of looking' and as 'the development of skills' and he distanced himself from Art teachers 'who would prefer culture to be the starting point in the classroom'. However, he did maintain that his approach to Art was multicultural in the sense that students were encouraged to represent their environment and perspectives in their artwork.

The Home Economics teachers pointed to the difficulties of integrating multicultural and anti-racist approaches into their subject.

Their approach was more orientated to the development of practical skills, hygiene, and notions of 'healthy eating'. They explained that many of the students preferred to cook 'westernized' food in school, and despite the fact that their subject inspector had encouraged them to introduce 'more than token gestures' they found it difficult to go beyond the occasional demonstration of food from different cultures.

Although these teachers did see aspects of their practice as multicultural and anti-racist their main objectives lay in the development of skills and knowledge which they saw as largely unconnected with issues of culture or race relations. These topics they thought should be the domain of other subject specialists. This parallels the findings of Troyna and Ball (1985) that teachers of English, History, Social Studies, Humanities, were more likely than Science or Creative Arts teachers to integrate multicultural education into their work.

What then of the teachers in these subject areas? The Modern Language teachers said that they were most interested in teaching linguistic skills, but maintained that teaching a language was in itself multicultural and anti-racist education because it involved teaching about another culture. The head of department said, 'We do quite a lot to encourage positive attitudes, by the mere fact that if you teach a language you can't divorce that from culture and you try to teach a tolerance of that culture.' As we shall see in the next chapter notions of multicultural and anti-racist education were heavily integrated into the work of the English department. They believed that an anti-racist approach influenced the way they related to students and they tried to adopt a 'child-centred' approach to pedagogy, based around discussion and creative writing. They deliberately selected a literature curriculum which they felt reflected the backgrounds and concerns of their students and which would raise controversial political and social issues for consideration. In the following chapter I shall describe some of the work of the Humanities teachers, who, whilst less influenced by the idea of anti-racist education, taught a curriculum which they felt represented a multicultural approach in that it reflected the backgrounds and histories of the students who attended Milltown High and drew its content from a variety of different world societies.

The teachers in the newly founded Integrated Curriculum department also claimed to have taken on board multicultural and anti-racist education. 'I think it runs through our whole approach, our choice of topics, our choice of books. It's at the back of our minds in everything that we do', said one of the teachers. They advocated a similar 'child-centred' approach to pedagogy as the English teachers, and the principle that all students should be considered of 'equal worth' and be given 'equal opportunities'. They described to me how in planning their new curriculum they deliberately sought out materials which would reflect the backgrounds and interests of the students and rejected those they felt had racist connotations or images associated with them. They had decided to use the 'World Studies 8–13' course (Fisher and Hicks 1985), a Humanities curriculum development project sponsored by the School's Council and the Rowntree Trust. This project attempts to 'promote the knowledge, attitudes and skills that are relevant to living responsibly in a multicultural and interdependent world' (Fisher and Hicks 1985) and encourages the study of different cultures and societies and major issues such as 'peace and conflict, development, human rights and the environment', through the use of 'active teaching methods'. In the second year of the Integrated Curriculum they were planning to adopt Jerome Bruner's 'Man: A Course of Study' (1968) which adopted a similar approach to the study of cultures and societies. They described how they had developed multicultural work on the topic of 'Festivals' in the first year of the course, which involved the students studying this idea from the point of view of several ethnic groups, and how they were working to increase students' awareness of apartheid in South Africa during the local authority's anti-apartheid week. They hoped to be able to slowly increase the political knowledge and awareness of their young students (only first year students at the time) by discussing with them current events and relating these to their own experiences.

The teacher of Drama also regarded multiculturalism and anti-racism as central to her work. She felt that Drama was 'one of the easiest ways of dealing with issues and problems and things about relationships'. She explained that usually she developed students' work from issues that arose or that concerned them, and that quite often this involved dealing with issues of race relations and racism. She generally employed 'improvization' techniques, and used the plays that students constructed to lead discussions about social situations and questions of controversy. Sometimes she would deliberately set up a role play exercise or a simulation in order to explore a particular issue, racism being one. For example, she described how she would ask students to role play a situation based around a mixed race boy/girl relationship, and how she set up a simulation based on a mixed race housing estate.

These then were the main examples of multicultural and anti-racist curriculum and teaching at Milltown High.[1]

Other multicultural and anti-racist initiatives

During my field work there were several other developments and events at Milltown High which were of significance to the area of multicultural and anti-racist education. First there were two 'special events' organized by staff during the year. The first of these was called an 'Asian Festival' which took place during the Autumn term of 1985. It was mainly organized by one of the school's 'Community teachers'. Her aim was to give local Asian people an opportunity to talk to students and staff about their culture and lives in Britain. She felt that, because of the preponderance of Afro/Caribbean students at Milltown High, Asian culture was rather neglected, and students often had negative attitudes to Asian people. Various events were organized over a week. They included talks on Asian religions, languages, and history given by a number of local Asian people, films about Asian people in Britain, demonstrations of music and cooking, and displays of books, photographs, costumes, paintings, and artefacts. Students from different classes took part in the festival at various times during the week.

A second event took place in the summer term of 1986. This was an anti-apartheid week which was sponsored by the local authority. A number of special events were organized by several teachers in the school and some students went out to take part in activities in other parts of the city. In the school David Benyon talked about apartheid in assembly, a bus with photographic displays and a video about South Africa was in the school playground for most of the week, and a number of speakers who had experiences or knowledge of South Africa came into the school to talk to small groups of students. For both these special events teachers in the Integrated Curriculum and English departments, who displayed the strongest commitment to multicultural and anti-racist education, were most involved.

Another development was the introduction of a short course in 'Black Studies' as part of the school's Alternative Curriculum. This was not a course put on especially for ethnic minority students who were turned off school. It formed part of the fourth year ACS which all students took for part of the week. The aim of the whole scheme in the fourth year was to introduce a number of different courses, which would include new curriculum and 'alternative' teaching styles, with the emphasis on greater student participation and more 'active' learning, for all students. The two teachers in charge had attempted to get as many people from the local community involved in teaching these courses as possible, so that class sizes could be small and a wider range of teaching skills could be drawn upon. A local 'Black Studies group', consisting mainly of Afro/Caribbean people involved in the local community, offered to take one of these courses. Their course centred around the histories and present situations of ethnic minority people in Britain and the teachers utilized a variety of different teaching methods from books to role plays. Unfortunately I was unable to observe these lessons. As the course and the teachers were new to the school, they were, perhaps understandably, unwilling to have me sit in on the lessons. The important point to note, however, is that this course took place thanks largely to the efforts of the organizing teachers and their willingness to introduce new approaches and involve local people.

A further development, which I have already partly described (see chapter 2), was the specific designation of three members of staff as 'Section 11' teachers. At the end of my field work these teachers had completed one term in their new positions. All three teachers had been initially keen to explore a new role, but by the end of their first term were uneasy because of the lack of a clearly defined job description and the unusual situations they were placed in. They were expected to provide for the needs of 'Commonwealth immigrants' and their children. In the case of some Asian students needs are often clear – English language tuition. But Milltown High had few such students. Although many of the school's students were of Commonwealth immigrant origin most were Afro/Caribbean. Their needs were more difficult to establish. For this reason much of the time of the three teachers in their first term was taken up with finding out where problems lay and where they could be of help. One teacher conducted a survey of staff to explore areas of need, but found that most of the teachers did not single out 'Commonwealth immigrant' students in this way. Most maintained that all the students had important 'needs', especially in language and writing skills. The teachers wanted general classroom assistance rather than specific help with 'Commonwealth immigrant' students. Another teacher explored the issue of Afro/Caribbean dialects, and whether these might be sources of special need, with local support teachers and the 'Caribbean English Project' in the nearby community education centre. The other began tentatively a process of consultation about the role of Section 11 teachers with ethnic minority groups in the local area. The results of such discussions were, however, rather inconclusive.

One of the stipulations of the new Section 11 role was that the teachers were not to teach mainstream classes. They were to act in an advisory capacity or to give assistance in the classroom. The three teachers at Milltown High over their first term attempted to broaden their own knowledge of multicultural and anti-racist education, of appropriate resources and approaches, by attending meetings and INSET sessions. They had begun to feed back some of this knowledge to the rest of the staff in a limited way. All three had also offered assistance to classroom teachers and had spent some of their time each week in classrooms. In class they provided extra individual attention for all students who were perceived as needing help, as it seemed totally inappropriate to restrict their activities to 'Commonwealth immigrant children'. To have done so would have been to contradict their belief in non-racially based classroom interaction. In practice they were often drawn into classrooms where teachers were having problems with classroom control. In these circumstances an 'extra pair of hands', as they were sometimes perceived by other staff, could be extremely helpful in maintaining classroom order. There was a danger, as one of the Section 11 teachers said, of them becoming a 'police service'. They all felt that other teachers thought they were on 'some sort of cushy number' as they had no set timetable. Two also explained that they found it difficult to adapt to the role of adviser or assistant to others. An advisory role meant they were sometimes seen as critics and therefore as threatening the autonomy of classroom teachers. An assistant's role meant they were no longer in charge of planning or reponsible for classroom activities, but had to work within another teacher's organization, which they did not find easy.

The three teachers were also involved in a number of other activities. One spent a lot of time in an evaluation of the school's ACS scheme, one, who had previously been a 'Community Liaison' teacher, continued much of his previous work involving attending meetings of various groups in the local area and communicating with parents and local people, and the other attempted to set up a 'link school' scheme with a suburban all-white school. They were thus involved in a variety of activities, but many were not directly related to the 'needs' of students of 'Commonwealth immigrant origin'.

Conclusion

In this chapter I have attempted to document the responses of teachers at Milltown High to LEA and school policies on multicultural and anti-racist education. Whilst most had favourable views towards the idea of policies on this issue some argued that they were being given too high a priority by the LEA and the school. They believed other matters were of more pressing importance. In terms of the policies themselves most teachers interpreted them as containing a commitment to teaching about other cultures in order to foster tolerance and better community relations and to adopting a non-racist approach in their relationships with students. A minority of teachers, mainly concentrated in the English and Integrated Curriculum departments, went further and interpreted policies as part of a broader commitment to reform which included a student-centred pedagogy, political education, and closer home/school links. In terms of curriculum practice most of those who claimed to be adopting multicultural and anti-racist approaches were concentrated in the English, Integrated Curriculum, Drama, and Humanities departments.

Chapter six

Multicultural and anti-racist education in practice – the English department

This chapter and the next contain case studies of two of the subject departments at Milltown High School which were most involved with multicultural and anti-racist education. I will describe at some length the sub-cultures of the two departments – the teachers, the context in which they worked, their subject perspectives and views on multiculturalism and anti-racism, and finally some examples of the teaching that I observed. The members of the two departments (especially the English department) spent a considerable amount of time talking to me about their work, informally, and in interviews, and allowed me to observe many of their lessons.

The English department

English was part of Milltown High's core curriculum and all students had four lessons from a twenty-five lesson week. All students followed a common curriculum taught in mixed ability groups, but in the fourth year a top set was selected which studied English Literature as well as Language to sixteen plus (later GCSE) level. The department occupied a suite of rooms at the back of the school with each of the four full-time English teachers having their own room. This was not the most salubrious location as the corridor was something of a thoroughfare. Lessons were often interrupted by the noise of passing students, and at lesson changes groups of students would meet up and socialize creating difficult supervision problems.

Although altogether six teachers taught English, four women teachers constituted the core of the department – Jennifer Green, the head of department, Susan Parker, second in the department and temporarily deputy head, Alison Mitchell, responsible for the library, and Jane Gabriel, a probationary teacher. The four formed a close knit group and shared a strong, common subject perspective. They had all chosen to work in the school (unlike several staff in other departments who had been re-deployed to the school at LEA re-organization) and were strongly committed to teaching there, seeing it as a place where they could develop their 'radical' educational ideologies. They also saw teaching in an inner-city working-class comprehensive as an expession of their socialist political sympathies. Alison Mitchell, for example, said she felt an 'intellectual and emotional commitment to an inner-city school' as a result of her political views, and at Milltown High she thought it was 'easier to take up the sorts of things that I am interested in' such as 'discussing political issues' and 'combating racism'. All were committed feminists and both Susan Parker and Jane Gabriel were active in womens' groups outside school. Indeed, Susan Parker explained that one of the attractions of the English department was that it was a group of women working collectively, sharing decisions, and supporting each other. All four teachers were heavily involved in curriculum development. Jennifer Green, for example, had a long and active interest in multicultural and anti-racist work and had been one of the key members of the school working party in the late 1970s, and Susan Parker had played a key role in developing anti-sexist work. They were also outspoken at meetings and INSET sessions and favoured many of the changes David Benyon was encouraging in the school. Their commitment, energy, and 'radical' educational views meant David Benyon frequently singled them out as the sort of teachers that he wished to have in the school. As one member of the department remarked, 'we're his radical babies'.

At breaks and lunchtimes the English teachers generally spent time together in the same area of the staffroom often with teachers from the Integrated Curriculum department. Conversation revolved around social and political issues, meetings and events, films, books, and the theatre. These common interests and commitments, combined with a shared belief in the nature of English teaching provided a strong subject sub-culture.

The English teachers' subject perspectives

The English teachers had very similar views about their 'subject paradigm', i.e. the nature of appropriate content of English curriculum, and 'subject pedagogy', i.e. 'the system of ideas and procedures for the organisation of learning in the classroom under specific institutional conditions' (Ball and Lacey 1980), or how it should be taught. They rejected the rationalist/functionalist conception of English teaching with its emphasis on the acquisition of basic skills of reading, writing, spelling, and grammar (see Ball 1983). Whilst they recognized that the teaching of basic skills was important, they saw these as the ability to use language, spoken and written, in a variety of different forms, not merely the ability to spell, punctuate, or comprehend a written passage.

They opposed the use of grammatical exercises and firmly believed that language skills were learned through the practical use of language, through talking and discussion, creative writing that could be drafted and re-drafted, and through reading literature and other forms of writing. Jennifer Green abhorred what she saw as the government's attempt to bring back the teaching of grammar:

> It's absolute nonsense. We all know from all the research and from years of being taught like that ourselves that it's a complete and utter waste of time . . . Taking language apart like that does nothing to give the children confidence in their own language, and to build on it . . . To work them rigidly through grammatical exercises . . . is just bad English teaching . . . Language isn't acquired like that. Language is caught not taught. It's caught by being in a rich language environment where you are reading and constantly talking and discussing and thinking.

The English teachers also felt they were more than just developers of language skills. They hoped that through reading and discussing literature students would increase their awareness of themselves and their relationships with others, explore moral issues and develop qualities of thoughtfulness, tolerance, respect for others, and empathy. Jennifer Green talked about what she called 'the hidden curriculum' of English teaching which involved 'developing them as people, to think and feel and act'. The students would, they hoped, become better people by reading and discussing the characters and situations they read about, and expressing and discussing their own views and experiences. In this sense they saw English as 'a curriculum for personal development' (St.John-Brooks 1983) and as a means of inculcating certain key values, one of which was anti-racism.

The English teachers stressed the importance of the 'relationships' that they established with the students. They expected the 'good' English teacher to have wide concerns – for the students' ideas, experiences, values and attitudes, and also for their personal welfare. This concern did not derive from a psycho/therapeutic model of the teacher's role in which they were attempting to compensate for the emotionally disturbed backgrounds of their students (cf. Stone 1981, Sharp and Green 1975), but from a view that English was essentially about developing students as 'people'.

The teachers also agreed that another of their main aims was to increase the social and political awareness of their students. Indeed, this was part of their commitment to social change and to working in an inner city school. They wanted to raise the consciousness of their students through the consideration of literature and other materials which addressed social and political issues. Thus many of the books and materials that they selected for classroom use were concerned with such issues. Susan Parker argued that it was essential that an English course raised 'the whole issue of oppression and injustice' and Alison Mitchell spoke of the need to 'raise issues and to raise consciousness'. Their aim was not to directly promote a particular political view, but to raise issues and viewpoints for discussion. They hoped that students would develop the ability to think critically and make independent judgements. However, they argued that it was impossible to conceal their own views and remain completely neutral in the classroom and they conceded that the material they presented to students and the issues they raised for discussion were often a product of their rather left-wing opinions. This was justified by Susan Parker by reference to the conservative bias of mass media and of many of the students themselves:

> I feel very strongly that the establishment line is already presented and you have to work very hard if they are to have a fair picture, if they are to have a balance, because they generally start off with an establishment view. So I do tend to present a strong alternative view and with a bright group I express my own views . . . but always leave them open to challenge . . . A lot of our kids believe it is right that they should have less money and fewer facilities than say someone from Sandhall (a middle-class suburb). They argue that someone with a lot of money is entitled to have it because they have worked hard for it . . . So I tend to put the alternative view. It's my job to make them question and make them be critical of the injustices in our society, but obviously what I see as an injustice someone else may see as fair.

Susan Parker's aim was more 'balanced learning' than 'balanced teaching' (Stradling *et al.* 1984). She recognized that students learned about controversial political issues in other areas of their life and she wanted to challenge their existing views by presenting alternatives to those she felt were dominant. This sometimes led her to play a 'devil's advocate' role, although the views she advocated tended, more often than not, to derive from her own political beliefs.

The aims of the English teachers can then perhaps be said to traverse what Ball and Lacey (1980) call the 'creative/expressive' and the 'sociological' paradigms. In practice these aims were reflected in the curriculum they selected and the pedagogy they employed. Most teaching in the department was organized around class readers, which were selected on the basis of 'having a good plot' in order to 'capture the kids' interest', 'relevance', which meant they had to reflect either the students' environment or the concerns of their age group and preferably include some ethnic minority or working-class characters, and 'raising issues for discussion', especially issues of moral, social, or political concern. In the second and third years (first year English was the responsibility of the Integrated Curriculum) the teachers liked to use historical novels like *Friedrich* by Hans Peter Richter, a story about a Jewish boy growing up in pre-war Germany, and *Underground to Canada* by Barbara Smucker, which was about the 'underground' escape routes used by black American slaves. Several books had adolescent relationships as their central theme and often issues of racism were closely interwoven. For example, all the teachers used *My Mate Shofiq* by Jan Needle, a story about the relationship between a white boy who overcomes his own racial prejudice and forms a deep friendship with a Pakistani boy, *Gowie Corby Plays Chicken* by Gene Kemp, about a white boy alienated from school whose life is changed by a black American girl who comes to live next door, and Rosa Guy's *The Friends* which concerns the experiences of a young West Indian school girl forced to join her father living in Harlem, New York. The classic story of culture clash, *Walkabout* by James Vance Marshall, about a white English boy and girl having to survive in the Australian outback with an Aboriginal boy, was also popular.

In the fourth and fifth years the teachers chose from a wide range of books. The English Language and Literature sixteen plus courses that the department used were based upon continuous assessment, which meant that individual students had to present a folder of completed work at the end of their fifth year to be assessed. Although the examination board provided a list of suggested reading materials there was considerable freedom. Certain books, however, were more often used than others. Two books from the Heinemann Caribbean Writers series were popular. *Green Days by the River* by Michael Anthony was one. Set in Trinidad, it is the story of a fifteen year old black boy growing up, coping with various family crises and forming a relationship with a young Indian girl. Its main theme is the boy's developing set of attitudes and values. Another was *The Humming Bird Tree* by Ian McDonald, which again is set in Trinidad and is about the relationship between a rich white farmer's son and two Indian children who are family servants. The theme is the deeply racist structure of Trinidadian society in the 1930s and the way the childrens' friendship is destroyed by their respective class/racial positions and cultures. The theme of racism was also common in other books used with this age group. *To Kill a Mockin' Bird* by Harper Lee, a story about racial oppression in 1930s America, *The Basketball Game* by Julius Lester, which concerns the relationship between a black boy and a white girl in a southern American town in the 1950s, and *Rainbows of the Gutter* by Rukshana Smith about an Afro/Caribbean young man moving into adulthood in London in the 1970s. More widely known books and plays were also used – *The Diary of Anne Frank*, Orwell's *Animal Farm*, Golding's *Lord of the Flies*,

Barstow's *The Human Element*, Miller's *The Crucible*, Brighouse's *Hobson's Choice*, *Macbeth* and *Romeo and Juliet*, for example, in addition to various short stories, plays, poems, and non-literary material such as newspaper articles and advertisements. Teachers drew from the department's large stock according to preference and what they felt was most appropriate for the ability and interest of individual classes. Their aim was to interest by being topical and 'relevant', to provide material that was exciting and good to read which related in some way to the students' world and experiences, and to create maximum opportunity for raising the issues that the teachers regarded as important.

The English teachers emphasized the importance of a pedagogy based on discussion and talk – whole class, small groups, and one-to-one discussion. 'Students actually learn by talking, they develop ideas and opinions by talking', Jennifer Green emphasized. Whilst silence was something that they would strive to achieve in certain circumstances, they said that they would suspect an English teacher whose room was always silent. Discussion was also at the centre of their ideas about the assessment of students' work. Work was corrected often with the student him/herself so that student and teacher could discuss the way it could be altered or improved and the teachers commonly wrote lengthy comments on a student's work so that it could then be re-drafted or re-written.

The English teachers also explained that they were attempting to move towards teaching styles which gave students greater control over their learning and more opportunities to express their thoughts and opinions. Susan Parker, for example, talked about how she was attempting to:

> Move away from teacher as instructor and moving towards debates which are genuinely open-ended, asking questions which are genuinely open-ended, asking students how they feel about something and there being no set answer that I'm expecting . . . Allowing a genuine openness in response . . . Moving towards a student rather than teacher-centred learning.

She also described how she hoped to create situations in the classroom in which 'the students run things for themselves' and her role was to provide resources, advice, support, and ideas, and to work with individuals and small groups of students. In this way, she suggested, students would learn skills of 'self-discipline, discussion, social awareness, and thinking'.

However, the advocacy of such styles was tinged with pragmatism. All the English teachers explained that it was often difficult to organize English teaching in this way at Milltown High. They often did not have enough time to prepare and organize appropriate resources, and the students could often exploit situations where traditional forms of classroom control were not used. In practice they advocated a flexible approach using a variety of teaching techniques. Jennifer Green, for example, explained how she used:

> The most efficient role for fulfilling the task or for getting across what I want to teach. If it's a class reader I take a very formal traditional approach of being the authoritarian teacher in control, in charge, keeping the discipline going, just so the reading can take place, but, if they're all working on an individual piece of writing, my role will be to give support and just work with individuals, and give the control back to them to take their work where they want to, but with my help and guidance. If it's a discussion with an older group my role is obviously more informal than it would be with a younger group . . . It might be just going between groups making comments and suggestions and letting them take it where they want . . . just guiding it and organizing it for them . . . I think the younger ones get more done with a more traditional approach. I believe they haven't got the skills of self-discipline yet. Some have, but a lot haven't . . . So for a while I have to impose it on them . . . But with the fifth years I've pushed them to the stage where they're now taking control of their own learning and disciplining themselves.

There was also often a gap between ideals and reality, or paradigmatic and pragmatic aspects of the teachers' perspectives (Hammersley 1977). As Jennifer Green explained:

> I think that's (the gap between pedagogic ideals and classroom practice) particularly true of this school. I think the reality of the students themselves and the discipline problems don't always allow you to teach in the way you want to teach.

Similarly Alison Mitchell conceded that she was concerned that the older students on exam courses were not 'getting through the work fast enough' and would not produce enough course work for assessment:

> I have a feeling that although I'd like to think I was operating partly in a facilitatory or advisory type role, and that the students played a more active part, that the tendency, and this is often because of the nature of the students and the difficulties that I sometimes have with discipline, that it ends up more like chalk and talk than I would want it to be. Well I'm sure it ends up like that . . . I'd rather it wasn't like that. A good example would be like with my fifth years. A bit back I decided I'd have them doing group work. I gave them all this Fay Weldon story to study. I gave them all two pages each and gave them a list of things they had to

find out and I had them doing it for three days and at the end of three days it just hadn't been worth it. Now I know that the answer to that is you start it early and you get it eventually, but at this stage in their lives I can't afford that sort of time, and I know that's what's going to happen now until the end of next year is when we do literature questions, yes there will be some discussion, but at the end of the day it'll be me coming back and saying, 'here's the notes, here's the quotes', and that's it. I'll try and elicit as much as I can about it, but at the end of the day I'll be doling it out.

She also argued that the students 'like a structure' because they were 'the sort of children that they are', and 'because they run rings round you if you don't give them a tight structure'. In practice this also meant being fairly 'formal' and sometimes 'quite authoritarian' in terms of classroom discipline.

The English teachers then favoured a discussion-based pedagogy, emphasizing oral work, student participation, and greater student control over at least some aspects of their learning. However, they stressed, because of the circumstances that existed in the school and the nature of the students themselves, that it had to be a flexible pedagogy flavoured with pragmatism.

The English teachers' approach to multicultural and anti-racist education

In the late 1970s the then head of English had become aware of the fact that whilst a substantial number of the school's students were Afro/Caribbean, very few of the books and materials used were written by Afro/Caribbean authors or were about the experiences of Afro/Caribbean people. Jennifer Green, then a junior member of the department, was given a Scale 2 post to read 'multicultural literature' and advise the department on how such materials could be incorporated into the curriculum, and several other teachers began exploring the issue. Subsequently a 'multicultural and anti-racist approach' became central to the department's working philosophy and the department gained something of a reputation in the city for its pioneering work in this area.

Multicultural and anti-racist education meant four basic things to the English teachers. First, it meant valuing and not denigrating the backgrounds and cultures of the students. Second, adopting a non-racist approach in their interaction with the students. Third, promoting the value of anti-racism in their teaching. And fourth, teaching about social and political issues and orientating teaching to 'political' aims. Jennifer Green argued that:

An anti-racist approach should come into everything you do. It isn't something which you just slot in as a single topic . . . looking at the 'problem'. It's something you as a teacher should take into every single lesson. So you're using the students' own culture in a very positive, strong way. So it goes right through the curriculum . . . But having said that I believe it's something more fundamental, deeper than that. It's your attitudes in the end, it's the teacher's attitudes to the students.

In this way, she emphasized, anti-racism was the basis of 'good' English teaching. By 'taking the strengths and positive things about the students' backgrounds and cultures and bringing them into the classroom and celebrating them', Jennifer Green hoped that ethnic minority children, who in the past often had rather negative views of their own ethnicity and blackness, would come to feel more 'confident' and 'positive' about themselves. This, she believed, would enhance their educational opportunities.

The English teachers' regard for the importance of the backgrounds and cultures of the students was reflected in their choice of curriculum. They constantly searched for books and materials which were written by ethnic minority authors or which contained minority group characters and reflected the history and experiences of minority group people. They also stressed the importance of students writing and talking about their own lives and experiences. A common language assignment in the fourth year, for example, was to write an autobiography, and in other years creative writing utilizing events and experiences in family and community life were encouraged.

The department's approach to the issue of Afro/Caribbean dialect (see Trudgill 1975; Richmond 1979; Edwards 1979, 1981) provides another example of the teachers' attitude to the backgrounds and ethnicity of the students. Whilst the English teachers stressed that they aimed to ensure students' competence in 'standard English', they felt that, as Afro/Caribbean dialects were 'part of many students' identity', their use should be encouraged and valued in school. Jennifer Green explained: 'I believe in getting kids to think that their dialect, in whatever form, is something that they should be proud of . . . to make them feel self confident.' She said the department's policy[1] was that non-standard dialect should and could be used by students 'when appropriate' and the aim was to encourage 'bi-dialectalism'. Often the English teachers would read and discuss poems that were written in Afro/Caribbean dialects. The work of Louise Bennett, Valerie Bloom, and Lynton Kwesi Johnson, for example, were used. Books were also used with dialogue written in non-standard dialect. Jennifer Green maintained that it was important that English teachers actually read such dialect aloud to their classes and if they did not feel competent that they should practise until they were. This, she felt, showed that they valued such language forms.

In students' writing the emphasis was on 'using the right form of English for the right purpose', so that students were encouraged to use non-standard dialect if they wanted to in writing poems, or personal reflections, or in stories, where it would form part of natural dialogue between characters, but not in more formal writing such as letters or reports. The policy was to correct errors which appeared to stem from 'dialect interference' if the teachers felt the mistake was spoiling the writing, given the purpose for which it was intended. In a formal letter or a piece of writing intended to express a point of view in a formal debate, then such errors would be corrected, but this was always done with an accompanying explanation. During my field work the department also developed a project with a community-based Caribbean Language Project to encourage a study of language and dialect. Students were offered the option of a six week course during their fourth year with two Caribbean teachers from this project.

Jennifer Green argued that this policy had been very successful. When she first came to the school, she said, the students did not use non-standard dialect in their work at all, it was primarily used on the corridor, often to abuse staff. Now its use in the latter way had almost disappeared, and the students were willing and able to use it in 'appropriate' ways in their work. Quoting the case of one student, who had written an account of her experiences on a recent stay in Grenada with all the family conversations in Caribbean dialect, she said, 'It works, it's appropriate, it's good. It didn't occur to Elizabeth not to do that . . . Hopefully we're getting to the level now where students are having more confidence in using language appropriately and more confidence to understand where it's appropriate to use dialect and where it isn't.'

As well as adopting a positive attitude to students' ethnicity the English teachers explained that they constantly strove for non-racist practice in their interactions with students. They saw themselves as 'inherently racist' because of their own backgrounds and upbringing, but they tried to reflect on their own attitudes and work in the classroom in order to guard against such racism affecting their practice. This approach was reflected in their conceptions of students. Although they saw many of the students as 'underachieving' or 'difficult to motivate', this did not lead them to a generalized or negative view of their academic potential. They were also reluctant to generalize about students on the basis of ethnic or racial differences and emphasized the importance of seeing and treating students as individuals. When they did generalize they pointed out the positive aspects of student ethnicity.

The promotion of the value of anti-racism was also central to the curriculum that the English teachers selected. Many of the materials they used were emphatically anti-racist. In most cases their message was clear – racism is fundamentally immoral, unjust, and divisive. The way materials were used in the classroom also reflected this aim. As a result the ethos of the deparment was strongly anti-racist, something which many of the students commented upon when I talked to them in interviews. 'One thing that you can say the English teachers are in favour of', one boy said, 'is race equality. They never stop going on about it!'

This commitment to the value of anti-racism was sometimes taken beyond the school. Jane Gabriel described how she saw it as 'a constant challenging of stereotypes, images, dominant ideas' and how she would challenge someone who told racist jokes. Jennifer Green came into the staffroom one day and recounted how she and her husband had walked out of a club where they had been with some friends when the performing comedian started telling racist jokes. The other members of the department present warmly supported her action.

Anti-racism was also central to their view of the political role of English teaching. It was part of talking about the whole issue of 'inequality, injustice, and resistance', as Susan Parker said. Again this was expressed in the department's curriculum, which involved what Susan Parker called 'a positive challenging of racism through literature', but it was also manifest in the pedagogy they espoused with its stress on debate, discussion, and student participation. Anti-racism meant taking issues like the riots in Handsworth in 1985 and, as Susan Parker explained, 'opening up the lesson and talking about why they happened and talking about what racism is and how it affects what's happening in the world'. It meant looking at the experiences of people reflected in literature and discussing issues concerned with the way societies were organized, and it meant talking about issues that were happening in the students' lives and how they were related to the way British society is organized.

This, then, was how the English teachers interpreted multicultural and anti-racist education. I now want to look at some examples of English teaching to see how these ideas were translated into practice.

The practice of English teaching

During the course of my field work[2] I observed over fifty lessons taught by the four main English teachers most of which they claimed were related to multicultural and anti-racist education. Whilst I make no strong claims about the representativeness of my observations, I hope that this description gives a picture of the sort of classroom practice that was common in the department, and also some examples of the ways that the teachers translated their ideas on multicultural and anti-racist education into practice. Where possible I tape-recorded the lessons, otherwise I took detailed field notes.

Whilst the English teachers each had their own particular approach in the classroom many of the strategies they used were similar. They all placed a great emphasis on 'building positive relationships with students' and went out of their way to be positive and friendly even to those who were the most negative towards school. Of course this was partly a control stategy. By cultivating 'positive relationships' they were attempting to develop binding commitments and a sense of loyalty amongst students which meant non-conformity was less likely. But it was also a genuine commitment to the students and a particular style of teacher/student relationship. They encouraged a relatively informal and relaxed classroom atmosphere, but all except Jane Gabriel, who, in her first full year of teaching, found classroom control difficult to achieve, kept a fairly tight reign on classroom discipline.

The English teachers all organized their teaching around literature. Of the lessons I observed hardly any were devoted specifically to grammar work or spelling. Students were expected to develop these sorts of skills through correcting and re-drafting their work following the teacher's help or marking. Sometimes teachers' would read a passage to a class and give them comprehension questions, but the bulk of their work was devoted to reading and discussing novels, plays, poems, and short stories which were then used as a basis for a variety of written assignments. Sometimes students were asked to write autobiographical or reflective pieces, at others more imaginative or empathetic ones. Polemical and persuasive writing was also encouraged. Indeed the teachers aimed to give students experience of writing in different ways, for different purposes and audiences. In several of the lessons I observed writing assignments were derived from the teachers' commitment to anti-racism. For example, Jennifer Green after reading a section of *My Mate Shofiq* set an assignment on 'urban myths'. She showed the students a TV programme containing several famous urban myths and then asked them to write and to read aloud their own urban myths. She hoped, not only to develop the students' language work in an entertaining and motivating way, but also to discuss with them the difference between fact and fiction, and the way rumours and myths develop.

The teachers favoured public class reading of literature, sometimes by the students, but more often by the teacher, believing that the books should be read aloud to the whole class so that students could share in a common class experience and enter into the collective enterprise of discussion and analysis of the text and the issues it raised. They also felt that this practice gave less-able students, who in the past had been confined to 'remedial' departments and to a stultifying and demotivating curriculum of reading schemes and language exercises, the opportunity to share 'real' English work with their peers.[3]

Whilst much classroom time was spent actually reading books aloud, the teachers would often break off the reading to explain the historical background or social context of the story. So, for example, when reading *Friedrich* Alison Mitchell went into the history of Nazism in pre-war Germany, and, when reading *My Mate Shofiq*, Jennifer Green explained to students the historical background to immigration in the 1950s and 1960s. When reading the latter novel Jennifer Green was keen to rectify any historical misconceptions that the students might have about the reasons for such immigration and the social status which many immigrants at that time were forced to occupy. The teachers also used opportunities in the texts to transmit factual knowledge about other cultures and societies to try to build up the students' awareness and break down prejudices they might have. On one occasion, for example, after reading a section in *My Mate Shofiq* which described the Asian community, Jennifer Green arranged for an Asian member of staff to give her class a talk on Pakistani culture.

They also used characters in the books as a basis for talking about peoples' attitudes to other social groups, showing how sometimes attitudes are based on preconceived ideas or inaccurate information. In *The Humming Bird Tree*, for example, the story describes the derogatory attitudes of a young, white, upper-class boy to the East Indians because they cook their food over fires fuelled with cow dung. After reading this Jennifer Green pointed out how these attitudes were misconceived and based on inadequate knowledge of the circumstances of the East Indian people. The racist attitudes of Bernard White, one of the main characters in *My Mate Shofiq*, were continually identified, held up to scrutiny and described as 'cruel and insensitive', 'nonsense', 'rubbish', or just plain 'racist'. Sometimes non-racist characters in the stories were presented as role models and teachers drew attention to characters who became more anti-racist. In the case of *My Mate Shofiq* the English teachers reinforced the clear intentions of the author to get the reader to share the experiences of the central character and learn from them, thereby becoming more aware, better informed, and anti-racist.

The texts were also used to encourage class discussion of racism. Students were often asked to speculate about why a particular character thought or behaved as they did or to talk about what they would have done in similar circumstances. The teachers preferred to raise the issue of racism indirectly through fictional characters and situations rather than to attempt to explore directly students' own perceptions and attitudes, because this avoided potential personal animosity and increased students' awareness of racism in other times, places, and societies. In these discussions the teachers sometimes attempted to explore the students' own experiences of racism. They related the issues raised in literature to experiences of their own, hoping that students would do the same, and thus could come to a greater understanding of the texts themselves and their implications for inter-personal relationships and social commitments. I observed Jennifer Green use this technique most often. However, sometimes these discussions were marred by problems of classroom control and the negative attitudes of some of the students, and had to be abandoned. At other times it was the teacher herself, as the most enthusiastic participant, who dominated and did most of the talking. The following lesson is an example of the type of discussion which the English teachers tried to encourage, and it illustrates some of these problems.

Jennifer Green's third year class, who were reading *My Mate Shofiq*, had come to the section of the book where a group of white children tell each other several racist stories about 'Pakistanis'. In this lesson a 'learning support' teacher had taken several students out of the class leaving eleven students – eight Afro/Caribbean (four boys and four girls), two white boys, and one boy of Asian origin. Jennifer Green broke off the reading, explained that the ideas voiced by the characters were 'absolute nonsense', and began a discussion.

Can we just stop there for a minute . . . Veronica, can you give me some examples of the sort of racism which, I don't know if you can tell us this, if you feel able to . . . that you as a black person have met in Britain? Can you tell us of an incident when you've met racism? Sh . . . now listen . . . because it's important that Veronica has chance to speak.
VERONICA(V) – What for?
JG – Because I want us all to discuss it, it's important.
V – Ask someone else then.
GEORGE(G) – Miss, I know one.
JG – OK, George you tell us about one, that's involving you is it? OK, now listen (to class) if you're not mature enough to discuss it I shall stop it.
G – This guy from Birchfield Lodge.
JASON(J) – Oh I . . .
JG – I remember this. It's most unpleasant.
G – Miss when we were just coming out of this shop . . . these lot here . . . Guy, just come up to me and said 'You black bastard and all this crap.'
JG – Was that when we were walking along the road?
BOYS – Yeah.

G – I was in a good mood, but if I was in a bad mood (waves his fist).

J – You'd have gone up to him and .....

JG – Well George how did you feel when that was said to you?

G – Miss I just felt like beating him up or something like that ... but I just couldn't be bothered ...

JG – That's a very very brave attitude to say don't waste you're strength. I think you're right. I think people who have that attitude are not worth wasting your strength on. Now I remember that I was walking along the road when that happened and we were ... I don't know if it was the same party ... but there was a school party coming our way, an all white school, and as I was walking along a child turned to a boy, it was a first year boy then he's in the second year now, and just turned to him and said, 'Oi you you nigger' and I just couldn't believe it. Mrs Freeman was with me, and he walked off as quickly as he could and of course this kid was here and he was, 'Let me at him, I'll teach him', and we sort of said, 'Look just cool it'. (Class laugh – they're very interested in the story.) Sh ... listen ... calm down ... and we went up to the teacher and we took the teacher on one side and said, 'Excuse me do you mind if we have a word with you?' and Mrs Freeman said to her, 'I think you ought to be aware that the children in your class have got really offensive views. One of your children has just called a black child in our group a "nigger".' And this teacher was horrified. She was absolutely shocked and she just said, 'I just don't know what to say, I'm so sorry, I'm really sorry.' She said, 'I'll take it up with him, who was it.' And we pointed the boy out and we said, 'We don't want a fight, we don't want trouble now, but we think you ought to have a serious word with that boy, because what he said was racist and offensive and you need to talk to him about it.' And she was extremely embarrassed and I'm sure she would have taken it up. Now I don't know about you, but me as a white person, because people know where I work, I'm always getting racist insults flung at me. Now if I'm getting it as a white person I don't know how some of you in the class feel because it sickens me. Would somebody else like to tell us about an incident they've been involved in?

At this point the discussion began to fragment and in order to hold the class's attention Jennifer Green told another story about the racism faced by an ex-student she had taught. Having regained control she again invited contributions from the class. Again George, one of the most talkative members of the group, took the lead and told the class about a time when he had been called racist names on a bus trip. Then, an Afro/Caribbean girl joined in the discussion.

ANN-MARIE(AM) – When we first moved down and we were living in (name) these white man, right, about sixteen, right, and me Mum was going out and she came back in, right. This was in the night about 10 o'clock. She was comin' in and they'd thrown chip papers in our garden and everything and beer cans. So me Mum went, 'You'd best pick them up right now.' So they started callin' her 'black bastard' and all of this and 'Get out of the country', and me Mum went in the house and came out (laughs) with a baseball bat.
JG – I can believe your Mum would as well (laughs).
AM – And then after that, right . . . one who started callin' her black bastard me Mum and him just don't talk.
JG – They just don't talk. (The girls laugh about the baseball bat.)
J – Miss.
JG – But why isn't it . . . you see I always, wait a minute . . . sh . . . Jason (much talking breaks out – JG settles them down.) Jason come on . . . sh . . .
J – Miss did you hear that thing just last night about that white lad, who stabbed a Paki to death – a Pakistani?
JG – Yes (numerous bids to speak). Wait a minute, wait a minute . . .one at a time please . . . sh . . . Arslam please tell us.
ARSLAM(A) – Miss, he had a fight the day before yesterday and the Pakistani guy won.
JG – Where was the fight?
A – (Name) School.
JG – That was in (Name) School listen . . . Sh . . . Beverley . . . listen.
A – Miss, right the white guy said to the Pakistani guy, 'Do you want a fight?', and the Pakistani guy said, 'All right.'
JG – So it was planned was it that the fight would go on?
A – Yeah, but Miss when the Pakistani guy came back the white guy pulled out a knife and stabbed him.
JG – Now that is a good example of what racism can lead to. (JG raises her voice above the rising class talk.)

The discussion again began to fragment at this point and Jennifer Green told another story about a teacher she had met on holiday who she felt had articulated racist views. However, Beverley, an Afro/Caribbean girl seemed uninterested and started to fool around.

JG – Well how would you have handled it Beverley? (numerous bids to speak and talking amongst themselves.) I'm interested, how

would you Beverley, what would you have done if you'd been me?
AM – She wouldn't bother you know.
V – You should have thrown your drink in his face.
JG – (Many students now talking at once.) . . . Wait a minute . . .
listen . . . one at a time. This is a good discussion. Beverley what
would you have done?
B – Me? (Inaudible.)
AM – I'd knock him down.
JG – Wait a minute, wait a minute (over student talk). Listen
Beverley what do you think I should have done?
BOY – (inaudible)
JG – Oh no if I'd have been black he wouldn't have said anything
. . . (inaudible), he wouldn't have been there.
J – He wouldn't have been near you Miss. (Girls laugh and
discussion gets very disorderly.)
JG – I must admit what actually happened was . . .

JG recounted another part of the conversation she had with the teacher
and when attention is restored asked:

What do you think I should have done? . . . because you had a
different reaction . . . sh . . . why do you think, do you think I
should have thrown my drink in his face?
MARK – Yes you should have given him a upper cut in his
eyebrow. (They all laugh.)
JG – Jason sh . . . what do you think I should have done?
J – Don't know really.
BOY – Walked off. . .
J – I would have walked off.
JG – But if I'd walked off. . .
AM – I'd have walked off come back again and boxed him down.
J – I'd have walked off dead cool and just left him to talk to
himself.
JG – You don't . . .
J – You'd have had an argument about racism.
JG – Well I did actually. We did actually get into a very fierce
argument.
G – (Inaudible.)
JG – George come on, battering him is not an answer really
because what I had to do and I couldn't do it because he was an out
and out racist, but what I had to do was somehow change his
attitude. That's what I felt I should do . . .
BOY – (Inaudible.)
JG – Well exactly. George go on.
G – Miss if I was you and he said that to me I would do this. If I

91

knew a black person who was black and they're nearby I'd just
walk up to the guy and say can you just wait there for a second . . .
JG – But is that fair because I'm just making their lives worse.
G – Now . . . (several students shout out at once.)
G – But he's the one who started it he should . . . I'd just go round
and get my friend and say you know what this guy called, said –
em (several students talk at once).
JG – Wait a minute . . . sh . . . sh . . .
J – Then just stand behind him when he's just talking.
JG – Beverley please.
AM – And then just tap him behind on the shoulder.
J – I'd do that miss. Say it was Paul here right, I'd say it was that
big man. Put him right behind him.
JG – But . . . it isn't always the answer to hit, is it?
J – It is if he's racialist (several bids to speak from the boys).
JG – What I actually did . . .
AM – Look how would you like it . . . (several students talk at
once).
JG – Well done Ann-Marie

The discusssion here became very fragmented and Jennifer Green again
began to lose control. A few minutes later the lesson was interrupted by
another teacher who was having discipline problems with one of her
students. Jennifer Green left the class to assist. As she returned the bell
went for the end of the lesson and she dismissed the class for lunch.

We can see clearly in this lesson how Jennifer Green tried to transmit the
value of anti-racism. Using examples from her own experience she
showed how racism can manifest itself in everyday life and, in a simple
way, she encouraged students to discuss appropriate responses. She also
encouraged students to talk about their own experiences. However, the
discussion was extremely difficult to handle. Several students, despite
attempts to involve them, were not particularly interested. In fact, they
sometimes viewed the concerns of teachers about racism as rather
eccentric. As students of thirteen to fourteen living in an area with a
large and well-established ethnic minority population, going to schools
where ethnic minority students were in the majority, they often had little
experience of racism, and mild racial abuse was common, even
acceptable in some circumstances, in their peer culture. Interestingly,
while Jennifer Green attempted to discuss the appropriate way of
responding to the racism that she experienced with the teacher she met,
some of the students began to fantasize about a fight situation of the sort
which characterized their peer group play. Throughout the discussion
some students used opportunities to begin their own conversations or

'mess about' and on several occasions Jennifer Green began to lose control. In order to re-establish control of subject content and re-focus student attention on the public class arena, Jennifer Green told lengthy, attention-grabbing stories. This, combined with her passionate concern that the students got the appropriate message, meant she dominated the discussion and student participation was limited. This is not to denigrate her attempt to engage students in a discussion about racism, but merely to point out some of the difficulties that she had in realizing her aim, and some of the strategies which students of this age use to make classroom talk their own.

With older students the English teachers sometimes attempted discussions about broader race-related issues in which students could articulate their own views and experiences and listen to those of others. For example, Susan Parker, in a lesson I observed with a fifth year class, used the book *The Basketball Game* which the class had just read to introduce discussion about race relations in Britain. Susan Parker felt this book was ideal anti-racist material as it raised questions of inequality and injustice and emphasized the way in which oppressive practices could be successfully resisted and challenged. The class were looking at an extract from the story where a black boy, who had recently moved to the racially segregated town of Kansas City, tried to borrow a book from the library previously reserved for whites. During the lesson I made the following field notes:

SP (standing at the front, students sitting in desks facing her in a rough sort of square) – Right, we're not just sitting and writing today. We'll have a change from work, not that talking isn't work. Can we have coats off please.

The usual ritual of reluctantly taking coats off begins. Following this SP asks them to get out the duplicated extracts that some of them read last lesson, and, after forcing the chatting to subside with the threat of extending the lesson after school, she explains to the class that she wants them to talk about the extract and then to answer some questions on it as a comprehension exercise and an assignment for their course work. She then explains the background to the story, the fact that it is set in the mid-west of America in the 1950s when there was quite rigid racial segregation, and that it is about the relationship between a black boy and a white girl. One or two students chip in briefly in response to SP's recall questions. SP then tries to broaden the class discussion out to compare the situation with Britain.

SP – Is it like that in Britain (i.e. racially segregated housing)? I suppose it is really a bit, what do you think? Norman shut up a minute.

The class are not really settled, although some are concentrating very hard, others have little conversations of their own. SP finds it difficult to keep them together to concentrate on the discussion.

STUDENT(ST) – It is like that in Britain, there aren't many black people live around my way (he is a white student living a fair distance away from the school in a mainly white area).
NORMAN(N) (Afro/Caribbean student) – No Miss I think people mix together more. I don't think there is as much prejudice today in England.
SP – (Says she agrees with the first boy.) Where do most black people in Milltown live? (She suggests some areas and the students suggest a few.) There are very few black people living in Kidsbrook. There's only one Asian family living in my street. Areas are dominated by different cultural groups. Why do you think that is?
N – Because black people might be called names and there are racial insults, so black people don't want to move.
SP – So black people want to move to areas where they are not insulted.
WAYNE(W) (Afro/Caribbean student) – But I think things are changing, people are mixing more now.
SP – So there's a gradual process of integration? What do you think girls? Amanda?
AMANDA(A) – Most of the people are mainly separate . . .
N (interrupting) – Miss, where there are more white people in an area then Asians are more accepted than black people.
SP – So you think there is more hostility to the Afro/Caribbean community? (The boys laugh at her use of this term.) What about Handsworth?
N – That was mainly black and Asian. The Asians used to get a lot of boot from the white, but it's not so much now.

SP pauses, the discussion is still unsettled, the girls chat and laugh and SP finds it hard to get them to listen to each other.

SP – So the situation in the story is still relevant today. Racial hostility leads to segregation.
W – But it's not so intense or obvious.
SP – And it's not legalized.
W – Some of the police do.
SP – Amanda (she can't hear what the boy is trying to say because Amanda is talking).

SP (to Wayne) – Is that fact or rumour?
ST – Fact, it has happened to me.
SP – Angela can you listen. What, the police pick on black people, fact or rumour?
ST – I know because I got flung in a van and they shouted insults at me. Well not exactly me (pause).
SP – Are you going to tell us?
RONY(R) (white student) – It has happened to me as well.
SP – So it happens to black and to white.
R – It's nothing to do with racism, the police pick up whites as well.
W – But the police pick up black boys and make racist insults.

At this point Amanda, a black girl, makes some gesture at Rony. Rony calls her 'a dick', she replies that he wouldn't know what one of them was!

SP (shouts) – Rony!

At this point SP decides that 'the discussion is getting far too personal' and after calming the situation and then getting Norman to read the extract to the class she restricts discussion to a consideration of the text. SP's questions become less exploratory and more directed to extracting information and meaning from the text. For example:

SP – What is the young librarian a symbol of?
W – A new age or generation.
SP – So is the future going to be better if people are more liberal. It's an unpleasant incident but has a happy ending. What word is used to put the boy down?
N – 'boy'.
SP – So words can be racist. For example 'boy' used in this way. What was the law concerning the use of the library?
ST – Anyone can use it.
SP – So what stopped him using it?
W – The fact that no blacks used it.
SP – And the way black people were treated. They were legally entitled to use the library, but an unwritten rule prevented them.

Following a short discussion of the text along these lines SP moved on to explaining the marking scheme and the comprehension questions that the students had to answer.

In the earlier part of the lesson Susan Parker succeeded in creating a situation where the students in the class could begin to talk about their own ideas and experiences. However, the discussion, as with many I observed, was rather short-lived because of discipline problems and personal animosities, and the comparison between race relations in America in the 1950s and contemporary Britain was only partially explored.

In a lesson I observed with Jennifer Green's fourth year class, students had more opportunity to put forward their views. The class had been reading the novel *Rainbows of the Gutter* by Rukshana Smith. They had come to a section which dealt with a young Afro/Caribbean boy's feelings about his schooling. After reading Jennifer Green split the class into two groups of about six or seven students, one with a student teacher and one with a learning support teacher. They had been asked to discuss the question – 'It is not enough that schools in inner city areas have multicultural education. Multicultural education should also be important in all white schools.' - in preparation for writing an assignment for their English Language course work. I was unable to record the discussions but they were relatively free-ranging and students played the main roles. Nearly all the students had a chance to participate and appeared to genuinely explore the meaning of racism, their experiences of it, and what they felt schools ought to be doing about it. The teachers played roles which were more akin to Stenhouse's idea of the teacher as neutral chairperson (see Schools Council Publications 1970), facilitating and guiding the discussion rather than playing a dominant part. Jennifer Green visited groups, listened to ideas and views, and asked for elaboration and clarification. At times the discussion became quite animated as students negotiated their ideas and interpretations. They were nearly all actively involved.

In the lessons following the discussion students wrote up their thoughts in the form of a persuasive piece of writing – a letter to a headteacher of an all-white school about why the school should adopt a policy of multicultural education. However, although the students were actively involved in classroom discussion the topic set tended to discourage consideration of the alternative view that multicultural education was not appropriate. This idea was in fact discussed amongst the students in their groups and rejected, but Jennifer Green did little to encourage its expression or elaboration. The agenda or framework of the discussion, which derived from Jennifer Green's commitment to multicultural education, was a strong influence over the arguments which were presented.

Another strategy that the English teachers used to try to raise the students' understanding of racism was to teach them certain sociological concepts. They had no systematic list of the concepts they wished to teach and often such teaching was implicit in their reading and discussions. However, occasionally they attempted to directly teach about specific concepts. For example, when I observed Alison Mitchell working with her third year class she tried to teach them about the idea of stereotypes. She produced a work sheet explaining the concept which she read to the students. In order to explore the students' own stereotypes she then asked them to do an exercise in which they related stereotypical characteristics of various national and ethnic groups from the work sheet to the names of the groups that she wrote on the blackboard. Following this they had to use their imagination to write an account of how they thought certain types of people (punks, skinheads, businessmen, pensioners, housewives, and vicars were among the list of suggestions) would spend their time. Finally the students were asked to go through a section of *My Mate Shofiq* picking out statements about 'Pakistani' people that were based on fact from those that were based on stereotypes. Unfortunately much of this lesson was marred by discipline problems that frequently bedeviled Alison Mitchell's work. Students messed about, shouted out, and interrupted the class discussion, chatted about anything but the topic and many appeared to do very little work. Alison Mitchell wanted students to understand the idea that much of peoples' thinking about other groups is based on preconceived images derived from the media. But several students appeared puzzled by the tasks she set them and her success in realizing her aim must be open to doubt.

In fact problems of classroom control were often a major constraint on the style of teaching that all the English teachers could employ. They forced them to cut short, abandon, or even not attempt at all, discussions of the sort they wanted. Their ideal of an interactive discussion-based pedagogy was difficult to realize and they often had to adopt styles of teaching and interactions with students that they found distasteful and frustrating. After one particularly difficult lesson with her third year class Jennifer Green said despondently: 'It was just a matter of control. I couldn't do any teaching. It was awful. Those kids are just not being stretched. The last few lessons have just been a waste of time.' She went on to say that one of the most frustrating things about teaching at Milltown High was that teachers were very restricted in what they could do in lessons by the 'behaviour and attitudes of the kids'. They were 'forced to compromise' and adopt more traditional, didactic, and teacher-centred approaches with a 'tight structure and a tight organization' in order to maintain classroom order.

Another constraint with the older students was the sixteen plus course work requirements. Students had to have a considerable amount of written work in their folders for course work assessment at the end of their fifth year. As a result much class time had to be spent telling students exactly what was required and ensuring they were adequately prepared. Some of the anti-racist work that the teachers attempted with these students became heavily didactic. This was the case in one of Alison Mitchell's fourth year lessons I observed. She decided to tackle a 'dub' poem, *Reggae Fi Dada* by Linton Kwesi Johnson, which is a political critique of Jamaican society based around a tribute to the author's dead father. After playing a recording of the poem she began to go through the text. With short student contributions in response to her questioning she drew out the main themes of the poem, writing them on the blackboard: '1) Hardship of his father – and poor people generally, 2) Exploitation by the government and ruling class, 3) Disintegration of society, 4) Political fighting – innocent people killed.' Each one required explanation which Alison Mitchell gave at some length. She then decided to go through the text of the poem. 'Right', she said, 'I'm going to go through it now and give you notes . . . This is what the poem's about.' She began and the students started to write from her dictation or make notes on her exposition. The following extract from my lesson notes illustrates the nature of the classroom interaction. Alison Mitchell had come to the third verse of the poem and was addressing the whole class:

> AM – Right verse 3, the next one (she reads the verse). There's a tremendous amount in that verse . . . (she reads the first part of the verse again). What's he describing in the first few lines?
> REBECCA(R) – The country.
> AM – But what about it? . . . There's a lot in there about trees being cut down, about the land being overgrown. It's happening in various parts of the world. People are cutting down the rain forest to make money and the land dries out and decays. It's happening in Jamaica and it's happening in places like Africa and India. The trees are cut down and what happens?
> ANNABEL(A) – The land dries up.
> AM – The land dries up and . . . (she goes on to explain soil erosion) . . . So in that one line you've got neglect. Who's cutting them down?
> A – The government.
> AM – The government and the big corporations . . . probably the big corporations . . . the big corporations exploit land for profit and people who farm the land are moved off, usually poor people . . . Look at the words thistle and thorn, what sort of plants are they?
> R – Hard.
> AM – If you get in there what will happen? What will happen if you try and grow things in there? (She answers the questions herself.) You're physically going to get hurt . . . If your livelihood is taken away, at the physical level you're going to be hurt, but you're also going to get hurt at the mental level. So he's talking

here at two different levels . . . You can look at the poor as
neglected, physically as well as mentally. It's a physical and a
mental wound. It's the same in this country . . . if you don't provide
work and give few benefits . . . if you haven't got a job it's almost
as if you don't exist . . . it's like another wound, a stab in the
back . . . The neglect of governments, even those who come to
power to improve the lot of the poor . . . He's saying their lot hasn't
improved. And contrasted with this you've got dangled 'glaring
sights of guarded affluence' . . . It's the same in his country with
the media advertising and shops full of things people can't have.
But if it's 'guarded affluence' what is it?
R – Rich.
AM – And guarded, it's referring to a small number of people in
the country who have wealth . . . You can draw another parallel
with this country . . . A small number of people own wealth . . . .
with the poor living on supplementary benefit (she quotes figures)
. . . The situation is similar in Jamaica, guarded affluence is
literally there . . . They literally guard their wealth and property . . .
All the poor can do is to look on . . . And then 'the arrogant
vices . . .
A (interrupts reading the poem) – . . . 'mocking symbols of
independence'.
AM – Slavery's past . . . colonialism is behind them . . . What is it?
R – Laughing.
A – But financially.
AM – Good. They're wage slaves, slaves to poverty. Nothing's
changed, despite the fact that the country has its own government
and runs its own affairs, there's still the division between the rich
and the poor. Independence hasn't made any difference.

Whilst on a few occasions in other parts of the lesson certain members
of the class did engage in more of a dialogue with Alison Mitchell about
the interpretation of the poem, their participation was limited. The poem
was, of course, a difficult one to interpret. It was read and written in a
Jamaican dialect and required some knowledge of Jamaican society. But
the students had little opportunity to actively participate in the process
of making sense of the poem or in drawing the sorts of parallels with
British society that Alison Mitchell clearly had in mind. Nor did they
have the chance to debate the Marxist-orientated political messages the
poem contained. Ironically students were being asked to consider a
radical message, but expected to play only a passive role in accepting
the ideas that Alison Mitchell had formulated for herself.

The Caribbean English Project

Before concluding this chapter I want to briefly describe a part of the English department's work which did not involve any of the English teachers in the classroom. In the 1985–6 academic year one of the school's Section 11 teachers made contact with two Afro/Caribbean teachers working in the local community education centre on what was called the 'Caribbean English Project', and arranged for them to come into Milltown High to conduct a half-term course with fourth year students in part of their English time. About twenty students, mainly, but not exclusively, Afro/Caribbean, opted to take the course. Unfortunately I was not able to observe any of the lessons, but I did talk to the two teachers about their aims and the sorts of material and teaching methods they were using.

The course focused around the idea of culture and the central role which language plays in culture. In the limited time they had, the teachers aimed to increase awareness amongst students of the linguistic structures and styles of Afro/Caribbean creoles and to develop their knowledge of the relationship between language and social structures. They were, they said, looking for ways to help students, especially those who were creole speakers, to become more proficient in 'standard' English by exploring their attitudes to their own language, and by going some way to clearing up possible confusions and insecurities which arose when they had to operate in a number of different language 'codes'. They hoped to encourage students (and teachers as they did a considerable amount of INSET work with teachers in the LEA) to re-assess their view of Afro/Caribbean language, to see it as linguistically valid. They did not subscribe, however, to a cultural relativist view that such language should be regarded as of equal worth and thus taught in schools. This, they realized would be a rather naive view in a society dominated by 'standard' English. Their aim was to clarify with the students the role and function of different language styles. They also tried to explain the use and importance of language in processes of social selection and, by examining the origin and history of Afro/Caribbean languages, the ways in which language is related to the social and political processes and inequalities. In fact, in a small way they were introducing the students to some quite complex sociological ideas.

Their teaching methods were similar to those favoured by the Milltown High English teachers. They explained that class and small group discussions, which focused upon pieces of literature and student writing, were the techniques they used most. In fact, judging from their account they appear to have had more success with these methods than the mainstream English teachers often did. This was perhaps because they were working with a relatively small, self-selected group of students, who were, as a result, well motivated. The literature they selected was often written or spoken Afro/Caribbean creole, either from one of their own published anthologies (they had published several books of their adult students' writing) or from established Afro/Caribbean writers, and was discussed and 'translated' with the students. They also asked students to write about their own experiences and ideas and to explore their own use of dialects in both oral and written form, and often typed this work up in preparation for the next session.

This was intended to be a one-off course with the students, but in fact it was repeated the following year. Whether it will become a regular feature of the English department's work is difficult to know as, at the time of writing, the future funding for the project was uncertain.

Conclusion

The English teachers were strongly committed to working at Milltown High and had all chosen to work there, regarding this as part of their wider commitment to social change. They had developed a curriculum and pedagogy in line with their aims of improving language skills, encouraging particular attitudes and values, and broadening the social and political awareness of their students. A key part of their philosophy was a commitment to multicultural and anti-racist education. They had positive attitudes towards students' ethnicity and tried to use literature which reflected the backgrounds, cultures, and concerns of their students. They also encouraged students to write and talk naturally about their lives, experiences, and ideas. In this way they hoped that students' self-confidence and achievement would be enhanced. This did not mean that the teachers encouraged the development of minority cultures and neglected to teach knowledge and skills which the students needed for success in mainstream society. Their primary aim was to enhance students' ability to use 'standard' English, but their view was that they were more likely to be successful if their teaching was conducted in an atmosphere where the students' backgrounds and cultures were respected and regarded as valid. They aimed to build bridges with foundations in their students' world in order to encourage their self-esteem and motivation, and enhance their chances of educational success.

Whether they were successful is difficult to judge. Certainly there was no feeling amongst any of the ethnic minority students that I interviewed that the English teachers under-valued their ethnicity or cultural heritage. In fact, sometimes the reverse was the case. Ethnic minority students occasionally complained about the amount of attention that was devoted to 'black issues'. Whilst clearly a number of students at Milltown High were alienated and lacking in motivation, the

English teachers did not adopt the sort of elitist approach to teaching which St. John-Brooks (1983) argued further alienated many of the working-class students she studied. Indeed, some students at Milltown High were encouraged to work harder because of the opportunity to express their ideas and experiences in their written and oral work, and because curriculum content was related to their concerns and world. For them their teachers' efforts to bridge the cultural gap did reap dividends.

The English teachers were also committed to developing the social and political awareness of their students, and this included educating them about and against racism. Much of the literature they used raised social and political issues and gave the opportunity to discuss racism. They wanted to encourage discussion and debate so that students could explore controversial issues and ideas from different angles and develop and express their own views and opinions. Unfortunately, in practice this style of teaching proved difficult to achieve. The teachers were often heavily constrained by the negative attitudes and poor behaviour of many of their students, and by the pressures of assessment requirements for sixteen plus courses. Discussions and debates did occur, but often they were cut short and tended to be teacher-centred because of these constraints. Moreover, the strong political commitments of the English teachers meant that they tended to present mainly left-wing material and views to the students which left other points of view unexplored.

Chapter seven

Multicultural and anti-racist education in practice – the Humanities department

The Humanities department consisted of three teachers. Stephen Barker, who took responsibility for Geography, was the head of department, Peter Mills was responsible for History and also head of fifth year, and Alan Moore was responsible for Religious Education. The three did not share the same commitment to the school as the English teachers. Both Stephen Barker and Peter Mills had been redeployed to the school during re-organizations and admitted that it was not where they would have chosen to work, and Alan Moore saw his stay in the school as a temporary one before he could move on to a promotion. Nevertheless, they were hard-working, conscientious, and experienced teachers who formed a strong department.

The Humanities department was based in three large classrooms on the second floor at the back of the school. It was a relatively quiet part of the school and the Humanities teachers had few of the corridor supervision problems that faced the English teachers. It was, however, rather isolated and doors and walls were often covered with graffiti and vandalized during lunch hours when few teachers were around. On the surface the department appeared well resourced, but a recent LEA dictat that any school-produced booklets or worksheets which contained copyright material should be destroyed had created shortages as the teachers had relied upon such materials in the past. The teachers had been forced to hurriedly buy commercially produced textbooks, which were often not ideal for their courses.

Humanities was part of the school's core curriculum and every student from year two to five took the subject for three lessons each week. Classes were taught in mixed-ability groups up to the third year, when upper and lower bands were selected in co-operation with the Science department. The teachers adopted an 'integrated' approach, but courses included elements of Geography, History, and Religious Education. The second year curriculum consisted of a series of regional studies from a historical, geographical, and religious perspective – Africa, the Caribbean, and India were the areas considered. The teachers

103

felt that such a content was more appropriate as it was important that the curriculum 'reflected the cultures and backgrounds of the different ethnic groups in the school'. The second years also studied part of what was called 'The Milltown Oxfam Project', a locally-produced course designed on similar principles to Bruner's 'Man – A Course of Study' (MACOS), and based on a case study of a community in Guatemala. In the third year students studied the theme of 'Development' and the teachers had devised three units of work, one based around 'Development in the Third World', another on 'The Industrial Revolution', and a third on 'Personal Development'. Finally in the fourth and fifth years the department utilized the Joint Matriculation Board's (JMB) Integrated Humanities O level course and the teachers had devised their own Mode 3 CSE to run alongside it. This meant that most students were studying the same content and there was the flexibility to move students between groups and to enter them for O level or CSE or both.[1] The course consisted of five units of work which were selected from the ten offered by the JMB. One term was spent on each of the following topics – People and Work, Poverty, Persecution and Prejudice, War, and Beliefs. Groups were rotated so that each teacher could, where possible, teach topics close to their subject specialism. Students were continuously assessed and, although the examination board outlined the 'qualities' on the part of the students which were to be assessed, the teachers themselves had considerable control over the means of assessment. They also enjoyed relative freedom to select curriculum content as the content of each topic specified by the syllabus was intended to provide a 'framework' rather a 'uniformity of content' (JMB 1983).

The Humanities teachers' subject perspectives

As with the English teachers there was considerable consensus amongst the Humanities teachers about 'subject paradigm' and 'subject pedagogy'. This was perhaps surprising given that they all had different subject backgrounds and, within the department, different subject responsibilities. But individual subject loyalties were not strong and the department did not appear to be an arena for competing subject interests. All three teachers agreed, mainly for pragmatic reasons, that the Integrated Humanities course was the most appropriate for 'this type of school'. They explained that the contracting size of the school and the poor academic ability of many students meant separate subject options at exam level were not really viable, and integration cut down on student movement around the school and made group rotation possible.

The teachers said that they had three main aims (though each gave slightly different emphases), apart from the general aims of literacy, numeracy, and social skills which Stephen Barker said 'is what I hope we're all doing all the time'. First they hoped to transmit a certain amount of knowledge about the social world and the variety of ways people interact with their environment. They did not see themselves as transmitting only knowledge about British culture, history, and society, and Christian beliefs and values, but wanted to give students knowledge about different cultures, religions, and historical events from around the world. Their aim was that students should have a deeper understanding of the variety of human behaviour and begin to formulate views and opinions based upon accurate information. As Alan Moore explained:

> I think we're trying . . . to give them some knowledge of what
> actually goes on in the world, how things are organized, how
> different people live, what different people think and believe in,
> and why things happen in the way that they do . . . And I hope that
> we do begin to challenge some of the ideas that they have. I mean
> they are very narrow some of them. They live in a very small world
> and they get most of their ideas from watching rubbish on the TV
> or from reading the Sun. I hope that we can give them more
> accurate information and that they can begin to think a bit more
> about the world that they live in.

In response to my question about whether they were trying to present a particular view of the world each of the Humanities teachers claimed to be presenting 'a balance' in that different explanations and ideas on social issues were considered. Stephen Barker said:

> I think it's important to look at several points of view and different
> explanations for things. For example when we look at something
> like why different industries are located where they are we
> consider all the different factors . . . or when we look at the
> question of nuclear weapons we try to put all sides of the argument.
> We wouldn't be doing our jobs properly if we didn't.

Their intention was to provide accurate information and a variety of viewpoints in order that students could formulate their own views and opinions. They aimed also to encourage students to look more deeply at social phenomena and become aware of the often complex factors which give rise to particular events.

The Humanities teachers' second main aim was to develop certain skills in their students. They all mentioned skills to do with the understanding and interpretation of information and evidence. For example, Alan Moore explained:

> I want them to be able to look at different sources of information
> and be able to understand them, first of all, you know documents,

105

diagrams, photographs, graphs, things like that, and then to be able to get from those sources the things that they need for whatever they're doing.

Peter Mills was in favour of the move in History teaching towards the use of primary sources and the interpretation of evidence, although he felt that the abilities of the students, and the LEA's ban on the use of copyright material, limited how much such an approach could be employed.

The teachers maintained that in order to develop these sorts of skills it was often necessary to teach about certain concepts or ideas. 'You have to explain to them things like population density or infant mortality or nuclear deterence or guerilla warfare', said Alan Moore. In fact the development of skills and key concepts was central to the department's syllabus and schemes of work.

A third aim was the development of certain attitudes and values in the students. They did not aim to encourage particular political views, but wanted to promote more general values such as open-mindedness, logical thought, and the use of evidence, tolerance, and respect for others. This they felt was part of their commitment to multicultural education. In fact it is worth outlining here how the Humanities teachers saw multiculturalism and anti-racism rather than considering it in a separate section as I did with the English teachers. Again there was little difference in their individual views.

The Humanities teachers all rejected the idea that they should attempt to foster cultural integration by emphasizing a narrowly 'British' cultural heritage. Instead they stressed the multicultural nature of British society and thought it was important that students learned about a variety of cultures, religions, and histories through the study of themes and topics which drew attention to common aspects of different societies.

Stephen Barker said that, whilst he was uncertain of the meaning of anti-racism, he took it to mean 'positive steps to end discrimination, and look carefully at materials and the ideas we are trying to put across', and that he supported this. But he felt a multicultural approach, which aimed to 'build up people who are tolerant, understanding, and appreciative of other peoples' backgrounds, beliefs, and traditions, to enable them to live and work together', was a more accurate description of the department's approach. Peter Mills agreed. He saw multiculturalism as:

to do with or having in school an education that is not narrow in that it just restricts the learning or the information giving to that of say England or Britain, in that it's an education which encompasses the history, the geography, the culture, and so on of as many different peoples as possible, and as far as we are concerned here, of those ethnic minorities that we would find living in this particular area.

He felt this was anti-racist in the sense that:

It's trying to educate those people who are bigoted . . . there are some youngsters who are very, very racist. And what we have got to do is that we have got to try and put into our education this business of tolerance and understanding of other peoples' backgrounds, customs, culture, and so on and try get out of some children, that just because they happen to be white that they're better . . . We musn't be insular in what we're doing . . . They've got to be tolerant of other people.

Alan Moore had a similar view. He regarded the department's approach as multicultural because: 'We educate about many societies, many cultures, many ways of life, and that's a lot of what we do in Humanities.' But he did have some reservations about the approach adopted:

The school in a sense has failed because it teaches about many cultures, but doesn't involve those cultures that are in the school in what it's doing. Because we're generally a white staff we look as outsiders at black culture, if there is one . . . and I suppose it could be perceived that multicultural education at Milltown High is charity from a white middle-class staff, and I wonder if there's some truth in that . . . whether our commitment is superficial in a sense . . . We're teaching about their culture, but in a plastic sense and not really using the kids so much as a resource.

He also felt they were anti-racist in that they were 'educating people to be tolerant and accepting of each other as a way of breaking down racism'. He suggested that multiculturalism could be used to create situations in which racist attitudes could be broken down:

When you talk about other religions, for example, Asian religions and you get, even though it's not shouted anymore, under the breath, sort of 'Paki this and Paki that' . . . I mean I challenge that. So in a sense the hidden curriculum that comes out of a multicultural curriculum can challenge racism.

One of the aims of the Humanities teacher, then, was to encourage the values of tolerance, empathy, and acceptance of others by teaching a multicultural curriculum. This, combined with their other aims, determined the curriculum content that they selected. It was based around regional studies in the second year and key themes in the third, fourth and fifth years, and utilized material from a variety of different societies and world contexts.

It might be useful here to describe briefly two of these themes to illustrate the type of curriculum that was selected. In the third year students considered the topic of 'Personal Development' as part of the broader theme of 'Development'. In this topic they looked at the socialization and role of children in different societies past and present and the variety of religious customs and traditions which marked the important stages in a person's life cycle. In the fourth year as part of their O/CSE course students studied a topic entitled 'Beliefs'. This topic aimed to give them some knowledge about the variety of religious, moral, and political beliefs and values, and so included information on the central beliefs of some of the main world religions – in this case Christianity, Islam, Sikhism, and Judaism. It also included information on the central values and policies of the main political parties in Britain, and looked at the beliefs surrounding important political figures and movements in other societies and times – Ghandi, Martin Luther King, the Suffragettes, and the Nationalists and Unionists in Northern Ireland were considered. The unit also examined the beliefs of opposing groups around moral issues such as abortion, vivisection, and private health care and considered the idea of 'pressure groups'. The unit was specifically designed to raise controversial issues in order to generate maximum interest and at the heart of much of the unit were important questions of social justice and conflict. Alan Moore, who designed the unit, said that he hoped that this curriculum content would also give students the opportunity to develop skills – 'language skills, study skills' and those concerned with the 'understanding and interpretation of evidence'. He also hoped to encourage an understanding of certain key concepts such as 'morality, democracy, and faith', and attitudes such as 'tolerance, empathy, and understanding'.

Let us now turn to the Humanities teachers' view of subject pedagogy. Turner (1983) has suggested that Integrated Humanities courses were established partly to encourage teachers to develop a pedagogy orientated to student-centred, independent, resource-based learning where 'the teacher is seen as less the purveyor of knowledge . . . but rather the enabler: the person who through interaction with the student, advises and directs the learner through his own chosen path', and where 'teaching and learning comes to be seen as more of a conversation between teachers and learner and their role-relationship to be egalitarian rather than authoritarian' (Turner 1983 quoted in Hammersley and Scarth 1986: 273). However, the Humanities teachers were very sceptical about the application of these ideas at Milltown High. Whilst they had some sympathy with more 'progressive' educational practices they were more than anything experienced pragmatists.

Peter Mills thought that such ideas were 'fine in theory', but in practice the lack of motivation and poor ability of many students made them impractical. Moreover, the other aspects of his role placed a constraint on the amount of time he could give to developing new teaching methods and materials. Stephen Barker and Alan Moore made similar points. Both identified student behaviour as a major constraint on the introduction of more 'progressive' teaching methods. Alan Moore said:

> The kids can be really very difficult if you allow them to be. If you give them an inch they'll take a mile, and so often you can't do the things that you would really like to do. I mean there's a great difference between how I'd like to run a lesson and how I do. The style is generally get 'em in, shut 'em up, talk to them, give 'em work to do, that could be very easy, very straight forward diagram copying or written question and answering, or it could be more demanding. It depends how well I get on with the group or how responsive they are to me as much as anything.

And Stephen Barker explained: 'So much of the time as far as I'm concerned is geared to keeping some kind of order and control so the teaching methods that I often use are intended to achieve that.' All three teachers explained how they thought independent student work with the teacher as adviser rather than transmitter of knowledge, small group activities and discussions, and more egalitarian teacher-student relationships were unsuitable given the reality of classroom life at Milltown High.

Stephen Parker advocated 'a more old-fashioned and . . . a more didactic approach'. He described his position in the classroom as a 'benevolent despot' and emphasized his role in providing a 'framework of order', a clear and consistently enforced set of classroom rules, so that students could work. His method was, he said, 'fairly formal' and he maintained firm control of curriculum content and student pace of working, generally spending the first part of each lesson addressing the whole class on the subject matter of the lesson before setting them individual written exercises. This 'more structured and formal approach', he claimed, worked best at Milltown High.

Peter Mills while stressing the importance of 'flexibility' in teaching style also said that he adopted a 'fairly formal' approach in the way he set out his room, approached students, and conducted lessons. He advocated class-based teaching where 'you as a teacher are in control' and where 'you can stand up there and show that you know what you are talking about and what you're doing'. There was a need to be 'structured and organized' and to lay down clear behavioural guidelines so that 'you start off from a controlled situation'. He felt lessons were best organized:

With a very formal content, which I choose . . . and then I talk to the whole class about what we're going to do, with I hope some involvement of the youngsters. Then they get on and as they work I move around the group asking questions, picking points out as they work, and so on.

Alan Moore claimed to adopt a variety of teaching techniques, but conceded that his overall approach was very similar to the others. He argued that he was 'willing to change in curriculum terms, but I still have a fairly authoritarian view of classrooms'. 'I still want to direct', he said. 'Generally speaking it's me organizing them and not too much leeway for them to do too much.' He too emphasized the importance of 'formality', of classroom rules and firm teacher contol over curriculum content, the pacing of students' work and interaction in the classroom.

The Humanities teachers advocated a more 'traditional' approach to pedagogy. They emphasized whole class teaching, often followed by individual, quiet seat work, in which they strongly 'framed' (Bernstein 1971b) curriculum content and controlled the pace of student work, 'formal' teacher-student relationships, and strong control over student interaction in the classroom. Whilst they made some concessions to 'discussions', they preferred these to be whole class affairs, teacher rather than student-centred.

Their conceptions of their students were, as with the English teachers, primarily individualistic and they were reluctant to categorize students or to talk about them in generalized ways. When we talked about students' ethnicity, they said they felt there were few significant differences between the students and certainly made no negative comments about students' ethnicity. All claimed to treat students as individuals. As Stephen Barker explained: 'The fact that there are children of different ethnic backgrounds makes me more aware of things I would say or the way I approach things, but I'm more concerned with the child as an individual.'

When the Humanities teachers did provide generalized descriptions of their students it was, as with the English teachers, often in terms of their common 'problems' – low ability, lack of motivation, emotional disturbance, and the like – which were explained by reference to a wide variety of circumstances in the students' environment and home background. But such a view was not used to justify a generalized low expectation of students' academic potential. 'We have children here who can do as well as any, if they would put their minds to it', said Stephen Barker, and Peter Mills thought that, 'some of the children here are very bright, it's just that they are often badly influenced by their friends and find it very difficult to break out of that'. All the Humanities teachers stressed the range of students that attended Milltown High.

The practice of Humanities teaching

In this section I want to describe two units of Humanities work that I observed in order to illustrate the teaching styles that were used in the department and the way the teachers incorporated ideas of multicultural and anti-racist education into their practice. I was restricted somewhat in my observations as the teachers were sometimes reluctant to have me sit in on their lessons, and again I must emphasize that this account is not intended to provide a comprehensive picture of the work of the department.

The first unit was taught by Stephen Barker and consisted of seventeen lessons with a third year class who were studying the topic 'Development and the Third World'. Stephen Barker explained that it was fairly representative of the department's multicultural approach. The lessons were always well planned and organized and were generally orderly. Often Stephen Barker spent ten minutes before the lesson setting out materials so that everything would be ready when students arrived and the minimum amount of class time was taken up with the distribution of equipment. Whole class teaching was the norm with Stephen Barker in full control of curriculum content. After 'settling them down' lessons generally started with a short talk to the whole class on the lesson's content, sometimes combined with a brief, recitation style, question and answer session.[2] Students were expected to 'pay attention' and 'listen', and answer questions when selected. Questions were usually designed to elicit from their memory knowledge of the previous lesson or knowledge of the subject matter under consideration, information known to Stephen Barker, rather than knowledge, ideas, or views, unknown to him. Stephen Barker often explained concepts that were to be introduced, went over the material (text, graphs, maps, etc.), and then set the tasks that he wanted the class to do in the lesson, usually putting instructions up on the blackboard. Frequently exercises involved copying diagrams, maps, or drawings, or transferring data from one form to another (e.g. from a table of figures to a graph), or answering comprehension questions on the text or on his talk. Students were expected to complete these exercises individually often in a specified amount of time as Stephen Barker tried to keep the whole class together as much as possible.

Blackboard instructions were of the type described by Barnes (1976), and served to, as Barnes says, 'isolate the learner with his task' and 'keep control firmly in the teacher's hands'. In this way Stephen Barker strongly controlled the content of his lessons and the pacing of students' work. Exercises were often designed to be rather mechanical, involving little thought, at least at their beginning, so that less-able or less-motivated students could 'get on' without the excuse that the work was too difficult. Students were expected to work by themselves with the minimum of interaction with their peers. During this 'working' time Stephen Barker generally patrolled the class or surveyed them from various positions around the room. He was quick to spot outbreaks of talking or potential disorder and moved quickly to defuse them either by directing students back to the task in hand, or questioning them about their work or by merely hovering around them.[3] Students were expected to ask him not their neighbour by raising their hand if they had a problem or query about the work or the nature of the task. This they usually did and much of Stephen Barker's time was spent moving around the classroom briefly answering student questions which generally concerned what they had to do or how a particular exercise was to be completed. In fact most individual teacher-student interaction was of this sort. Stephen Barker rarely initiated individual interaction on the subject matter of the lesson and he rarely marked work during lesson time preferring to leave himself free for the roles of 'policing' (A.Hargreaves 1979), task supervision, and answering questions. As a result his lessons were usually quiet and calm with students working away at their individual tasks.[4]

The following lesson was typical of those I observed:

The class have come straight up from registration together. SB is by the door as they come in, exercise books are out on the tables. Students sit down and there is an air of sleepy calm about the room, first lesson in the morning I suppose. One girl complains that a boy has taken her seat. 'It's not your seat, it's where you usually sit, find another place, come on it's not musical chairs', says SB . . . .The class settle. SB, standing at the front facing them, begins . . .
SB – Right. Think back a long time ago, last Thursday. We were looking at the Third World and we talked about what that meant and why it might be a better name than something like the Underdeveloped World. We looked at all the words that are used. Then we looked at the Third World, at some photographs, and we talked about some of the features of Third World countries as compared with richer countries, and we spent most of the time talking about food. Now the Third World is short of food. You have seen pictures of Ethiopia and the Sudan on TV. But is the world short of food? What can we say about the distribution of food? Clifford is there enough food in the world to go around? Is something the matter Darren?
DARREN – I haven't got a pen.
SB – You don't need a pen now. Clifford's telling you something (no response from Clifford). Oh, he's obviously forgotten. Pamela you tell him.

PAMELA(P) – Yes, er I mean no.
SB – Do you mean yes or do you mean no?
P – Yes.
SB – Did you hear that Darren or were you too busy talking? She
said that food supplies are not distributed equally. There are
inequalities, it's not shared equally. Which gets most Trevor?
TREVOR – The North.
SB – Right and we said that if there were twenty-one bags of grain
how would the bags be shared out? How are they divided Patricia?
(No response from Patricia.) Billy-Joanne?
BILLY-JOANNE(BJ) – There would be eleven in the North and
ten to the South.
SB – Yes that's right, but that's fair isn't it? (Several hands go up.
A boy shouts out.)
BOY – There are more people in the South.
SB – So it's not a fair share is it. Those were the main points we
were talking about. We finished off looking at a diagram which
compared what an average American and an average Indian person
eats. Do they eat the same Jason? (No response.) Who ate the most
Vincent?
VINCENT(V) – The American.
SB – Right I want to go on from there today. Can you find page 15
. . . Come on Carvil page 15 (some chatting starts). Sh Sh . . .
There's the diagram. If you look at it we're saying not only that the
amount of food varies, what else varies?
DARREN – The variety.
SB – Very good . . . These are the points we discussed. Most of you
seem to have remembered them well. Now to make certain I want
you to write them down . . . Put the heading 'Food' and from the
blackboard answer those questions in your own words. We have
been talking about them all so you should know the answers. (He
reads the questions written on the blackboard.) (1) Is there enough
food in the world to go around? (2) Why do some people go
hungry? (3) If the world's food supply is represented by
twenty-one bags of grain how are they divided between North and
South? Right make a start please. The date is the 15th. I know
people need pens. Put your hand up if you need a pen (he
distributes pens). Right any problems put your hand up and ask me.
You don't disturb anyone. When you get on you really work well.

While the class work quietly SB writes further questions on the
blackboard, occasionally turning and surveying them, shushing
anyone who talks. The questions are: (4) Why is the division of
food not equal? (5) Copy the drawings of the scales with food on

from page 15. He then wanders around the class, occasionally helping students who ask for assistance and distributing equipment. If students start talking or appear to go off the task set he moves over to them, hovers, or asks them where they are up to. After several minutes he writes a further two questions on the blackboard: (6) What do you notice about the amount of food eaten in the two countries? (7) What do you notice about the variety of food? After twenty-five minutes of individual work several students begin to get a little restless and some chatting starts. SB declares . . .

SB – It would appear that many in the class are close to finishing. You have worked very well. Two or three minutes to finish off now. Nobody waste time. If you have finished get on with some reading. Read pages 15 and 16 . . . (The chatting subsides. SB moves to the front of the class and surveys the room. A few minutes later . . .)
SB – I would like us to spend the last few minutes looking at a map on pages 16 and 17. Can you spend a few minutes looking at it now. It's a funny map. Try to understand how the shapes are drawn . . . (pauses for thirty seconds) . . . Let's look at it those who have finished . . . It has been constructed not as the shape of the actual countries. What they have tried to do is to draw a map to match the population of the country. So a bigger shape means a bigger population. Britain is bigger than normal size and so is India. Countries with a smaller population are much smaller. Then it is shaded to show the amount of food per person in calories . . . (he continues explaining the map for the next couple of minutes until the bell goes and he dismisses the students one at a time).

Most of the lessons that I observed in this unit were similarly organized. The exceptions were three lessons where the class watched films from the LEA film library. Following viewing Stephen Barker held a brief question and answer session based on recall of the film's contents. The films themselves whilst related in some way to the subject matter of the unit appeared also to provide light relief from ordinary classroom work for Stephen Barker and the other two Humanities teachers who brought their classes along. They were, perhaps inevitably, somewhat dated. One consisted of a comparison between the natural environment and farming economies of the Swiss Alps and Peruvian Andes. The film, rather like a tourist brochure, focused on local farming methods, customs, and crafts, presenting an unproblematic, conflict-free, even romantic picture of community life. Modern technology, we were told, was the main factor in accounting for the different adaptations made by the respective communities to a similar natural environment.

A second film was entitled *Our Asian Neighbours – Harvest at Nong Lub* and showed, in a very similar way, life in a rural Thai village during the rice harvest. The focus was on farming methods and the village economy. Again a consensual image of village life was presented. A third film, *Miners of Bolivia*, presented a less rosy picture focusing on the problems of tin mining and the poverty of mining communities in the Andes. Difficulties were created, the film suggested, by the altitude, mountainous environment, poor communications, and primitive technology, and the miners themselves were presented as victims of a harsh environment, exploitation, and lack of opportunities.

However, these films were really interludes in the unit of work. What about the overall curriculum content? There was no scheme of work for this unit so individual teachers largely planned their own programme around the resources available. Stephen Barker used two basic text books, *Different Worlds* by Tony Crisp (1975) and *The World Now* by Andrew Reed (1984). The first book was clearly a product of the development of the 'new' geography with its emphasis on quantification, graphicacy, etc. However, practice in the manipulation of statistics, graphs, tables, and maps appears to have taken precedence over the understanding of issues and problems. The students were provided with a range of material indicating inequalities in food supply, health, and wealth, but little in way of explanation. Explanations that were provided were sometimes rather facile. In a section on apartheid in South Africa and Rhodesia (the book was first published in 1975 and reprinted several times, the last time in 1983) for example, under the heading 'Birds of a feather flock together' students were informed that 'many of the world's problems are caused by people flocking together because they have the same skin colour, religion, politics, language, and customs'. The second book was far more detailed and sophisticated in the analysis offered. It provided a wealth of data, case studies, analyses and explanation of issues affecting the 'Developing World'. Stephen Barker's practice, however, was not to follow the sections in a text book (he did not use the section quoted above, for example), but was to dip into each book for a graph, map, diagram, or section of text which he thought was appropriate.

He began with three lessons, which I did not observe, in which he described differences in wealth and population between the 'North' and 'South', talked about the different terms used like 'development', and 'Third World', and listed some of the 'Symptoms of Inequality' such as amount of food, number of doctors, and different life styles. Students did exercises in which they coloured world maps showing the rich north and the poor south, and compared their homes with that of a poor family in Nairobi. The first lesson I observed was the one described above which concentrated on inequalities in world food supply. The next two lessons were devoted to the same issue. This appeared to provide plenty of opportunity for the analysis and drawing of maps, graphs, and diagrams, and the calculation of comparative statistics highlighting north/south inequality. The different types of inequality between developed and developing countries was the basic idea that Stephen Barker wanted to transmit in these lessons. However, he did not offer or discuss with the class potential explanations for these inequalities. He seemed content to describe them and get students to understand the statistics. The possibility for speculation and discussion of competing explanations about why such inequalities exist was not taken up. Such a descriptive approach has been criticized by Klien (1985) and Hicks (1980, 1981) because of its concentration on the symptoms of inequality and neglect of explanations. They argue that the central issues are ignored and the way left open for simplistic, even racist, explanations to develop in the students' minds. Stephen Barker justified his concentration on description because he felt that the low average ability and the behavioural problems of the class would make it difficult to tackle such complex issues effectively. He also said he did not wish to pre-empt work on this topic which was planned for the fourth and fifth years. But interestingly he did, in the lesson described above, introduce the idea of 'fairness' in the distribution of world resources. He implied that the present inequality was unfair which, of course, is a political judgement and perhaps open to alternative interpretations that were not in fact raised.

The next two lessons consisted of a case study of a farming family in Zambia based on material in a book called *North-South Lifestyles – Case Studies from the South* by Arnold Turner (1985). This book appeared to adopt the approach which Klien (1985) calls a 'non-racist perspective' focusing in some detail on the everyday life of individual families in various parts of the developing world. Its intention was, as the introductory notes to teachers explained, to 'illustrate patterns of life (of families) which have been influenced by their economic and social status and by their beliefs' and to 'give some idea of the diversity and range of lifestyles within a category as well as their commonality'. Each chapter contained a case study of one family, combining photographs, graphs, tables, diagrams, and text into an attractively produced book. Unfortunately, on reading the case studies contained in the book one is left with the impression that most of the families live in an unproblematic, conflict-free world. In an effort to portray the lifestyles of people in other countries in a positive way, the book presents a rather rosy and optimistic view of the families, and, whilst there is a lot of technical information about how families make a living, the sorts of food they eat, and the sorts of houses they live in, we are told little about the social structures or political organization of their communities, about conflicts within those communities, or about social change and how this affects the families. In short, the image presented is de-contextualized and consensual. Interestingly, also, eleven of the twelve case studies are centred around the life of the *male* head of the family.

Stephen Barker chose to spend two lessons getting the students to read and answer a number of comprehension questions on this case study mainly focusing on the ways in which the Zambian family produced food. Following this he went on to spend two lessons considering the idea of what sort of technology might be appropriate to farming in the Third World and introduced the idea of 'intermediate technology'. Either side of these lessons he showed the two films on farming mentioned above. He then moved back to the notion of inequality, teaching a lesson which focused on a comparison of Britain and Bangladesh through the consideration of a variety of facts and figures – size, population growth, population density, calorie intake per head, number of doctors per head, etc.

Following this he taught two lessons on population growth and finally four lessons on urban growth and rural/urban migration in the Third World. Here he considered push/pull factors affecting migration, the interpretation of population statistics, and some of the problems young migrants face when they arrive in Third World cities, the latter through a moving story of the life of a poor teenage street vendor in Dar es Salaam taken from a booklet produced by a local 'Development Education Project'. Again most of the content of these lessons was descriptive and provided plenty of opportunity for copying drawings and graphs.

The curriculum selected, then, began to raise some of the issues surrounding the relationship between the developed and the developing world and presented examples of cultures in different parts of the world. Although in some of the materials students were presented with a consensual, conflict-free image of Third World communities, Stephen Barker emphasized the problematic nature of the inequalities which exist between rich and poor countries. Thus he introduced the students to an important and controversial question of social justice. Unfortunately the teaching style he adopted (or felt he had to adopt) with the group did not allow very much discussion of the issues involved. He concentrated on description and the skills of data interpretation, and used exercises such as copying maps, graphs, and diagrams primarily as a means of enhancing classroom control. This meant that the students had little opportunity to ask questions, raise issues, or voice their own ideas. Their perceptions and understanding of development issues remained largely unexplored and their engagement with the curriculum was limited.

The second unit of work I want to describe was taught by Peter Mills. This was with a fifth year top band group who were studying 'Persecution and Prejudice' for their O/CSE exam. This topic involved a whole term's work and was divided into four main sections. First, there was a brief introduction in which basic terms were defined. Then there were studies of apartheid in South Africa, Nazi Germany, and the struggle for women's rights in the late nineteenth and early twentieth centuries. I observed twelve lessons mainly from the first and second sections of the topic. The work was historical in orientation and utilized materials from a variety of sources.

In the section on South Africa Peter Mills used a set of materials entitled 'Segregation by Race' that the ex-head of department had obtained from a London school. It included basic background information on the racial categories of the South African population, the history of the country, laws passed by the South African government to control political protest, newspaper reports and extracts from novels concerning the system of racial segregation and discrimination, views of apartheid from a black person and a white person, extracts from Mandela's statement from the dock during his trial in 1964, and a series of source materials on the Sharpeville shootings in 1960. Whilst the material was somewhat dated, failing to provide information on or to utilize more contemporary developments, and suffered because of the poor quality of the reproduction, it did provide a fairly accurate and personalized, if simple, description of South African society and its inequalities and conflicts. In fact issues of inequality, conflict, and social justice were clearly central to the curriculum content of this section. Moreover, an emphasis on black protest meant that a view of black South Africans as passive victims of an oppressive system was avoided. The section, however, lacked any clear explanatory framework. Students were presented with interesting stories, information, and case studies regarding racial segregation and discrimination, but were not helped to understand very much about why such a system came into being, about the complex historical development of the country, or about the relationship between the economy, the political, judicial, and ideological systems, but perhaps this is expecting too much of a short course at this level.

During my observation, which covered half a term's work, Peter Mills taught lessons on the meanings of the terms persecution and prejudice, and then a series of lessons on South Africa covering the system of apartheid and its implications for black/white social relationships, an analysis of population figures and infant mortality rates, black and white views of apartheid, different forms of protest, and an exercise looking at historical evidence on the Sharpeville shootings.

Peter Mills presented a generally critical view of South African society. Perhaps one criticism that could be made of the content of the unit is that it did not examine in any depth ideas which have been put forward in support of apartheid. Whether such views should be presented as legitimate political opinion in the interests of balance is, of course, a controversial issue. My view is that such views would generally be racist and, although they should be examined and discussed, they should not be presented by teachers as acceptable opinion in a non-racist society.

He described the class as 'a fairly amenable bunch', who, though 'not very bright', were 'quite keen to get on and work'. The teaching methods employed were heavily dominated by the examination requirements of continuous assessment. As with the other units on the Integrated Humanities O/CSE course students were given marks for their completed unit folder, for a number of exercises completed during class time, and for a unit project which they worked on in their own time. Peter Mills constantly reminded students of the need to complete folder work 'because the marks go toward your final mark' and often parts of lessons were taken up with an explanation of the mark scheme for the particular exercise.

The lessons that I observed were class taught, Peter Mills taking responsibility for curriculum, and closely supervising student work activities. When most of the students had arrived Peter Mills would deliver a short introduction standing at the front to the students who faced him sitting in rows. Sometimes he included a brief question and answer session mainly employed to elicit student knowledge or understanding of a particular term or idea, often following with a brief explanation himself. Occasionally he would lead brief discussions on value issues, but these never formed a major part of the lesson, and student participation was generally confined to a small group of girls who most often volunteered answers and comments. When opportunities arose for students to take a more active role in the interpretation of curriculum materials or to engage in discussion or collaborative forms of learning, as for example with the primary source materials on the Sharpeville shootings, Peter Mills did not take them up. The emphasis was on the production of written work for assessment.

Following his introduction Peter Mills then usually explained the exercise he wanted the students to complete, which was listed in worksheet form in the appropriate section of the prepared booklet, dealt with any equipment shortages, and expected the students to work quietly by themselves for the rest of the lesson. During this individual work he wandered the class, supplying paper, answering student questions, and generally surveying the group, occasionally glancing over a student's shoulder to inspect their work. The class usually worked quietly, if unenthusiastically, with the minimum of disturbance. Students were expected to take home work to complete if they did not finish during class time. This lesson format was fairly standard and was used for general class work and special sessions devoted to completing assessment work under 'exam' conditions.

The following lesson was fairly typical. The students were asked to work on an extract from a novel called *The Evidence of Love* by Dan Jacobson about the return to South Africa of a white woman and a 'coloured' man who have married in England.

> Last lesson Tuesday afternoon. Five boys and two girls are present when I arrive three minutes after the bell. PM is on the corridor waiting for others to appear. A few minutes later four girls arrive. PM decides he is going to start. The students have helped themselves to folders as they come in and sit down quietly. PM gives out the work booklet.
>
> PM – Right could you turn to page 6 please. (A girl arrives followed by a boy. His friend from another class tries to accompany him. PM ushers him out.)
>
> PM – Sorry about the interruption. Can you turn to page 6. I'll explain what we're going to do after we've read through this together. It's an extract from a novel. It's not true. It hasn't actually happened, but it could have happened. It highlights the problems that face people of different colours in South Africa . . . (he reads the title of the extract and explains where it is from) . . . I'll make a start to prove I can read then I'll ask for volunteers or press gang someone. So 'Coloured Husband, White Wife' . . . (He reads. About half way through he stops and asks if anyone would like to carry on. Rebbeca(R) and Sharon(S), two Afro/Caribbean girls offer. PM choses Sharon and she continues with the passage for a few minutes. Then R has a turn, followed by Elizabeth(E) another Afro/Carribean girl. PM stops the reading two or three times to explain the meaning of several words that he thinks they might have difficulty with. They finish the passage.)
>
> PM – Right thanks to our three readers. Does anybody have any observations?
>
> (No response.)
>
> PM – Well what briefly has happened? What incident is highlighted? What do you think the author is trying to convey?
>
> R – If you are married you are going to be banned.
>
> PM – Right co-habitation between whites and those classed as coloured is banned. Why did the couple decide to go back to South Africa? What was the driving force?
>
> E – They're both South African.

PM – Yes, they're both South African. What did they know before
they left England Elizabeth?
R – That it would be a problem.
PM – Yes, they knew that they'd be breaking the law. What is
there in the extract which shows they were aware, Susan?
(No response.)
PM – Have a look on page 7 . . . (pause) . . . Anybody found it yet?
Have you got it Darren? You won't find it on the wall.
S – Where it says welcome home.
PM – Yes. (He reads a short section) They were very concerned.
They were afraid to open their mouths. It took a bit of time before
the officials realized that they were going to be breaking the law.
Why do you think it's got to a situation where the lounge is empty?
GIRL – Because they have been left 'til last.
PM – Why?
E – Because . . . (inaudible).
PM – Yes. Perhaps they have been expecting a confrontation so
they would rather stay at the end of the queue, so that it would be a
private thing. Now on page 10 there are three standard form
questions. The fourth question carries far more marks. (He reads
the question.) 'Do you think that forcing races to live apart is right?
Write 100-200 words for or against.' You need to find reasons for
whatever stance. I've got a rough idea what the majority of you
would stand for, but you've got to try and back up your stance.
What could be one answer?
R – No.
PM – Why shouldn't they be forced to live apart? Why should they
be allowed to live together?
E – If it's two groups then one of them might not like it.
PM – Yes, the stigma of segregation. Right, it's grossly unfair. Are
there any other reasons, what's the main one, what is the principle
we should all work for? (Pause, but no response.) . . . Well
irrespective of race, or colour, or where you come from, all people
should be treated equally . . . Number 4 will take some thinking
out. Start off with number 1 and work from there. Start from the
same page as 'A Vicious Act' (a previous exercise).

PM then explains about how much they should write on each
question and the marks that are allocated. He gives out marked
work from the last lesson with odd comments on tidiness, spelling,
questions missed out and length of answers. He then tells the
students to work on their own for the remaining twenty minutes of
the lesson. After a little chatting they settle down to their work. PM
stands at his desk and surveys the class or gazes out of the window.
On several occasions students put up their hands and PM goes to

them to answer their questions. A few minutes before the bell is due to go PM tells them to pack and to take the work home if they haven't finished, explaining that they will start the next section of work on Thursday.

Conclusion

Although the Humanities teachers were ambivalent about teaching at Milltown High and lacked the political commitments which had drawn the English teachers to the school, they adopted a calm and consistent approach to their work, based upon long years of classroom experience, and succeeded in establishing an ordered working environment which did not characterize some areas of the school, and which some of the students I interviewed appreciated. They thought many of the students were 'difficult' and 'disturbed', but maintained a commitment to individualism in their perceptions of students. Their main aims were to teach basic skills and concepts derived from the disciplines of Geography, History, and Religious Studies, and to increase student knowledge of the variety of human cultures. They also aimed to provide a 'balanced' examination of important social issues and developments by presenting a range of different explanations and viewpoints. It is difficult to judge whether they succeeded here, partly because of the problems of defining and assessing 'balance', but also because I was unable to observe the full range of the department's teaching and curriculum. In the units I did observe, whilst I felt a rather rosy picture of contemporary social organization and relationships was presented in some lessons, in others a more critical view was transmitted. The unit of work on 'Persecution and Prejudice' was certainly unbalanced in the sense of being specifically anti-apartheid and anti-Nazi, but I would regard this form of imbalance as being acceptable and necessary in a society committed to the values of non-racism and democracy.

Multiculturalism was a central organizing principle in the selection of curriculum content in the department. The idea was to reflect the history and background of the students in the curriculum and to use different world cultures to illustrate key concepts and common themes. In this way the teachers hoped to enhance the self-esteem of their students and encourage a greater awareness and tolerance of different cultural forms. A unit on 'Persecution and Prejudice' was also taught in the fifth year. However, unfortunately a consideration of racial inequality and racism in Britain were absent from this unit and from the rest of the department's work.

The teachers felt the 'progressive' pedagogy, advocated by some Humanities teachers, was inappropriate given the realities of classroom life at Milltown High. Here their most pressing need was the maintenance of classroom order and they developed teaching styles orientated primarily to this aim. Their approaches were dominated by whole class teaching in which the teacher strongly 'framed' (Bernstein 1971b) the knowledge transmission in the classroom. In every lesson the teacher alone was responsible for the selection and presentation of subject content, and exerted strong control over the pacing of students' work. There was little differentiation of tasks according to the ability level or interest of students. Lessons were generally 'aimed at the middle' and basic work tasks, written on the blackboard or on work sheets, were intended to be completed by all students. The only modification that had been made to practice as a result of the introduction of mixed-ability grouping had been to begin each set of work tasks with a simple exercise that all students could perform and to provide extension tasks for those who 'finished first'. Teaching was usually didactic in form with an emphasis on teacher exposition interspersed with short question and answer sessions heavily dominated by the teacher. This was followed by individual seat work in which student/student interaction was discouraged and the teacher 'policed' the classroom. Group work and small group discussion, which might have permitted a greater degree of student participation, and co-operation, or project work which could have increased student control over the pacing of work were rarely used.

Chapter eight

Racism, social differentiation, and equal opportunities at Milltown High School

It has been suggested that within-school processes frequently disadvantage ethnic minority students in British schools. In particular it has been argued that some teachers have negative views of ethnic minority students, especially of Afro/Caribbean students, and that these views can affect their behaviour towards them in the school and classroom. Moreover, it is claimed that such students are more likely to be allocated to low status positions in school and classroom social structures and accorded less favourable treatment and opportunities as a result. I was interested in whether I would find such processes in operation at Milltown High or whether, as a result of having a school policy on racism, they would have been eliminated or avoided. In other words I was interested in whether the staff at Milltown High had succeeded in creating the non-racist environment that their policy advocated.

In order to address this question I will present data from a number of sources. First, there are my own informal observations during the year of my field work. Second, there is data from interviews that I conducted with thirty-two of the teaching staff. Third, there is information from interviews and small group discussions that I conducted with a sample of fifth year students. Fourth, there is an analysis I conducted of the school's procedures for formal differentiation, its division of students into ability groups, and its option system. Finally, there is data from a case study of differentiation within one mixed-ability class by five of their teachers.

Racism in school – an ethnographer's overview

One of the strengths of the ethnographic method is the observation of social action as it occurs in 'natural' settings. The ethnographer is able to study what people actually do in 'real' life rather than what they do in a laboratory or what they say they do in answer to survey questions. Such observation is generally conducted over a relatively long period of time and the researcher becomes a participant in some way in the setting in order to minimize what has been termed 'reactivity', i.e. the effect that the researcher has on whatever he/she is studying. Thus at Milltown High I was able to study the attitudes and behaviour of staff and students in 'naturalistic' settings. Several of the teachers and some of the students also became key informants supplying me with information about the attitudes and behaviour of others in the school. Furthermore, because of the length of time I spent 'in the field' I became an accepted figure in most areas of the school and the influence of my presence over social interaction was minimized. This does not mean, of course, that my observation of social behaviour and attitudes at Milltown High was totally accurate. It is possible that views were expressed and behaviour occurred which were different from that which I observed. It also does not mean that reactivity was totally eliminated. This is, of course, never the case (see Hammersley and Atkinson 1983). It is possible that because of my presence actors did not express the views or behave as they would otherwise have done. We can only say that the ethnographic method made this less likely to happen than would be the case with other methods.

During the course of my field work I encountered very few naturally expressed attitudes from teachers which could be said to be racist. Unlike the staffroom described by Hammersley (1980) staffroom talk at Milltown High (and also naturally occurring teacher talk in other situations) was not characterized by derogatory remarks about 'immigrants' or about the threat to 'standards' and discipline posed by 'immigration', nor were there references to ethnic minority cultures as 'alien' or 'inferior'. Whilst there was much talk in the staffroom about individual students in which information and perceptions were 'traded' (Hammersley 1980), few references were made to students' ethnic or racial group. Students who posed problems in terms of behaviour were featured more frequently in staffroom talk, but there seemed to be roughly proportionate numbers of black and white students who came into this category. Moreover, although sometimes staffroom talk did result in premature categorization of certain students, there were several staff who would challenge the conceptions of others, especially where they sensed unfair or inappropriate labelling.

The only times that I came across racist attitudes was from a small number of 'supply' staff. During the teachers' pay dispute the school was desperate for supply teachers to cover for staff absence. They were difficult to obtain and often the school had to take whoever was available or send students home. It was not possible for the head to interview such staff and therefore explore their attitudes before they came to the school. A few of these teachers were clearly working 'just for the money' and had negative and preconceived views about ethnic minority students. One retired ex-teacher whom I spoke to informally in the staffroom explained how she found 'these black children aggressive and threatening' and how she 'avoided confrontation with them at all costs'. Another, when I asked him how teaching at Milltown High compared with other schools he had worked in, said: 'The big difference is the black kids. They're just bone idle and lazy.' Another came up to me in a lesson I observed and said, 'You get plenty of jungle talk here, but not much in the way of work.' However, the majority of supply teachers were not of this ilk, and certainly these comments were not characteristic of the talk of permanent staff at Milltown High.

In terms of behaviour in classrooms and around the school I did not observe any situations which I felt were patterned by racist attitudes from staff. There were no incidents of the type described by Wright (1986) in which a teacher's insensitive attitude towards his ethnic minority students created a situation of conflict. I did see many conflicts between staff and students, but they seemed to be largely unrelated to issues of race and uninfluenced by racist attitudes. The one exception to this was an incident with a supply teacher which was reported to me by another teacher. A black student had become embroiled in a confrontation with her and she had in a fit of temper called him a 'nigger'. The staff I spoke to about this were horrified and the boy's complaint was speedily and sympathetically dealt with. The teacher did not return to work in the school.

I did not observe any racist behaviour by staff in their interactions with ethnic minority students. Classroom rules and codes of conduct were on the whole flexibly and fairly administered and in the lessons I observed interaction patterns appeared to be unrelated to students' ethnic group. However, on isolated occasions, according to my informants, racially differentiated patterns of interaction did occur in classes. One example was given to me by Susan Parker, one of the English teachers. She described a class that she took over from Jennifer Green who went on maternity leave. The students were apparently very angry that their 'proper' teacher had left them in the middle of an examination course. They had not been taught by Susan Parker before and it seems that the Afro/Caribbean students in the group were particularly annoyed, as they had developed a close and loyal relationship with Jennifer Green. They responded by behaving badly and being extremely hostile to their new teacher. Susan Parker explained that she found herself interacting more often and more positively with the white students in the class. The situation was made worse by the fact that she decided, partly on Jennifer Green's advice, to study Ian MacDonald's novel *The Hummingbird Tree* which contains in it racist dialogue. When Susan Parker read the text to the class, hoping to explore the anti-racist message of the book, she was accused of racism herself by the Afro/Caribbean students. Only after a long session of discussion involving one of the deputy heads was the situation eventually resolved. Perhaps this incident serves to underline that it is important to take student attitudes and action into account in explaining classroom interaction. And again it is important to emphasize that this situation was very much the exception. I myself did not observe any examples of such clear differential treatment.

The types of inadvertent differential treatment that Driver (1979) observed were also not apparent at Milltown High. Whilst many of the students perplexed, confused, and posed management problems for the teachers, this did not seem to relate strongly to their ethnic backgrounds or characteristics. Afro/Caribbean students were not markedly over-represented in the disciplinary incidents that I observed. Teachers did not take longer to get to know Afro/Caribbean students, nor were they more likely to confuse their identities. In fact it appeared to be unstated policy at Milltown High for teachers, where possible, to continue teaching the same class of students in consecutive years. As a result many of the teachers 'knew' their students very well. Teachers did not, so far as I was aware, confuse the non-verbal communications of their Afro/Caribbean students, nor did they fail to interpret derogatory expressions used by them. In fact cultural signals of this type were far more ethnically uniform at Milltown High than appears to have been the case in Driver's study school. White students, for example, would sometimes suck their lips in the same way as black students to signal dissent. In an established multi-racial area like Chesham and Richmond Hill there was considerable mixing of peer group cultures and ethnically exclusive behavioural forms were less common.[1]

It is important to realize that Driver's research was conducted in the early 1970s. Some of the students he studied may have been fairly recent arrivals from the Caribbean and certainly the teachers cannot have had much experience in dealing with students from diverse cultural backgrounds. The situation in his school must have been ripe for the sorts of cultural confusions he described. At Milltown High this was not so much the case. Not only was there less ethnically exclusive behaviour, but also teachers had had far more experience in recognizing and dealing with such behaviour when it occurred. This applied to the use of 'patois' which Driver noticed was used by black students to insult teachers or deny them access to communication. Although a form of 'patois' was used sometimes by black students in this way, it was very much a Milltown youth version and as such was sometimes used by white students, especially those with strong black friendships. The use of 'strong' patois, unintelligible to teachers, was relatively rare. Furthermore, I did not see any negative or derogatory treatment of students by teachers in response to the use of dialect or patois. Thus the sorts of confusions which Driver argued provided 'obstacles to confident relations between West Indian pupils and English teachers' were not apparent at Milltown High. Afro/Caribbean students did not appear to be treated differently from their white peers as a result of cultural confusions.

On the surface, then, it did seem that the teachers at Milltown High had created an environment which was free of the expression of racism by staff and where students were treated equitably. It is possible though that racist attitudes whilst proscribed in public staffroom talk could still be important in teachers' private views and attitudes towards students from different ethnic groups. I address this question in the next section.

Teacher attitudes

To examine teachers' racial attitudes more closely in the interviews that I conducted with thirty-two of the staff I asked two open-ended questions. First, I asked what teachers felt were the main characteristics of students of different ethnic groups. Second, I asked whether the teachers adjusted their approach in the classroom to suit students of different ethnic backgrounds. These questions were similar to the ones asked by Carrington and Wood (1983) in the secondary school they studied and resulted in several staff there revealing derogatory stereotypes of ethnic minority students. I have already described the responses of the teachers in the English and Humanities departments to these questions. These teachers were reluctant to categorize and generalize about students in terms of their race or ethnicity. They explained that they saw students as individuals and whilst it was important to understand students' ethnic backgrounds this was relatively unimportant in their day-to-day interactions with them. When they did generalize it was usually in terms of positive attributes deriving from ethnicity. They said that they adjusted their approaches in the classroom to, as far as possible, cater for the needs of individual students, but this was not dependent upon ethnic group. To what extent were these attitudes characteristic of staff as a whole at Milltown High?

A large proportion of the teachers that I interviewed (twenty-four out of the thirty-two) either refused to generalize or explained that they thought there were no or only very small differences between students of different ethnic groups. A number were well aware of the dangers of stereotyping and were therefore reluctant to attribute characteristics to students on the basis of their ethnic origins. 'I don't think about students in those terms' or 'I think it's very dangerous to start thinking about kids in that way', were very common replies to my question. Two teachers, perceptively, challenged the ethical basis of my question, arguing that by asking it I was perhaps encouraging teachers to articulate stereotypes that might not have featured centrally in their thoughts and that I might thereby legitimate such views. The majority of these teachers argued that there were as many differences between students of the same ethnic group as there were between ethnic groups, and that really it was 'individuals' who were different.

Several teachers made the point I raised in the last section, that in a multi-ethnic area like Chesham or Richmond Hill there was considerable mixing of cultural forms, and that nearly all the students at Milltown High had been born and brought up in the area, and so ethnic differences were far less pronounced than they were fifteen years ago. These teachers all maintained, in answer to my second question, that they did not adjust their approach to suit students of different ethnic groups. They adjusted their approach to suit 'individuals' or what they knew of the individuals in their classes. Differential treatment, they argued, was not related to ethnic group. Students were typed on the basis of their classroom performance and general behaviour around the school, and if differential treatment was necessary it was on this basis. Ethnicity, they maintained, was not a factor in their judgements.

The majority of teachers who did offer to generalize (eight out of the thirty-two) did so very tentatively, often prefacing their comments with statements like – 'You do realize I'm generalizing like mad' or 'I'm not saying they're all like this, it's only a tendency'. Their comments in reference to ethnic minority students displayed a mixture of positive and negative attitudes. Afro/Caribbean students were generally held to be more 'volatile', 'excitable', in their behaviour and, especially the boys, 'laid back' in their attitudes to school work, but they were also seen as 'lively' (in a positive sense of playing an active part in lessons), 'better attenders', and by one as 'better dressed'. Two of these teachers made distinctions between Afro/Caribbean girls and boys. The former were held to be 'grafters' and 'dependable', the latter as having a more 'easy come, easy go attitude'. The few Asian students in the school were regarded as 'more willing to work' and 'better behaved', but also as 'tending to be rather arrogant'. These teachers certainly did not have negative attitudes towards their ethnic minority students, and as I have said they were extremely cautious in their generalizations. Indeed the typifications that they did produce were, perhaps, more a product of the interview questions than an indication of their active attitudes. In answer to my second question they all maintained that they did not vary their approach in the classroom according to the ethnicity of the students, but adopted common standards and expectations for all students.

Only two teachers out of the thirty-two interviewed appeared to attribute exclusively negative characteristics to ethnic minority students. One, a Craft teacher, said that Afro/Caribbean people were 'an underachieving nation, on the whole', and Afro/Caribbean students 'don't make much effort'. 'I think basically it is just their culture . . . and their family set-up', he explained. He also thought many of the white children at the school were 'lazy' and 'un-disciplined', but Afro/Caribbean students were more so, he suggested. The other, a Science teacher, argued that, 'Afro/Caribbean boys tend to be more aggressive than white boys in this school. That's largely to do, so far as I can see, with their nutrition at an early age.' He also commented that:

> Afro/Caribbean attitudes to society and life in general are much more laid-back than typical English attitudes . . . Afro/Caribbeans have got a different attitude to life, to their behaviour, I mean generally they are less likely to want to sit still and write, they're more likely to be up and doing things. They don't take discipline so easily, they're not disciplined in that sort of sense. That's not making any inferior statement about them, it's a recognition of their racial differences.

However, even these teachers maintained that in the classroom they did not adjust their approach to suit students of different ethnic groups. They both said that they treated all the students equally, and made judgements and based their actions on the same standards for all.

On the basis of these interviews, then, it appears that the vast majority of staff at Milltown High did not subscribe to racist views of ethnic minority students and were well aware of the dangers of attributing characteristics to students on the basis of their ethnic group. They did not appear to operate on the basis of what Figueroa (1984) calls 'a racial frame of reference'. To what extent this awareness was a product of the school having adopted a policy statement and having engaged with the issue of multicultural and anti-racist education is difficult to say, but a number of the teachers explained that their awareness of such issues had been heightened by informal discussion of school policy in this area.

Interestingly two teachers described how their attitudes had changed since arriving at Milltown High. They had both previously taught in mainly white schools in other parts of the city. When their colleagues there heard that they were going to work at Milltown High they were told by several to 'watch out for the black kids'. The impression they got from 'the grapevine' was that Afro/Caribbean students were 'difficult', 'excitable', and even 'explosive', and that they had to be 'handled with kid gloves'. They therefore arrived with certain preconceptions regarding the nature of Afro/Caribbean students. One of the teachers explained how he deliberately treated Afro/Caribbean students less strictly than their white peers as a result during his first few months in the school. However, after discussing this issue with other staff at Milltown High and experiencing the school, he had come to the conclusion that his view was erroneous. He now treated all the students equally irrespective of their ethnic group. It seems that informal gossip within the teaching profession can sometimes lead to the transference of racist myths from one institution to another. This perhaps, combined with impressions gathered from the media, can influence teachers' attitudes which may influence their initial actions when they arrive in a multi-ethnic school, or indeed their decision to work in such a school at all. But the fact that staff at Milltown High had engaged with the issue of multicultural and anti-racist education and discussed it informally helped to dispel these myths once the teachers arrived in the school.

Students' views

So far the evidence that I have presented seems to indicate that Milltown High was characterized by a non-racist ethos. I was interested in whether the views of students would confirm this. To find out I conducted six small group discussions involving twenty-two fourth year students and interviewed thirty-one fifth year students from different ethnic backgrounds. Of the latter group I selected roughly equal numbers of students whom class tutors felt were pro-school, anti-school, or ambivalent to school. Interestingly Afro/Caribbean boys were more likely to be seen as anti-school than might have been expected given their numbers in the year. Most of these discussions and interviews were tape recorded with the students' permission. By the time I did this work I had got to know many of the students quite well. Most had come to know me as 'the person who was writing a book about the school' and did not see me as a teacher, although I was, of course, someone whom they knew spent a lot of time with the teachers. I reassured all of them about the confidentiality of what they said to me, and this most seemed to accept. On the whole they seemed to welcome the opportunity to talk openly, express their opinions, and to help with my project. It is, of course, impossible to tell how much the data from these interviews was affected by the students' perceptions of me as adult, male, white, and 'teacher-like'. Within obvious constraints I did my utmost to minimize such reactivity.

I have not got the space here to report the detail of these interviews. What I mainly want to focus upon is students' perceptions of racism within the school. I began all the discussions and interviews with general questions, asking students what they felt about the school and the education they received, and what they thought were the good and bad things about the school. I then went on to ask them about their attitudes to and relationships with the teachers, and what they felt were the good and bad things about the teachers. By not raising specific issues at the beginning of the interview I hoped to get at what the students felt

131

were important. If, for example, racism was seen as a significant issue then I thought the students would raise it in response to these early general questions. Later in the interview I asked more specific questions about their perceptions of racism in the school amongst the teachers and students, and the extent to which they felt relationships were influenced by race and ethnicity.

Responses to my questions varied considerably according to the student's general orientation to school. Unsurprisingly, those who had been categorized by their teachers as pro-school were more likely to respond positively and favourably to school life and to their teachers. Such students from both main ethnic groups explained that they were happy on the whole with the school and their education. Some said that they felt that the school had got an unjustified bad reputation in the local area, largely as a result of the activities of a small minority of 'unruly' younger pupils. The trouble and disruption caused by such students and the inability of some teachers to deal with it effectively was their biggest complaint. Others expressed concern about the lack of adequate facilities and extra-curricular activities, the poor quality of many supply teachers, and 'falling behind because of always being sent home'.

Most of these students had a fairly sophisticated typology of teachers which expressed their clear expectations of how they thought teachers ought to teach and act. Students of both main ethnic groups had very similar views which resembled closely the opinions of school students interviewed by other researchers (see Nash 1976; Furlong 1976 and 1977; Beynon 1985). Teachers were expected to be 'strict' and not 'soft', keep order in the classroom, deal with them fairly and consistently without undue aggression, and be reasonably friendly, showing they had the ability to 'have a laugh' (cf. Woods 1979) and share a joke. They were also expected to set work and teach in a way which was interesting, and to give explanations which were clear and easily intelligible. On these criteria teachers were judged or 'typed' and it was largely around these criteria that the students I interviewed focused their comments. Their biggest criticism was of teachers who were 'soft' and failed to control their classes, or who provided 'boring' work with inadequate explanation. But these pro-school students felt that the majority of their teachers were competent and fair and that the work they set was interesting. Several specifically commented favourably on the openness and friendliness of many of the teachers. Racism from teachers was not something that any of them raised themselves as an issue.

When questioned more specifically about racism in the school pro-school students of both main ethnic groups argued that it was relatively limited. None of the students said that they had come across racism from any of the teachers at present at Milltown High. One Afro/Caribbean boy explained that he thought teachers who were racist would not come to work at Milltown High anyway. However, one ex-teacher's name was quoted with monotonous regularity in response to my questions. He was a Craft teacher who had since left the school and every student appeared to have a story to tell about him. An Afro/Caribbean girl described him:

> That Mr Stone he was racist . . . He did little things like always put you by yourself and other people from a different part of the class would talk and he would directly pick on you. He would take you out of the class and start givin' you lip. And he mainly seemed to pick on black children. I stayed out of his way . . . Most of the kids didn't like him because of the way he acted towards them. He was really out of order. For example, if he accused you of something you did not do and you argued back he would shout in your face and point at you and push you around. He was randy as well. He used to come up to you and put his arm around you. He shouldn't do that.

This teacher was accused of racism by nearly all the students (pro-school and anti-school) I interviewed. In a sense his reputation had entered into student mythology and may have been exaggerated as a result, but from the students' accounts he does appear to have been particularly inept in his dealings with many students, especially Afro/Caribbean. He apparently had a short and explosive temper and regularly got into confrontations with students. Several of these resulted in physical violence from students to him and vice versa. On occasions racist insults were exchanged. On many occasions he over-stepped the limits of what students regarded as fair and acceptable teacher behaviour and was disliked by many students as a result (cf. Werthman 1963; Woods 1979; Beynon 1985). However, several of the pro-school students I interviewed used the case of Mr Stone as a means of highlighting what they saw as the non-racism of the present staff at Milltown High. 'None of the other teachers are like him', one said. Another explained how he thought the teachers had got rid of Mr Stone because he was racist. Mr Stone was very untypical of teachers at Milltown High, they maintained. On the whole these students did not feel that racism was very significant in their relationships with teachers. Similarly none of them quoted any instances where they felt ethnic minority students had been unfairly treated or examples of practices they thought disadvantaged them. They felt that generally students from different ethnic groups were treated equally and fairly.

There were only four students of Asian origin in the fifth year all of whom were perceived by their teachers as pro-school. I interviewed two of these students together. Their views were very similar to those of the students I have just described, but they were even more critical of the inability of their teachers to handle the students who 'mess about' and 'waste everybody's time'. In their opinion teachers were far too 'soft' and 'tolerant' and they thought such students ought to be 'expelled'. Apart from this they explained that they got on very well with their teachers and did not feel that any of them were racist.

Those students who were described by their teachers as anti-school or ambivalent to school not surprisingly were less positive about their experiences in school and about their teachers. These students were more likely to describe the school as 'rubbish', 'a waste of time', or a 'right dump'. They often thought that the 'standards' of work and behaviour in the school had 'gone right down' and mainly attributed blame to the teachers who 'don't really care' or 'can't handle us'. Many of these students could find very little that was good to say about the school, and often produced a string of complaints ranging from poor school facilities to petty and childish rules, an indication of the extent of their alienation. Some believed that it was pretty pointless to come to school anyway as they were not going to get any qualifications and even if they did there were few jobs for them to go on to. Many, however, and this especially applied to Afro/Caribbean students, maintained a strong belief in the value of academic qualifications and although rejecting much of what was on offer at school said they were planning to go to college to 'get qualifications'. They displayed a similar 'contradictory' attitude to their education to that noted by Furlong (1984) in his study of a group of disaffected Afro/Caribbean students. On the one hand they valued 'education' and the potential upward mobility that it offered, on the other they were strongly attached to a peer group culture which rejected many school norms.

These students operated with similar conceptions of teachers to the ones I discussed above. If anything they were more discerning and more prepared to be critical if teachers did not live up to their expectations. They criticized many teachers for being 'soft', 'unable to control us', 'not making us work', for setting low standards of work and behaviour, for giving dull or incomprehensible work or activities they regarded as pointless, or for being 'moody' or unfriendly. At the same time teachers who tried to impose their authority too forcefully were often seen as 'pushing their luck' or 'gettin' above themselves'. Teachers had to tread a very narrow line to win the respect and compliance of many of these students.

Only three of those that I interviewed complained, without being asked, about what they felt was racism from their teachers. When I asked one Afro/Caribbean boy who had been in a lot of trouble in school, what he thought were the bad things about the school he said:

> The teachers . . . they treat you really bad. I'm sure there are some racist teachers in this school. Like last time I got suspended Mr

Benyon asked Paul Jones (a white boy in similar trouble) to sit down while he told me to stand up. There were a load of chairs there, but he made sure I had to stand up.

However, when we discussed this instance further he explained: 'I don't really think it was prejudice against colour, just prejudice against me. He doesn't like me at all.' When we discussed teacher racism more generally he said that there was 'racism between some of the teachers and the pupils', and he quoted the infamous Mr Stone as an example: 'He got Peter Miller in his woodwork room and he locked his door and he had a stick and he was trying to hit him. And Peter picked up another one and fought his way out and Mr Stone didn't report it. That's just racialism . . . ' But he explained that he did not think it was always possible to tell if a teacher was actually racist or not. As far as he was concerned he felt that he had been labelled and 'picked on' by the teachers, but he was unsure whether this was related to race or whether 'it's just me'.

Two other anti-school Afro/Caribbean boys interviewed together also raised the issue of racism:

DAVID – A few of the teachers are prejudiced. For example Mr Stone he always used to act aggressive to black kids when they used to do something wrong. I got told that he called a black girl a black slag . . .
PF – Are there any other teachers you would say are prejudiced?
DAVID – Na
EDWIN – Mrs Woods
DAVID – Yeah, I don't like her attitude . . . She's aggressive all the time . . . It's the way she carries on. I mean you can tell someone . . . They don't need to show you what they're like, you can just read them as they go along, as they do certain things, you can just read them.

When pressed further these boys found it difficult to specify exactly what they meant and to give examples of incidents which they felt showed 'prejudice'. They appeared to use the accusation in a generalized way in order to signify their profound alienation from the school and the teachers. 'Racism' here was used as a slogan to criticize the school.

But these students were unusual even amongst the anti-school students in complaining of racism. Most students did not raise it as an issue. When I introduced the topic the majority agreed that, with the exception of Mr Stone, they did not feel their teachers at Milltown High were racist, or that any of the systems that operated put ethnic minority students at a disadvantage. The following discussion with a group of

135

Afro/Caribbean students was typical of many of the conversations I had. We had been talking about the issue of racism in general and one of the boys had described an incident on recent bus journey where he and some of his friends had been called 'a nigger' by a local bus driver.

PF – Is there any racism in school like that?
CHRIS – No way, there can't be, none of the teachers here are like that.
JUNIOR – I don't see nothin' me personally.
PAUL – The teachers here are alright in that respect.
PF – Are there any teachers who you would say are prejudiced?
JUNIOR – Na, not really. It's difficult to tell.
PAUL – I don't think there are. I don't think there's much racism in this school. In some schools there is though.
PF – Do you think black kids get a worse deal than white kids in this school?
PAUL – No I think we get treated more or less the same here. But I don't think we go on as many trips as we used to . . . Now we just don't go nowhere. That's probably why a lot of people don't like school no more. You know we used to like goin' on a trip, like an outing. Teachers don't say nothin' like that no more. So they just wag it or whatever.

The hostility of most Afro/Caribbean students to school did not hinge around perceptions of racism from the staff or the disadvantages they felt they faced as a group in the school. It appears to have derived largely from a more general dissatisfaction with students' subordinate position in school, what was on offer in school and their poor post-school prospects. As such Afro/Caribbean students' feelings were similar to those of many of their white peers. Occasionally the hostility of Afro/Caribbean students was expressed using the vocabulary of 'racism', but such accusations rarely specified incidents that were racist in terms of the definition I have used. Most of these students, whilst critical of many of the practices at the school, agreed that students of different ethnic background were treated equally and fairly. Milltown High in this respect seems to have been very different from the schools that Wright (1986) researched. Many of the Afro/Caribbean students that she talked to believed that the teachers were negative and antagonistic towards them and the school system worked against them. As a result they felt 'resentment, bitterness and frustration' towards the school. This does not appear to have been the case at Milltown High.

In terms of their relationships with other students, again both Afro/Caribbean and white students argued that racism was relatively insignificant. Nearly all said that on the whole black and white students mixed and got on very well in the school and that there were very few conflicts which were influenced by racism. Girls especially pointed to the large number of ethnically mixed friendship groups that there were amongst students. This was largely confirmed by my own observations around the school. Whilst friendship choices were clearly influenced by ethnicity and both boys and girls tended to choose friends from within their own ethnic group there were many exceptions. A large and dominant group of fifth year girls, for example, had many Afro/Caribbean and white members who shared common attitudes to school and youth cultural interests. Similarly, a dominant group of fifth year Afro/Caribbean boys included several white members. During my field work there were very few inter-student disputes or conflicts which were patterned by racism. In fact the only time I observed such a dispute was in Susan Parker's English lesson described in the chapter on the English department and this was perhaps more a personality clash than anything.

Whilst some of the students complained about racist name calling they said this was mainly confined to 'young' and 'cheeky' 'little kids', and ironically to Afro/Caribbean students themselves. An Afro/Caribbean girl explained:

> I say it's equal in this school . . . You think when you hear of prejudice in the school you think it's the whites callin' the blacks or the whites callin' the Pakis, or whatever . . . but it's not it's the black people callin' the black, they're always callin' each other black this and black that, it's ridiculous really.

A number of teachers explained that amongst the Afro/Caribbean students there were status divisions which sometimes hinged around skin colour. On discussion with the students these appear to have taken contradictory forms. On the one hand students with a lighter skin tone, especially those of mixed-race parentage, were insulted or made fun of because they were 'breeds', i.e. half-caste. On the other hand the term 'black' could be used as a term of abuse. On the whole though, such abuse was regarded as fairly harmless and did not result in overt conflicts.

I think there are three possible reasons for the lack of racially motivated clashes between Afro/Caribbean and white students at Milltown High. One, a point that I have made before, is that the area in which the school was situated has been multi-ethnic for a considerable number of years and has a long history of fairly co-operative and tolerant relationships between the two main ethnic groups. Students have generally been brought up in the area and attended multi-ethnic schools for the whole of their school careers. Anti-racism amongst both black and white youth was a dominant attitude. Second, those white

137

students who did subscribe to racist beliefs, and there were some who voiced their prejudices to me in the privacy of the interview situation, were extremely reluctant to voice their views publicly in the school. Afro/Caribbean students enjoyed a slight numerical superiority and were often dominant in peer group cultures. As one white student, who at the weekend associated with a gang of white youths outside the area put it, 'the best thing to do is to keep quiet in school or you'll get your head kicked in'. A third reason is that the teachers at Milltown High had succeeded in conveying the importance of anti-racism. A number of the students that I talked to were clearly very conscious of the stand of the majority of the staff on the issue of racism and agreed with it, sometimes censoring their peers for their racism. Clearly the teachers had been influential to some extent.

However, they had not been completely successful in eliminating racial abuse. The two students of Asian origin that I interviewed complained that they were sometimes subject to abuse, name-calling, and hostility from other students, both Afro/Caribbean and white. The term 'Paki' was often used by students as a word of abuse around the school, despite attempts by staff to stop it. But although such abuse was clearly significant and offensive to these individual students, because they were such a small minority in the school it did not appear to affect relationships in general. Relationships between students from the two main ethnic groups were relatively amicable.

Social differentiation at Milltown High School

In most schools students are differentiated by their teachers on the basis of their academic ability and behaviour. In streamed or banded schools this differentiation is formalized into a fairly rigid social structure (see Hargreaves 1967; Lacey 1970; and Ball 1981) and there are systems for allocating students to different status groups soon after they arrive in the school. In other schools students are taught in mixed-ability groups[2] for the first few years and formal differentiation is postponed until the age of thirteen to fourteen (or sixteen in a small number of schools). In both systems differentiation also occurs more informally at the classroom level (see Lacey 1970; Ball 1981). It has been argued that both formal and informal differentiation often result in higher status students being treated more favourably and given superior opportunities within schools.

There has been increasing concern about the way ethnic minority students fare in processes of differentiation. At the formal level this concern has focused on the extent to which minority students are allocated to low status positions because of teacher prejudice, cultural bias, or cultural confusion (see, for example, Coard 1971; Driver 1979;

Wright 1986; and Tomlinson 1986), and on the inferior and demotivating treatment they might receive when allocated (on whatever basis) to such groups. In assessing whether Milltown High provided a non-racist environment I was interested in whether the system of formal differentiation operating in the school disadvantaged ethnic minority students in these ways.

I was interested first in the system of formal differentiation operating in the school and the ways students were allocated to different status groups, and whether minority students were treated less favourably than white students in the process of allocation. Second, I was concerned with the distribution of students from the various ethnic groups in that system and the extent to which groups were treated differently. Of course, a disproportionate number of ethnic minority students in low status groups does not in itself necessarily mean that minority students are being disadvantaged by practices within the school. Such students may enter a particular school with lower achievement levels, perhaps because of the peculiarities of the school's intake, or because of home background disadvantages, or differences in achievement in primary school, and be allocated to low status groups on fair, meritocratic criteria. In order to identify disadvantageous treatment we would need to show that, given an ethnic imbalance in the formal social structure, low status classes with higher proportions of minority students were treated less favourably by, for example, being given less teacher time and effort, poorer resources, or less-effective teachers.

The formal system of differentiation at Milltown High

The system of banding that was in operation at Milltown High was abandoned shortly after the arrival of David Benyon as headteacher in 1984. He was fundamentally opposed to any formal, rigid system of ability grouping, and attempted to move as much as possible towards mixed-ability groups. This he had succeeded in doing in the first three years, so that all classes here were mixed-ability, with the exception of Languages where students were divided into ability sets at the end of the second year. The system of selecting out a 'remedial' or 'bottom' group was also abandoned and the Remedial Department became the 'Learning Support Department'. Students with 'special needs' were taught alongside their peers in mainstream, mixed-ability classes, sometimes with the help of a Learning Support teacher. Formal differentiation of students had been postponed until the end of the third year at Milltown High.

This meant that the school avoided the situation described by Ball (1981) in the banded Beachside Comprehensive where students were 'labelled failures' by a system 'that had not given them the opportunity to show their worth'. Teachers were not encouraged by the system at Milltown High to make hasty or premature judgements and students had time to develop and display their talents through the study of a common curriculum which did not place restrictions on their choice of courses at thirteen plus.

At the end of the third year each subject department adopted its own system of setting. The English department selected a 'top' set which could be 'pushed' through both English Language and English Literature, thus gaining two qualifications at sixteen plus instead of one. Other English groups were 'mixed ability'. The Maths department adopted a hierarchical system of setting. Students in the top group had the opportunity of entering O level. Others took CSE, with the exception of those in the bottom group who did not work for public examinations. The Science and Humanities departments operated a joint system of banding. Together they divided students into an upper and lower ability band. In Science the top band students studied either Physics or Biology to sixteen plus level whilst the lower band studied a general Science Studies course to CSE. From within this lower band the Science teachers sometimes selected a 'difficult' group of students who were regarded as behaviour problems and, they felt, unlikely to achieve even a low grade CSE. In the 1985–6 fourth year there were relatively few girls in the lower band and so they were concentrated in the three 'non-difficult' groups. The 'difficult' group was all male. In the Humanities department both bands followed the same basic Integrated Humanities course. Those in the top band had the opportunity of entering for O level, but in fact the vast majority of students were entered for CSE. A 'remedial' group was selected from the lower band and followed a non-examination course, taught by 'Learning Support' teachers.

The other school subjects (with the exception of Social Education which was taught in years 4 and 5) became options at the end of the third year and students 'chose' three of them. Although in theory all options were of equal standing, Spanish (O/CSE) and Chemistry (sixteen plus) were regarded as the 'academic' options and were reserved for 'high ability' students. They were placed in different 'option blocks' so that these students could chose both subjects if they wanted to and less academic subjects were set against them. With the exception of Spanish and Chemistry all option subjects operated on the basis of mixed-ability groups as most had only enough students for one group. Because of the relatively low student numbers in the school setting in option groups was not possible and thus differentiation through the option system was not marked.

Thus the system of formal differentiation which began at the end of the third year was rather complex. There were, in fact, several status hierarchies. Some students were concentrated in the top groups and others in the lower status groups, but most occupied a variety of positions in the different status hierarchies. The system of differentiation was also fairly flexible as block timetabling allowed the English and Maths departments to move students from set to set without affecting their positions in other subject areas.

Given this system the students often found it difficult to identify where they or their peers stood in the school social structure. Although some that I talked to had a fairly accurate conception of their standing in each of the subject areas, others were confused about which set or band was which. It must be said that, as far as I could see, teachers did little to clarify these matters. Several of the teachers explained that to draw attention to the relative standing of the various groups would be 'unfair' as it would make a public statement of a student's worth and expose them to the scorn of their peers. It would also serve to demotivate further many students who were already difficult to motivate, by publicly labelling them. Many of the staff were committed to an egalitarian educational philosophy and were therefore reluctant to emphasize differentiation when it occurred. Differentiation was therefore concealed or at least not publicly declared. Sets and groups, for example, were not referred to by the words 'top' or 'bottom' or the numbers 1, 2, 3, but by the name of the teacher and when students were divided up into sets at the beginning of the academic year no mention was made of the relative standing of such groups. As Furlong noted in his study of a group of Afro/Caribbean boys in a 'liberal' comprehensive school, 'the school had learned the lessons provided by social science of the 1960s. It had abandoned explicit streaming . . . and the pupils were therefore shielded from the full reality of their *public* evaluation' (his emphasis) (Furlong 1984: 232).

The relationship between the process of 'polarization' and formal differentiation consequently appeared less marked at Milltown High than in the schools studied by Hargreaves (1967), Lacey (1970), and Ball (1981). In these schools there was clearly a strong link between allocation to low status positions in the school social structure and 'anti-school' attitudes and behaviour, although as Hammersley (1985) notes the question of causation is problematic. At Milltown High there was a relationship between attitudes to school and low status position in the fourth and fifth years. In the interviews that I conducted with students those in low status positions were far more likely to express anti-school attitudes and were also more likely to truant and get into trouble with staff. But the school, by postponing formal differentiation and adopting a flexible and fairly concealed system when differentiation was introduced, made it less likely that students would come to see themselves as rejects early in their school careers and develop anti-school attitudes and behaviour as a result. Moreover, friendship choices were less restricted by formal status differentials within the school. In fact two large and dominant friendship groups that I observed in the fourth year included students from a number of different positions in the school social structure. Mixed-ability grouping and banding also allowed staff to switch potentially troublesome combinations of students from class to class thus reducing the opportunities for coherent anti-school groups to emerge (cf. Ball 1981).

Allocation to groups

How then were students allocated to different groups and was there any evidence that ethnic minority students were treated less favourably? As might be expected each of the main departments at Milltown High adopted their own procedures (Science and Humanities worked together). Unfortunately I was able to observe only the English department closely, but I attempted to reconstruct the processes in other departments following discussions with the staff involved. It did seem that the methods adopted had quite a lot in common.

The English department did not set a formal exam, but based their decisions about which students were to be in the 'top' group on teachers' subjective views. Decisions were made at a meeting of all the teachers of third year English groups held in the summer term of the students' third year. At the meeting I observed, Jennifer Green, the head of department, proposed that they divide the students into four possible categories: (1) those who could definitely do Language and Literature, which she called 'the definite copers', i.e. those who were top group material,[3] (2) those who could possibly do Language and Literature, that is those who 'have the skills and really ought to be in, but are lazy', (3) those who are 'just capable of GCSE Language' (which was to be introduced in the 1986–7 academic year), and (4) those who 'really need learning support'. The teachers then went through the tutor group lists and together divided students into these four groups. There appeared to be three main criteria for judging a student's potential, although these were never made explicit. First, there was the perceived ability of the student which was based on the written and oral work that he/she had completed for the English teacher(s) during previous years, especially the last. Second, was the perceived motivation of the student which was based on past behaviour and general demeanor in class, the amount of work completed, and attendance. Third, was the perceived psychological state of the student which was important in judging whether he/she could 'cope' with the 'stress' of being 'pushed' for two examinations rather than just one. Again this was indicated by students' previous behaviour and orientation to school, teachers, and school work. For most of the students their placement was decided by their present third year teacher who indicated their suitability for one of the four groups, sometimes with a short accompanying explanation such as: 'He's a good worker, but not really a highflier, not very forthcoming, but should cope alright with GCSE.' For some, especially those who were in the borderline group of 'possible Lang/Lits' there was more of a discussion. The opinions of other English teachers who had taught or knew the student came into play here and a decision was negotiated (see Hammersley 1980 and Beynon 1985 for descriptions of a similar process in staffroom talk).

It is difficult to know how much weight was attached to each of the three criteria in these decisions. It is clearly possible that individual teachers varied or indeed that the emphasis placed on each criteria differed for each student. A significant consideration was which teacher was to take the top group. In the year prior to my field work one of the more inexperienced teachers in the department was to take the group. She was perceived as rather weak on classroom discipline and it was thought unwise to place too many 'difficult' students in the top group. Thus the behaviour of students became a more significant criteria and a number of students who were defined as 'bright enough' were ruled out because of their record of past misbehaviour. Interestingly these students were nearly all Afro/Caribbean boys, which perhaps accounts for the fact that there was only one Afro/Caribbean boy in the top English group in that year. In fact, considerable importance was attached to the attitudinal and behavioural make up of the top group because it was regarded as crucial that the group as a whole were successful, and a hard-working, academic atmosphere with the minimum of disruption was established quickly. As Afro/Caribbean boys were somewhat more likely to present behavioural problems to the teachers and therefore to be regarded as unmotivated, then it is possible to infer that they found it more difficult to secure a high status place than would have been the case if students had been allocated solely on the basis of measured 'ability' (as also did individual Afro/Caribbean girls and white students who were perceived as behavioural problems).

In Maths all students took a common examination and then at a departmental meeting the teachers would consider the students' 'suitability' for the different sets, special attention being given to the selection of a top set. The criteria used were 'ability' based on performance in the common exam and work completed during past years, and 'motivation' which was judged by attendance, behaviour, and attitudes displayed towards Maths work and teachers. Again great emphasis was placed on the judgements of the class teacher who would make an assessment of the student's 'suitability' for the top set, but this

143

was compared with the student's performance on the common exam. Again it is difficult to estimate the relative weights given to these two assessments. The head of department explained that there was a tendency for 'poorly motivated' or 'badly behaved' students who were 'quite able' to be allocated to lower positions in the set hierarchy than might be expected on 'ability' because: (1) it was often difficult to distinguish 'ability' and 'motivation' and (2) that it was important that students in the top group were 'motivated' in order to do well in public exams.

The allocation to positions in Science and Humanities involved a process of negotiation between the two departments. Each met separately and each divided students into two bands. In Science this was done mainly on the recommendation of third year class teachers who based their judgements on 'ability' displayed in class work and half termly tests and on perceived 'motivation' based again on past student behaviour. In Humanities the upper/lower band division was based on: 'the class teacher's comments on whether the child is an upper or a lower band type – very unscientific!' (head of Humanities). The class teachers appeared to base their recommendations on similar criteria to those used by the other teachers. However, no common examination was taken by all the students and so teachers' views were paramount. Following these departmental discussions the two heads of department met together and negotiated the final band allocations. The Science teachers then created their male class of 'difficult' students, the majority of whom, in the 1985–6 fourth year, were Afro/Caribbean, and the Humanities department selected a 'remedial' group of 'those who need most help'. Again the majority were Afro/Caribbean boys.

Differentiation through the option system was not marked at Milltown High. Most options consisted of only one mixed-ability group and only the Spanish and Chemistry options were considered higher status. Entry to these groups was not particularly restricted. Staff who taught them preferred students who they thought were able and motivated, but often, because of low numbers, they were prepared to accept students whom they felt 'really didn't stand much of a chance' in order to ensure they had a viable group to teach. They generally had the space to be able to give a borderline student who wanted to take the option 'a chance to have a go'. In fact the majority of students, I was told, made 'sensible' choices in the option system and, as a deputy head said, 'streamed themselves'.

Was there any evidence that ethnic minority students were treated less favourably in these allocation processes? In my observations and my discussions with teachers I certainly found no evidence that allocation was influenced by racially prejudiced views of minority group students. Given the generally positive attitudes of most teachers at Milltown High to students' ethnicity I think it was highly unlikely this would have been the case. Allocations were based on a number of criteria the most important being teachers' conceptions of student ability, based on test performance, classwork and homework, and motivation, based largely on past behaviour and work output. I also found no evidence that teachers' assessments were based on irrelevant, culturally biased criteria, such as knowledge of particular cultural practices or dress, or family circumstances. The question of whether teachers were more likely to make misjudgements about the ability and motivation of Afro/Caribbean students as a result of cultural confusions is difficult to answer. It seems to me that this was unlikely, given the relatively late stage at which formal differentiation occurred and the awareness of most teachers of Afro/Caribbean culture.

Teachers have been criticized (see Wright 1986) for using behavioural criteria in their allocation decisions. These, it is implied, are irrelevant considerations in selection for what are primarily *ability* groups. It is suggested that this can sometimes work against Afro/Caribbean students who may be more likely to be (or to be seen as) poorly behaved. It could be argued that this was the case for Afro/Caribbean boys at Milltown High. They did seem less likely to secure places in high status groups (see below), often for behavioural reasons. However, such a criticism is, in my view, unjustified. It seems to me that both academic ability and motivation (which is, I would think, most reliably indicated by past behaviour and work output) are important in deciding which students are likely to make best use of a place in a high status group, and this is what teachers must decide. Teachers must also consider the optimum make-up of classes, given their teachers, in order to maximize the achievement of all students. These are complex decisions and I think it is unreasonable to imply that academic ability should be the only relevant criterion.

The distribution of ethnic minority students in the school social structure

When I examined the distribution of students from different ethnic groups in the formal social structure of Milltown High in the fourth and fifth years[4] I did not find a marked division of students on ethnic lines. However, there was a tendency for Afro/Caribbean boys to be under-represented in high status groups given their numbers in the year. They formed 28 per cent of the 103 students in the fourth year, but only 4 per cent of the top English set, 22 per cent of the top Maths set, and 16 per cent of the Science/Humanities top band. However, Afro/Caribbean girls were over-represented in such groups. They formed 23 per cent of the students in the year, but 44 per cent of the top English set, 26 per cent of the top Maths set, and 35 per cent of the Science/Humanities top band. The same gender difference was true for white students – boys were less likely to be in top groups, girls more likely, although the trend was less marked. Similarly boys, especially Afro/Caribbean boys, were more likely to be placed in low status groups. However, it must be emphasized that in all these groups we are dealing with very small numbers and differences.

There could be a number of explanations for these patterns. First, they could have been an accurate reflection of student ability. It was difficult to check whether this was actually the case because of the variety of methods used in the different departments to assess ability, and because records of test and examination results taken at the end of the students' third year were often unavailable. Given the fact that motivation was also an important criterion for group allocation, I think that it is likely that differences in student behaviour were also influential. As Afro/Caribbean boys were somewhat more likely to be seen as poorly behaved this may well have been a major factor in their under-representation in high status groups.

Whatever the explanations, we need to ask whether the tendency for boys, especially Afro/Caribbean boys, to be placed in lower status groups meant they were disadvantaged by the process of differentiation (and, of course, girls advantaged). The answer to this depends partly on whether lower status groups received inferior treatment. This was difficult to ascertain, not least because of the problems of defining and assessing the idea of 'inferior treatment'. Certainly there was no evidence that low status groups received less teaching time or poorer resources than other groups, or that they were allocated the least-experienced teachers. In fact the situation tended to be the reverse – low status groups were often much smaller and therefore enjoyed a more favourable teacher/student ratio, and they tended to be taught by more-experienced teachers. However, my impression was that low status groups were often regarded less seriously by teachers than high status exam groups. It appeared more common for teachers to accept lower standards of work and behaviour from them because they were anticipating that students were not going to succeed in public examinations. In contrast they were far more conscious with high status groups of the need to insist on high standards, set homework, and generally encourage students to work hard and succeed academically. Of course, given ability differences, one would anticipate some differential expectations and treatment of different status groups, but my impression was that in some low status groups expectations and standards were lower than might have been anticipated. One might also speculate that the self-esteem and thus motivation of students allocated to low status groups would decrease (though, of course, this is not necessarily the case), further reducing their chances of academic success. Unfortunately, I did not have the opportunity to systematically test this hypothesis. My rather tentative conclusion is that boys, especially Afro/Caribbean boys, were slightly disadvantaged, and girls slightly advantaged in the formal system of differentiation at Milltown High.

Differentiation in the classroom – a class case study

Concern has also been expressed about the way ethnic minority students fare in the processes of differentiation within classrooms. I speculated that if teachers were operating on the basis of (perhaps unadmitted) racist views then it would be likely that ethnic minority students would be allocated to low status positions in classroom social structures and differentially treated as a result. It was also possible that ethnic minority students could occupy lower status positions because they were less highly regarded in terms of the traditional notions of the 'ideal student' that teachers typically employ. If this was the case and the ethnic minority students were treated less favourably, then they would be indirectly disadvantaged.

On the basis of my general observations of classrooms at Milltown High this did not seem to be the case, but in order to examine these questions more closely I conducted a small case study of a third year class, consisting of fourteen boys – eight Afro/Caribbean and six white – and eight girls – four Afro/Caribbean and four white – and five of their teachers – English, Maths, Humanities, Science, and Art.

I first interviewed the teachers about the teaching strategies they employed, and how they saw each of the students in the class. I have not got the space here to discuss individual teachers' typifications in detail, many of which were long and elaborate. Two points, however, are important. First, their typifications were strongly evaluative and revealed clear positive and negative views of students based on the extent to which they conformed to their notion of the 'ideal student' (Becker 1952b). In the main the teachers typed the students in terms of two key constructs of academic ability, and classroom behaviour, the latter being used as an indicator of a student's motivation, orientation to school, teachers, and school work, and personality. In fact the constructs that the teachers used were similar to those which researchers have found other teachers use (Nash 1973; Hargreaves, Hester, and Mellor 1975; Ball 1981). The second point is that none of the teachers made reference to racial or ethnic features in order to typify the students. These characteristics appeared to be unimportant to teachers' typifications of students. This is not to say, of course, that they did not in their *unarticulated* conceptions of the students attribute certain characteristics to them on the basis of race or ethnicity, merely that in typifications revealed in interviews with me this was not apparent.[5]

I then asked the teachers to rank the students in terms of: (1) academic ability and (2) behaviour. This gave me a complex picture of the class social structure. Whilst there was considerable overall similarity between the rankings of different teachers, several students were at different levels of the hierarchy in different subjects, and although there was a strong relationship between academic and behavioural positions some students varied quite considerably. Overall there was no tendency for the Afro/Caribbean students to occupy lower status positions. However, there was a tendency for boys to be ranked on average lower than girls, especially in terms of behaviour. The four white girls in the class were consistently highly perceived, especially in terms of behaviour, as was one of the Afro/Caribbean girls. One of the white boys and one of the Afro/Caribbean boys, who interestingly was the only 'middle-class' student in the class (his father was a polytechnic lecturer), was also well thought of. At the other end of the scale four white boys, three Afro/Caribbean boys, and one Afro/Caribbean girl, were fairly consistently poorly perceived. The other seven students lay in between these two groups.

After interviewing the teachers I began to observe a sample of their lessons. However, after two lessons the Maths teacher asked me not to observe as he felt my presence placed him under too much stress. Thus my observations were confined to Humanities, English, Science, and Art and I saw at least eight lessons of each. I was mainly interested in whether differential treatment occurred on the basis of student status or ethnic group and so I used the Brophy and Good Dyadic Interaction System (Brophy and Good 1970, 1974, 1984) observation schedule which allows the observer to record teacher interactions with individual students. Most of the teaching that I observed was class based. Students were all expected to complete the same tasks with the same curriculum materials, although those who finished work first were usually given extension work. Thus there was no obvious differential treatment such as the singling out of high status groups to do different types of activity or to study different curriculum materials. In most of the lessons there was also little difference in the extent of interaction (both public and private) teachers had with students from different status or ethnic groups. One exception to this was in Humanities. Here the teacher tended to favour the high status white girls in the number of public reading turns he allocated and in the questions he asked. This could be explained largely by the strategies the teacher used to enhance classroom control which involved focusing classroom interaction on the students he perceived as most able in order to maintain the flow of classroom discussion and convey the curriculum points quickly. Another exception was in English where the teacher tended to favour boys, especially Afro/Caribbean boys, in public class discussion. This was mainly because such students were far more vocal and visible in her classroom (perhaps because she enforced classroom rules less strictly) and thus made themselves more available to participate, but also because the teacher directed questions to the boys more frequently as a means of controlling their rather boisterous behaviour. She also tended to give less able students more individual attention as she felt they found class work more difficult to cope with.

Occasionally there did seem to be a tendency for teachers to have more positive interactions with students of high behavioural status, but this often appeared to be a reaction to the poor behaviour and frequently hostile attitudes of some of the students themselves rather than something which sprang independently from the teacher. There also seemed to be a tendency for teachers to be more demanding in terms of the questions they asked of and written work they demanded from students whom they perceived as high ability, although this might, of course, be anticipated.

However, on the whole there was little significant differential treatment of students on the basis of status or ethnic group.

Conclusion

In this chapter I have argued that within-school practices and procedures which many authors have claimed work to the disadvantage of ethnic minority students in British schools did not do so at Milltown High. I found little evidence of racial prejudice in the attitudes of teachers. In fact the majority of teachers had fairly positive views of ethnic minority students and were well aware of the dangers of generalizing about and stereotyping students on the basis of ethnicity. I also discovered no marked differential treatment of students on the basis of race or ethnicity and the types of indirect discrimination identified by researchers such as Driver (1979) were also absent. Most of the students I interviewed confirmed these views. Whilst a small number spoke of racism in the school, their criticisms were generally reserved for an infamous ex-teacher, and few identified racism as a key area of concern. Similarly relationships between students of the two main ethnic groups were not marked by conflict. In fact here, it seemed, was a school where race did not divide (cf. Ward 1979). I think we can conclude that the teachers at Milltown High had succeeded in creating a non-racist environment in the school. Racism did not influence social relationships and, on the whole, both Afro/Caribbean and white students enjoyed equitable

149

treatment. This appeared to be reflected in the output of the school. If we take exam results as an, admittedly rather crude, indicator of the success rate of different groups, Afro/Caribbean students did as well as their white peers. In fact in the 1985–6 fifth year they did significantly better – Afro/Caribbean girls achieved an average of 1.2 O/CSE Grade 1 passes, Afro/Caribbean boys 0.59 passes, white girls 0.15 passes and white boys 0.22 passes (cf. Driver 1980).

Chapter nine

The inner city school and the
problem of teacher 'survival'

There was no evidence that ethnic minority students were disadvantaged by the internal practices and procedures of Milltown High School. But, of course, Milltown High was not a school in isolation. It was part of a wider educational system which still tends to favour students from particular social groups (Halsey, Heath and Ridge 1980; Heath 1987). Students from different social class backgrounds often enter different educational institutions at the age of eleven, if they have not done so earlier, and selection often depends directly or indirectly on the possession of economic resources. Those who have such resources can secure places for their children in independent schools, or houses in suburban areas served by 'better' schools.

A substantial proportion of Milltown's middle-class children attended independent schools in the city or surrounding area, or, if they lived in the small middle-class enclaves of the city, the local comprehensive schools of, in the words of an ex-Secretary of State for Education, 'proven worth'. In fact it had become common for middle-class families to move house into these suburban enclaves or into neighbouring, more suburban LEAs in order to secure places for their children at a 'better' comprehensive school. Non-Catholic working-class children generally found themselves in neighbourhood comprehensive schools. Social background was thus a fairly powerful factor determining educational routes through the city's school system, and the social backgrounds of students entering secondary schools in Milltown were far from heterogeneous. The intake of Milltown High School was predominantly from the inner city and was therefore almost completely working class. In fact many of its students were drawn from what some authors have referred to as an 'underclass' (Rex and Tomlinson 1979).

On a number of occasions during my field work it became starkly obvious that the educational experiences that many students received at Milltown High were very different from those that they would be likely to receive in certain other sectors of the local educational system. I am not in a position to present a systematic comparison of the educational provision or effectiveness of different schools in Milltown (as did Rutter *et al.* 1979 and Mortimore *et al.* 1988). My study was basically a case study of one school. However, during my work, I gathered a certain amount of data, mainly from interviews and informal conversations with staff, which supported my view that there was a difference in the quality of education experienced by students at Milltown High.

I want to emphasize here that I am not setting out to criticize the teaching staff or individual teachers at Milltown High. I would, in a sense, be pleased if I could do that because it would mean that the educational disadvantages faced by the students could be put right if their teachers only pulled their socks up and performed their jobs properly. Alas things are not so simple. In fact many of the teachers at Milltown High, as we have seen, were hard working and committed to the education of students in the school. What I will argue is that many of them were caught up in a vicious spiral which resulted in declining morale and low expectations and the consequent impoverishment of the educational experiences of many of their students, a substantial proportion of whom were from ethnic minority backgrounds.

Many of the teachers at Milltown High developed similar work and career perspectives to the Chicago teachers described by Howard Becker in 1952. He argued that for many teachers 'horizontal' (movement to alternative jobs at the same status and salary level) rather than 'vertical' career mobility (movement to jobs at a higher status and salary level) was important. Teachers, originally allocated to positions in 'slum' schools, catering for 'lower class' and black students, often sought 'easier' work at the same level of the job hierarchy in 'good' schools in middle- or upper-class areas, rather than seek promotion in 'slum' schools. A minority of teachers, however, remained for some reason or another in the 'slum' schools. Here they were forced to 'adjust to the particular work situation' (see also Becker 1964). This involved first 'learning new teaching and disciplinary techniques which enable her to deal adequately with "slum" children', second learning 'to revise her expectations with regard to the amount of material she can teach' and 'to be satisfied with a smaller accomplishment', and third finding 'for herself explanations for the actions of the children which she has previously found revolting and immoral' which 'allow her to "understand" the behaviour of the children as human' (Becker 1952a). Becker also argued (1952b) that teachers generally orientate their perspectives, their view of how the job of teaching ought to be performed, around an image of the 'ideal client', and in a highly stratified urban society there will be 'many groups whose life-style and culture produce children who do not meet the standards of this image'. These children, who largely attend 'slum' schools, he suggested, will present the greatest problems for teachers in terms of teaching itself, classroom discipline, and 'moral acceptability'. The adjustments that their teachers are forced to make in order to deal with these problems have strong implications for the educational opportunities made available to such students.

The data that I collected led me to conclude that similar processes occurred in the educational system of Milltown and at Milltown High School, and these had similar implications for the educational opportunities of the students in that school.

Staffing problems at Milltown High

As with Becker's teachers the idea of 'horizontal' mobility had become more important to many teachers in Milltown in recent years as the school system contracted because of falling rolls and the opportunities for 'vertical' mobility lessened. Many teachers also operated with similar preferences regarding jobs in the various schools in the city to those described by Becker. The teacher 'grapevine' provided them with the knowledge of which schools would be 'easy' and rewarding to work in and which would be more 'difficult' and potentially unrewarding. Such knowledge was influential in decisions about which school to apply to teach in and in patterning expectations of the nature of the work situation in a chosen or allocated school. Thus some teachers in Milltown would not even consider applying for a job at Milltown High. Others were prepared reluctantly to accept posts for a short period at the school in return for higher salary scales which they hoped would lead to 'better things'.

These preferences were revealed most clearly when Milltown re-organized its county secondary sector in 1982, scrapped school sixth forms creating sixth form colleges, and reduced the number of comprehensive schools. In order to ensure a fair disribution of teaching posts the LEA adopted what was called an 'all out – all in' system in which all teachers 'lost' their current jobs, but were guaranteed a job somewhere in the city and were free to apply for any job in any school or sixth form college. This provided a great opportunity for horizontal mobility. Jobs in the colleges and the 'better' schools proved by far the most popular attracting large numbers of applicants. A number of 'good', well-qualified teachers left Milltown High.[1] Their places were, however, difficult to fill as jobs at Milltown High and other similar inner city schools attracted few applicants and sometimes the local inspectorate, whose job it was to staff the schools, were forced to employ subtle pressures to persuade teachers to go to such schools. A number of staff came to or stayed at Milltown High rather reluctantly.

The school had experienced similar, though less severe, problems over staffing since 1982. Eighteen months after the re-organization the headteacher resigned. He explained in an interview with me that he had felt under increasing pressure as he was expected to support staff, who were finding it very difficult to cope in the school, without appropriate resources and support from the LEA. Many staff experienced 'discipline problems' which they expected him to deal with in an 'authoritarian way'. This, he explained, was at variance with his personal philosophy which emphasized 'co-operation and relationships'.

The new head, David Benyon, felt he had been lucky since his arrival in the school as most of the jobs that had become vacant he had been able to fill with what he regarded as good candidates, and no jobs had remained vacant for long. But when a job was advertized the number of applicants was usually small and the choice therefore was limited. The position of head of Music, for example, became vacant in June 1985. A local teacher was appointed temporarily for September whilst the job was advertised, but there was only one applicant, the incumbent temporary teacher, who was automatically appointed. Staffing the school was not always easy and suitably qualified and committed teachers were sometimes difficult to find.

In the year of my field work, however, by far the biggest staffing problem was that of supply teachers. The teachers' industrial action meant that permanent teachers in the school refused to 'cover' lessons when their colleagues were absent. Because of the stresses and strains involved in working at Milltown High (see below) there was rather a high rate of staff absence. Thus the need for supply teachers was great. The preference of the limited number of supply teachers available for work in the 'easier', 'better' schools meant that Milltown High frequently could not obtain enough teachers to cover all the classes of absent teachers. Thus many classes were sent home or in reality out of the school to wander the local area. In the absence of appropriate LEA provision of supply teachers, schools like Milltown High were hurt far more severely by the teacher industrial action than those in more suburban areas.[2]

The problem of teacher 'survival'

Many of the teachers that I talked to, especially those who had not taught before in similar schools, described their initial classroom experiences at Milltown High as a 'baptism of fire' or a 'culture shock' (cf. Grace 1978; Cole 1984). In interviews and conversations they frequently described their early experiences and feelings. The following example illustrates:

> I'd taught in a number of other schools and in all those schools I loved teaching . . . And then I came to Milltown High and I just

couldn't believe the difference. The first thing I found was the childrens' behaviour towards each other and how they talked to each other . . . The second thing was their lack of respect for teachers. I could not get over the cheek and the rudeness. And I couldn't get over the fact that I couldn't get a class to sit down and listen and do as they were told . . . That first year was very hard . . . I had all sorts of problems because I didn't know how to cope with these sorts of children . . . They'd get up to all sorts of tricks like when I wasn't looking taking things out of the cupboard . . . I had my purse pinched . . . Things used to be thrown out of the window . . . After two weeks I had a real fight in the class, blood flying everywhere . . . I felt absolutely helpless . . . Having got over that within days I had another horrible incident where a boy just went up to a girl and stabbed her with a pair of scissors . . . And I found it impossible to cope with twenty children demanding your attention at the same time and getting really nasty and stroppy if you didn't, you know, drop everything and see to them . . . I'd always taught in an environment where they stood around and watched you and you could talk to them and explain what you were doing and why you were doing it. Not so here. They wouldn't stop talking long enough for you to be able to explain anything, with the result that you'd come out at the end of the lesson thinking, 'What have I done? I've done absolutely nothing. And what have they learnt? They haven't learnt anything because they haven't been quiet enough.' (Home Economics teacher)

Such experiences were particularly common for the staff who came new to the school following the re-organization in 1982. A number of established teachers, noted for their 'good discipline', had left the school. Within only a few weeks the new staff had to get to know each other, the new courses they were to teach, and a new school with many different practices and procedures. Many of the students apparently felt betrayed by the disappearance of their familiar teachers, and others made the most of exploiting the difficult situation for their own amusement. The weeks following the re-organization were particularly fraught for the new staff struggling to establish themselves as the following comments from a new, but experienced, Science teacher illustrate.

The weeks after re-organization were horrific . . . The major thing was the discipline in the classroom . . . I couldn't get them to shut up long enough to launch them on the prac. or whatever. As soon as I got them quiet and started to talk, somebody would fall off their chair laughing and poke someone else. It was just as if I wasn't there . . . I'd send a kid out and go out to talk to them in the corridor and try to knock them back into some kind of shape so that they can come back into the room, but they'd just go dumb, they'd refuse to answer anything, or they'd have a right stand up argument with you on whatever you said . . . some kids would throw stuff about when I wasn't looking, some would throw stuff about when I was looking, the noise level was very high . . .

Even teachers experienced in working-class comprehensive schools frequently had similar stories to tell about their initial experiences. Some were perhaps not as extreme as those I have quoted, but nevertheless the first few months at the school were often cited the most difficult in their career.

That such experiences were not uncommon was reinforced by my own observations. My field notes are littered with descriptions of incidents in which students challenged teachers' authority and disrupted lessons by boisterous and difficult, sometimes hostile and aggressive behaviour. Of course this was not the case in all lessons. Particular individuals, groups, or classes, and particular times were more difficult. But for the majority of teachers, even the most experienced and committed, classroom control was never easy to establish, and was frequently contested. Often class atmosphere, unlike the mixed-ability classes described by Ball (1981) at Beachside, was not dominated by pro-school students, but by a significant number of poorly motivated and anti-school students.

The source of such attitudes and behaviour is, of course, highly complex. To some extent the social organization of schools, which differentially allocates power, status, rights, and territory to teachers and students, offering prestige and rewards to some students whilst rejecting others, encourages such resistance. And, as Waller (1932) noted, conflict is almost written into the nature of the teacher/student relationship because of the different interests and desires of the two groups. The lengthening of the years of compulsory schooling combined with the development of adolescent culture, also clearly play a part. But particularly significant at Milltown High appears to have been the development of distinctive working-class and ethnic youth sub-cultures in and around the school. These sub-cultures have complex roots in parental culture (see Pryce 1979), the social and economic position of working-class and ethnic minority youth (see Cashmore and Troyna 1982; Cross and Smith 1987), and wider class and youth cultural forms (see Miller 1958; Hall and Jefferson 1976; Willis 1977). Their development has been given an added twist in recent years by mounting youth unemployment and declining economic opportunities in areas like Milltown.

Such sub-cultures have been most studied amongst boys. Willis (1977), for example, described the sub-culture of a group of white working-class boys he studied. They rejected school and the authority of their teachers, spent most of their time 'mucking about' and 'havin' a laugh', and celebrated toughness, aggression, verbal smartness, and the masculinity of manual labour. Such a style, Willis argued, mirrored a wider working-class culture, and was a means by which the boys expressed their own collective identity. However ironically, its acceptance by the boys made it more likely they would move into low status manual work. Furlong (1984, 1985) provides a more recent analysis of a 'culture of resistance' amongst a group of Afro/Caribbean boys in a London comprehensive school which, he argued, resulted in the boys adopting a contradictory stance to their school life. On the one hand they accepted the need to obtain qualifications in order to 'get on', but on the other they spent much of their school time 'messing about', flouting school rules, socializing, and 'establishing a reputation for being a man'.

In fact the attitudes and behaviour of a substantial number of male students, both Afro/Caribbean and white, at Milltown High, was similar to that described by Willis and Furlong. Their peer group culture was often anti-academic, emphasizing instead the values of physical toughness, verbal smartness, non-conformity, and 'havin' a laugh'. A number of girls had similar attitudes and also displayed behaviour which challenged school values and norms, but, as McRobbie (1978) observed in her study of working-class girls, this was often expressed in less overtly aggressive and challenging ways. This is not to say that all, or even the majority of students, at Milltown High were orientated to such sub-cultures. As in most schools there were a number of different student adaptations to school life. But in many respects the anti-school orientations of the minority were more dominant at Milltown High than in other schools I am familiar with.

What is important for my argument is the effect of the attitudes and behaviour of such students on the teachers at Milltown High and the quality of educational experience they were able to provide. As David Hargreaves (1975) notes the job of teaching contains two main sub-roles – the establishment of order and discipline in the classroom and the organization of instruction and learning, the latter being almost impossible without the former. For several teachers at Milltown High classroom control was extremely difficult to establish and they were faced with a serious challenge to their conception of themselves as competent role performers. The result was what might be termed a 'survival threat' (Woods 1979; Pollard 1980; Riseborough 1985). By this I mean that their conception of themselves as competent practising professional teachers and thus, given the importance of occupational identity in our society, their basic identity, self-esteem, and status was challenged and placed under threat.

In order to 'survive', to avoid what Pollard (1980) terms 'personal and career bankruptcy', teachers, as with most other workers, must feel that they can perform their role adequately (or at least to an acceptable level of inadequacy) and that there is some degree of congruence between their conception of themselves and the nature of the role they are required to perform. Few teachers could continue for long believing that they were total failures and that their view of themselves was totally at variance with the type of work that they were expected to do. Of course definitions of 'adequacy' (or acceptable inadequacy) vary. An individual's definition is largely dependent on his/her conception of how the job ought to be done which is derived from a number of background factors, the influence of training and socialization into the occupational culture and the work place. It is also dependent on the extent to which the individual is willing to make compromises between their conception of how the role ought to be ideally performed and how it actually can be performed in practical circumstances, what Pollard (1980) terms the 'ideal-self/pragmatic-self tension'. The level of acceptable incongruence between a teacher's conception of themselves and of their role performance will also vary for similar reasons.

Where their survival is threatened teachers must develop strategies which allow them to perform, or allow them to believe that they perform, their roles adequately, and to establish acceptable levels of congruence between their self-image and the nature of the role. These strategies often involve learning new teaching practices and techniques, re-defining notions of 'adequacy', and re-defining their conceptions of themselves as teachers. It is these responses to 'survival threat' amongst the teachers at Milltown High that I want to describe now.

Responses to survival threat

Breakdown

A small minority of the teachers at Milltown High became what Riseborough (1985) terms 'sinkers'. They failed to 'survive' and sometimes suffered the pain of mental exhaustion or breakdown. Following school re-organization, for example:

> The guy who was in the department with me, John White, was a complete and utter disaster. He just couldn't stand it. He kept phoning in and saying he'd fallen off his motor bike and he'd lost all his stuff and he couldn't come. And he didn't arrive and if he

did arrive he left early, and there were problems with his classes not being looked after and chaos even when he was there. He only lasted until Christmas. In the end he gave in. He was forced to give in his resignation. (Humanities teacher)

During my field work two of the staff new to the school in the September suffered nervous breakdowns, partly the result of the considerable stress they faced during the first few months at Milltown High. As one of them later explained to me:

> The illness was very definitely the result of the pressure here. I'm a worrier ... I was starting to be pressured and pressured and pressured, and getting ill without really realizing it, until in the end it all got on top of me ... So yes, no two ways about it, the job was just too much ... What finally happens is that you just cop out, you're just totally unable to cope any more. (Music teacher)

Other staff came perilously close to giving up or suffering similar breakdowns:

> I know this sounds strange, but I think it's taken me until now (2nd year at the school) to cope, because my reaction to spending this first half term of hell, which it was although I was determined to beat it, was in the following half term I was off a lot with various illnesses ... It took its toll of me health-wise and I just lost weight and after the Easter holidays I just went downhill, and although the lessons got a bit easier, the kids weren't quite as obnoxious ... it was still an intolerable situation. (English teacher)

Others, whilst eventually surviving, went through what they often described as the most difficult periods in their teaching careers, experiencing considerable stress:

> The first two weeks here I went home, sat on the sofa, and vegetated. I couldn't bear the T.V. on, I wasn't eating, I wondered what on earth I'd done ... to come here and find that you were struggling to keep them in their seats or even in the room in some cases, and certainly silence was out of the question ... The shock of all that was unbelievable ... I couldn't do anything. I dropped out of politics (he was a local party agent). All I did was to come here and go home and be shocked really. I couldn't believe that such places existed or that we as adults were tolerating it ... the shock was incredible. (Humanities teacher)

As Riseborough (1985) vividly reminded us the working-class school can be as much an institution that 'processes' teachers as it is one that 'processes' students. Indeed, as he argues, working-class students can be powerful 'gatekeepers' in teachers' objective and moral careers.

Retreat

There were also some teachers who left the school, and in some cases teaching altogether, because they were unable or unwilling to make the adjustments required in order to survive at Milltown High (cf. Woods 1981). Either they found the necessary strategies difficult to master effectively or they were unwilling to re-define their conceptions of adequacy or make the appropriate changes to their conception of themselves as teachers. One such teacher was the English teacher, Jane Gabriel. She came to the school as a relatively inexperienced teacher and saw herself as a radical, committed to 'progressive' educational ideals. During her initial year at Milltown High she experienced many of the difficulties I have described and found her view of teaching and the sort of teacher she wished to be under threat. She compromised to some degree by adopting survival strategies, but she was never satisfied with the way she was forced to work and with the changes in her personality that the school appeared to be forcing. After two years she decided to leave the school and seek a job in community education.

Adjusting to the inner city school

The majority of staff at Milltown High stayed and 'survived'. They could not leave teaching, their 'investment' (Woods 1979) in the job was too great, horizontal mobility was not often possible or, in some cases, was ideologically undesirable, and their personalities did not incline them to mental breakdown. They thus had to 'adjust to their situation' (Becker 1952a), adapt to the inner city school, and cope with its constraints in order to 'survive'. What adjustments did they make?

As the main threat was to their competence in maintaining classroom control, the disciplinary rather than the educational aspect of their role became the primary concern of many of the teachers. This concern was displayed in talk in the staffroom and in meetings where disciplinary problems were a common topic of discussion. In fact classroom control often became the central and over-riding goal of some. Their aims often became 'getting through the next lesson' without 'losing control', without a 'confrontation' or 'incident', and with the minimum of stress. As one teacher said: 'Most of the time it is just survival here, a matter of control, getting through each lesson or each day with the minimum of trouble. We don't think about actually teaching the kids very much' (Science teacher).

To achieve classroom control, which is central to the self-esteem of most teachers and therefore to 'survival', they often had to learn new disciplinary strategies and modify their established or preferred teaching style. In fact often the need to avoid classroom disorder by the use of disciplinary techniques became far more important than any pedagogic ideology (cf. Denscombe 1980). These techniques involved many of the strategies described by Woods (1979) and Denscombe (1985). They sometimes included 'domination' strategies such as the use of punishments, verbal (and very occasionally physical) aggression, 'showing students up', threats, and a heavy emphasis on rules and regimented routines, the aim being to force students to conform by using fear and intimidation. But given the relatively liberal climate of Milltown High and the recalcitrant nature of many students domination strategies by themselves tended to be rather ineffective. What Denscombe terms 'classwork management strategies' were often more important. These frequently involved tightly structured lessons with a strong teacher control of content, pattern, and pace of student work, a close surveillance of classroom talk, student positioning and movement, combined with the subtle use of spoken and body language by the teacher. Given also that the motivation of many students to complete classwork was low, what Denscombe terms 'co-option strategies' were also important. A variety of techniques were used in order to win student commitment to the classroom order. These involved the judicious use of assessment (Scarth 1983) (records of achievement and 'unit credits' became very popular during my field work), reasoning and 'talking things through' with students, negotiation and bargaining, persuasion, and increasing the entertainment, interest value, and 'relevance' of lessons. As we saw in the English department they also involved 'building relationships with students', and what Woods termed 'fraternization', in order to strengthen students' sense of obligation to the teacher. Some teachers also adopted what Woods calls the strategy of 'absence or removal' which included unofficial and official absences, getting rid of or unloading trouble-makers, ignoring truancy, wasting time at the beginning and end of breaks, and avoiding potentially difficult situations and students.

Even experienced and established teachers had to devote a considerable amount of time and energy to the development and use of such techniques in order to achieve classroom control at Milltown High. The following extracts from interviews provide some illustrations of the adaptions teachers had to make:

I've got to concentrate on individuals all the time. I give general instructions and hope that two or three will follow them, then I have to go to each one and tell them what to do, because they're not listening properly . . . We try to do a lot of oral work as well . . . which is how they learn the language, but it's a real uphill struggle . . . I always try to do some oral work. But if it breaks down I end up getting them to write it which is totally the wrong way to learn the language. They ought to be listening to it and speaking it first before they even see it. We do far too much written work. (Languages teacher)

In the end I stopped having conclusions at the end of lessons. I launched the lessons and they did the prac., and I threw some kids out and every now and again if it got too noisy and too uncooperative and silly I'd stop it altogether and give them books out and they'd copy out of books . . . What I did at one point was . . . we had a circus of experiments with maybe twenty experiments on it. When they came in they just took one off the tray and just got on with it by themselves, so I never had to speak to them as a group ever, and I just walked around and talked to them a few at a time. And that worked very well. The trouble is it's an incredibly slow way of working, but the kids who were getting on with the Chemistry O.K. I could spend more time with, and the kids who were still totally disruptive I threw out, and the ones who were learning nothing I just let learn nothing. We've got some books called 'Reading about Science' with a very low reading age, really jolly books with lots of good Science background information, and they read it . . . and I write ten questions out on the board and it always starts off with 'Copy the first paragraph out', because that gives you five to ten minutes peace and quiet . . . Then 'Draw the diagram half way down the first side', and then half a dozen questions which the answers are really just re-writing a sentence, and then maybe a few harder ones at the end. I do that with second years and I did it with third years a lot. (Science teacher)

The bulk of the time I can't teach the way I want to teach. I mean I ought to be doing far more teaching than I actually do. But so much of the time they won't listen or I can't get them together because they're all over the place. So I tend to try and work informally with individuals getting in the odd bit of teaching here and there, but a lot of the time it's just entertainment, we keep them amused. (PE teacher)

Well I tried all sorts of things. I've tried the dictatorial approach, because that had worked in the past and once you've established yourself well then you can ease up. So I tried that, and then with some I tried the more softly-softly approach, you know trying to get to know them, taking an interest in them, hoping that they would start to trust me. But now I suppose I'm somewhere in the middle. But it took me a couple of years to establish that, to find out what works. At the end of the first year I felt it was a total waste of time and I felt that I was never going to get anywhere. (Home Economics teacher)

I think you have just got to persevere . . . In my first year I was always keeping kids in, giving lines, talking one-to-one for ages and ages which is very tiring when you're tired already because of the stress . . . I believed in the end it would pay off and it has. I still do detentions, etc. especially with a new class. I have a blue book in which I monitor everything. I write down what they've done wrong with the dates and the times and who I've seen and what I've done. It's very important to keep on top of everything . . . .I don't let anything go. There are lots of examples here of things being ignored, for example you have a bit of a do with a kid and they say, 'Oh fuck off', and people ignore it. Well I don't and my hearing is too good for my own benefit sometimes . . . If a kid answers me back I'm ready for throttling them and I won't let them get away with it without me really going on about it, and in the end I think that works. (Humanities teacher)

Playing things down, not reacting, keeping cool, even when you're burning inside to explode, don't. And that's what's so tiring . . . Not to rise to the bait, not to interpret everything as aggression . . . To respect the kids making them feel that they have an important part to play . . . They like to feel that they are special to you as an individual. It's very important to give them individual attention and get them involved, bring them into conversations, talk about their experiences, care about them, their interests and their needs . . . then they like to work *for me*. I also try to get to know their social workers. If they realize you're one of a network of people working together and that what is said and done won't be ignored, part of the network of people trying to help them out, then that helps . . . You also have to cajole a lot, you have to negotiate and bargain with them and they're extremely skilled negotiatiors most of them . . . You have to put up with a lot and try not to rise to their provocation . . . If you follow everything through you could spend half an hour and just drive yourself round the bend trying to make one kid take his jacket off. So you have to adapt the rules . . . And you can't really say if you do this you're going to get such and such a job, because the jobs aren't there anymore. So you have to make the experience itself as exciting as possible . . . you have to make the experience inherently interesting. (Integrated Curriculum teacher)

For several teachers what they felt were important aspects of their teaching – oral work in Languages, end of lesson summaries and sometimes experiments in Science, coaching in PE, discussion work in English – frequently had to be restricted. They were often replaced by what Woods (1979) calls 'occupational therapy' - copying, simple written exercises, drawing, watching television programmes, and walks in the park – activities designed to 'keep them occupied' and 'get their heads down' rather than educate. On the other hand some teachers were also given a strong incentive to search for new, more interesting, and 'relevant' teaching techniques and materials, and in this sense the 'survival' problems of the inner city school did have positive spin offs.

Many teachers explained that another strategy they adopted was to lower their expectations of the amount of academic work the students could get through and of the standards of that work. The following quotations illustrate:

> Attainment as a goal for most of the kids for most of the time, I think, has gone. The only strategy is containment. At one time if a kid had done nothing in a lesson I think I would have done something about it . . . but now if a kid did nothing and he didn't annoy me I would consider that pretty O.K. So in a way we've let standards go I think. (Science teacher)

> In the end you have to accept that you will get through less in a lesson than you expected . . . and you often end up expecting less of the children here, which leads to more stress. The feeling that you're not getting through what you should do and yet you start perhaps planning to get through less and you're expectations start slipping. You can't help it . . . as the term grinds on and you're wound down further and further. I do think you come to expect less of the kids. (Languages teacher)

> We do tend to have low expectations here because, in a sense, we're grateful if they do anything, if they finish a piece of work off or something. We do that because we're having to cope with difficult children in the classroom by ourselves. (English/Social Education teacher)

Although the school officially had a policy of setting homework very few of the staff actually did so on a regular basis. An English teacher explained:

> They don't do as much work as a kid in another school where they have two or three homeworks a week . . . I've lost so many books. It's been so much of a hassle to get the homework in it's just not worth it . . . You can't cope with getting through the day and having to run around, and what it means is that if they haven't got

their books for the next lesson, then your next lesson's going to be
a right bloody mess and you're going to have confrontations over
homework . . . and you avoid the confrontations.

For several of the teachers this reduction in expectations also applied to
the standards of behaviour they demanded from the students. The norms
of classroom behaviour which they negotiated with students were often
lower than they had been accustomed to in other schools. A Science
teacher explained:

> You inevitably let far more go than you should do. You don't see
> things that you should see, and you're happy sometimes if
> everyone sits down and doesn't start throwing things. You've just
> got to accept a lot of the minor things that go on, otherwise you'd
> go bananas trying to chase everything up.

And an English teacher commented:

> I think the standards of many staff have become very low. It's
> understandable the way some classes behave. People just have not
> got the stamina to keep up. If you tried to follow up everything that
> you should do according to the system then not only would you not
> be able to cope, but the whole disciplinary system would become
> overloaded. As it is the heads of year find it almost impossible to
> keep up. And many staff just get ground down with it all and they
> take the easy way out which is to ignore it or forget it.

Those teachers who tried to maintain high standards of behaviour had to
accept that often large amounts of teaching time would be spent or
'wasted' on behavioural negotiations and disciplinary matters. They had
to continually fight 'battles' over issues that in other situations were
taken for granted as 'won'.

> You've got to get used to the fact that sometimes two or three
> lessons each week will be lost because the kids just won't behave
> or are being awkward. If they're like that well I just won't start a
> lesson until they are prepared to co-operate, and sometimes it takes
> a whole lesson. (Science teacher)

> You'd just waste a tremendous amount of time getting them into
> the classroom reasonably, getting them to sit down quietly,
> checking if they've got pens, and dealing with those who haven't
> got them . . . In the classroom if any of them misbehaved and had
> to be sent out you'd have to fill in a slip, give them work, and send
> them to 201 (the school's withdrawal unit), and later you'd have to
> follow that up. And then there'd be constant interruptions, late

165

arrivals, and sometimes kids wandering in and out. You just spent
so much time dealing with all these disciplinary things.
(ex-Languages teacher)

Many also felt that norms of behaviour around the school had become
low because staff ignored student deviance or avoided situations where
they would have to deal with it. A Maths teacher was one of several who
explained:

I think many of the staff, and I include myself in this here, have
retreated to their classrooms. They 'don't see' things on the corridors anymore, they avoid going out at lesson changes, they 'forget'
to do duties at break times. You can't blame them. I mean if you
tried to pick up on everything you saw on the corridors you just
wouldn't be able to cope with it. But it does make a difference to
the whole school. Kids don't get to lessons on time, they're high
when you get them in the room and so you've got to spend the first
part of every lesson calming them down or dealing with
latecomers.

The changes that teachers had to make in teaching methods and in
expectations of the students also meant that they had to adjust their
expectations and conceptions of themselves. For example, one of the
Integrated Curriculum teachers explained:

JP – I suppose I have re-assessed what the role of a teacher is
especially in relationship to the type of children who come to
Milltown High.
PF – And how would you say it has changed?
JP – That I'm not just a class teacher preparing them for academic
success . . . I feel there are a lot of social skills they need. Little
things like sitting down and listening to each other and respecting
and tolerating each other. You've got to try and develop those
things . . . You've got to be more of a counsellor than a traditional
teacher.

Several other teachers explained how they had become less of 'an
academic sort of teacher', as one put it. Others talked with pride of their
ability to 'handle difficult children' and to achieve classroom order in
difficult circumstances. Some also came to judge their own success less
on the basis of students' academic progress, and more in terms of
increasing student 'maturity' and conformity to social norms.

Collective teacher strategies

Teachers also adopted collective strategies to ease their problems.
'Other staff' were frequently mentioned as a source of support and a

considerable sense of comradeship, reinforced by mutual adversity, developed in the school which helped many staff cope. This seemed especially marked in the larger subject departments which acted as socializing groups for new members of staff.[3]

> The English department helped me a lot. At the end of the lesson I used to say to Mary and Alison, there was really just the three of us then . . . the support we gave each other . . . we used to have our coffee down there and we'd always have our break together. I'd just say, 'Oh this is awful', and they'd come in after the end of lessons, I think because they knew I was devastated, and we'd sit and have a cup of coffee and talk about it and each of us had a horrible class that we had difficulty coping with, and we'd give each other a lot of back up, and that was very important, and I felt I could say, 'I find that class very difficult' and not feel any sense of failure. (English teacher)

What was particularly important for many staff was the realization that they were not alone in experiencing problems, that they were not to blame, and that their competence as teachers was not automatically in question if they experienced difficulties.

> I did find it very difficult at first and I got depressed. I thought it was me . . . But I remember a staff meeting during my first term when (ex-headteacher) said that he couldn't cope with his first years, and that we all ought to share ways of managing and help each other, and that took a great weight off my mind. (English teacher)

Re-assurance from colleagues fulfilled an important function in defending the teacher's identity and self-esteem from attack and 'survival' threat.

This social contact also provided an arena where alternative explanations of student attitudes and behaviour, 'the problems we are all facing', could be developed. These appeared to focus mainly around students' backgrounds and family circumstances (cf. Stebbins 1975), which amongst the more 'radical' members of staff were extended into more politically orientated critiques of the deprivations of the inner city or the structure of society. Stories about students and their families were swapped (Hammersley 1980, 1984) and provided evidence which enabled staff to 'understand' the 'reasons' behind the problems they were facing. However, whilst the emphasis was upon the students and their 'problems', a small number of staff did question their own role, but such views, which meant challenging their own position and function as teachers, were not common.

Other teachers also provided an invaluable source of advice on possible coping strategies for new members of staff:

I had a long talk with Susan in the staffroom the other day (about the problems I've been having with my second year). She said the best thing to do was to set them piles of written work, nothing too difficult or too experimental or different, but just get their heads down, and watch them all the time, and that does work. (English teacher)

It was often these socializing experiences which helped teachers to 'survive' at Milltown High and adjust to the prevailing norms and self-definitions of staff or subject culture.

Humour was also common (see Woods 1979; Stebbins 1980; Hammersley 1980). Lampooning and making light of serious and difficult situations often served as a form of tension release. It promoted solidarity and strengthened the attachment of individuals to the group. The use of ridicule also conveyed explanations for common problems. As such, humour was often a way of coping at Milltown High. As one member of staff rather poignantly said, 'If you didn't laugh you'd cry!'.

There were also more obviously collective staff strategies. In a year characterized by teacher industrial action, not surprisingly, co-operative action to defend working conditions was high on the agenda. Union meetings were frequent, and these were discussions not just concerning the pay dispute, but also about how to protect and improve the situation of classroom teachers in the school. The problems created by disruptive students, supervision of corridors, and security for staff threatened by student assaults were often raised, and questions were put to 'management', i.e. the headteacher and senior staff, about what they intended to do about these issues. On one occasion the school was thrown into turmoil when the members of one of the unions collectively refused to teach a boy who the head and school governors recommended should return to school following suspension for an assault on a member of staff. This threatened to develop into a 'Poundswick' like situation in which teachers refused to teach students following suspension and were suspended themselves by Manchester LEA in 1985–6.[4] However, a compromise was suggested by the head in which the boy was referred to a local Intermediate Treatment Centre and the union members, realizing their weak situation, subsequently backed down.

Collective refusal to teach like this was rare, though the fact that it occurred was an indication of the strength of feeling amongst some staff about the difficult circumstances in which they worked. Other collective strategies included the persuading of 'management' to organize and staff a 'withdrawal unit' (called 201 after the room it was housed in), a permanently staffed room where students who were badly behaved during lessons could be sent and supervised. Troublesome students could be removed and isolated, although on occasions the staff supervising the unit had problems with the concentration of such students in one place. I discovered also the existence of an informal agreement between some of the heads of department that certain students who appeared to be flouting the disciplinary system by refusing to do detentions, etc., would not be taught, but sent to 201, thus effectively suspended internally, until they conformed. Staff had also succeeded in persuading 'management' to mount what was called 'patrol' in which a senior or experienced teacher patrolled the building during lesson time directing students to lessons, dealing with students truanting from lessons, and generally being available to help deal with problems that arose. An 'emergency' system where classroom teachers could contact a senior teacher immediately to summon help should they need it was also negotiated. These strategies were, of course, all part of the school's disciplinary and control system which in many comprehensive schools, as Denscombe (1985) points out, has become central to, in fact synonymous with, the system of 'pastoral care'.

Conclusion

In this chapter I have argued that attitudes and behaviour of many of the students at Milltown High, deriving from class, ethnic, and youth sub-cultures, were hostile to schooling. As a result teachers often found it extremely difficult to establish classroom order and were faced with a 'survival threat'. Some solved this problem by horizontal or vertical mobility when the occasion arose, which meant at times the school was difficult to staff. But those who did stay in the school, were forced, as were the Chicago teachers Howard Becker described, to adjust to their situation and 'cope'. This generally involved modifying their teaching practices, learning new disciplinary strategies, and reducing their academic and behavioural expectations of students. For some it also meant re-defining their expectations of themselves as teachers and their conception of the sort of teacher they were. Many teachers developed what Stebbins (1977) calls a 'custodial orientation' to school life in which they placed 'emphasis on control at the expense of teaching'. As with the teachers Woods (1979) studied, 'survival' rather than education became their predominant concern.

This inevitably affected the educational experiences of students at Milltown High, and in some cases further alienated them from their schooling. *All* students were likely to experience an atmosphere of low rather than high expectations, and an emphasis on behaviour and conformity rather than academic achievement (cf. Bowles and Gintis 1976). If other schools serving ethnic minority communities are similar it may be that the disadvantages faced by minority students in the educational system stem, not from their treatment at the hands of 'racist' teachers or from within-school processes which discriminate against them, but from the simple fact that they are more likely to attend what Roberts *et al.* (1983) call 'low achieving schools'. The evidence of this study certainly supports this view. It is interesting to note that the O level/CSE Grade 1 pass rate at Milltown High was one of the lowest in the city at 0.52 passes per student in 1986.[5]

The irony of all this, as writers like Willis (1977), Weis (1985), and Riseborough (1985) point out, is that it is not just the teachers or the administrators of the educational system who produce this situation, but the students themselves, who through their 'resistance' succeed in helping to create the unequal educational outcomes which ensure many of them remain disadvantaged. In fact to some extent both students and teachers are trapped in a spiral of alienation and underachievement. The structural 'underclass' location of many of the students at the school produces a peer group culture characterized by low academic motivation, low self-expectations, and rejection of school values and norms. The resulting behaviour of these students creates 'survival' problems for the teachers who cope by adopting strategies which contribute to the underachievement of their students and the perpetuation of their 'underclass' status. As Riseborough (1985) lucidly comments, with reference to Althusser's educational ideological state apparatus illustrated as a 'pupil mincer/processor' (see Open University 1977), 'The paradox is the more efficiently they (the students) mince teachers, the more they ultimately ensure the efficacy of the pupil mincer.'

Chapter ten

Conclusion

This study has had two main aims. First, to describe the way teachers in one secondary school responded in terms of policy and practice to the fact that they were educating students from and for a multi-ethnic society. Second, to shed some empirical light on certain theoretical questions in the sociology of education about the role of schools in reproducing the social characteristics of modern society.

In this chapter I want to summarize my findings on these two themes, then discuss the policy implications of the study, both for schools and LEAs, and finally point to other possible areas of research that may lead to a greater understanding of the way in which the educational system caters for the needs of ethnic minority students and prepares all students for the task of creating a non-racist society.

Policy and practice in multicultural and anti-racist education at Milltown High School

Milltown LEA and Milltown High School had developed policies on multicultural education in the late 1970s and more recently on anti-racist education. The emergence of these issues on the LEA and school agenda was the result of a number of factors. On the one hand there was an increasing concern about the threat to order, both in school and out, from young, especially Afro/Caribbean, people. Multicultural and anti-racist education was, in one sense, an attempt to co-opt this group into the school system. It aimed to win greater commitment of ethnic minority youngsters to the school system and increase their self-esteem and motivation by reflecting their cultures and concerns in the school curriculum. This was part of a more general move by teachers to reduce the alienation and consequent disruption of (mainly) working-class students by introducing more 'relevant', 'interesting', and 'student-centred' curriculum and school practices. But, it would be wrong to see moves to multicultural and anti-racist education as merely the school's response to a threat to social order (Carby 1982), and as the introduction

171

of new, more subtle forms of social control. Milltown High School's commitment arose from a genuine concern amongst a number of more 'radical' teachers to enhance the life chances of ethnic minority students, and encourage all their students to be non-racist. They were concerned with social justice in education and wished to educate their students to be thinking, politically aware, and skilled adults capable of viewing the world critically, and they saw reform of the school's curriculum and practices as a way of achieving these ends.

The LEA and school policy statements were intended to facilitate and encourage the development of multicultural and anti-racist education, but they did not set out specifically how staff were to incorporate it into their practice. How then did teachers in the school respond? David Benyon, the headteacher appointed to Milltown High in 1984, was strongly committed to LEA and school policies. He saw multicultural and anti-racist education as part of a commitment to equal opportunities, education about a variety of different cultures, and the social and political education of students. It was central to his egalitarian and progressive educational ideology and to the way he wanted Milltown High School to change and develop.

Most classroom teachers were in favour of multicultural and anti-racist education. They thought that the school should encourage cultural tolerance amongst students and that they as teachers should adopt an individualistic, non-racist approach in their relationships with students. A minority of teachers, mainly concentrated in the English and Integrated Curriculum departments, felt that multicultural and anti-racist education also involved the broad social and political education of their students and the development of more 'progressive' curriculum and pedagogy. There was considerable difference of opinion amongst teachers about the issue of racism in education. Some teachers were hostile to the implication contained in policy statements that they might be racist in their attitudes or practice. They felt that they were being accused of something they regarded as unprofessional on the basis of very little evidence. Others felt that there might be, and certainly had been in the past, instances of racism in school curricula and in teacher attitudes, and they attempted to guard against these in their own practice. A small number of teachers thought that school practices and the working of the educational system as a whole could disadvantage ethnic minority students more indirectly, but found it difficult to establish meaningful implications for their individual practice as teachers.

In terms of practice in education for non-racism several departments had made efforts to include aspects of the history and cultures of minority groups in their curriculum content and to teach about the variety of human cultures. In the English department, for example, the teachers had included literature written by and about ethnic minority people, especially Afro/Caribbean people, and attempted to increase awareness of linguistic variety and stress the linguistic validity of different language forms. In the Humanities department the second year curriculum consisted of regional studies of the history, geography, and religions of the main areas from which their students' families had originated, and in subsequent years topics and concepts were generally illustrated with content drawn from a variety of societies in different parts of the world. In the Integrated Curriculum similar approaches were adopted.

Specific teaching about racism was also concentrated in these departments. The English teachers often chose class readers which directly raised the issue of racism and used them to teach about how racist attitudes are formed and can influence social relationships, and to encourage non-racist attitudes and behaviour. Here too the teachers attempted to include the issue of racism within a curriculum orientated to teaching about broader political and social issues. They were also committed to a pedagogy designed to encourage discussion and debate of a variety of ideas and viewpoints, although sometimes their own strongly held views resulted in them presenting predominantly critical views of contemporary social arrangements. Again the Integrated Curriculum teachers adopted a similar approach with younger students. In Humanities the teachers were less willing to raise the issue of racism directly, but in their fourth and fifth year courses they did teach a unit on 'Persecution and Prejudice' which dealt with racism in South Africa and Nazi Germany, and much of their curriculum was concerned with social and political issues. Outside of these departments there were one or two attempts to introduce anti-racist work into the curriculum. The Science department had developed a unit of work in their third year curriculum which stressed the non-elite nature of Science and the role of 'Third World' people in the significant scientific revolutions. The head of department was also searching for ways of introducing curriculum elements which stressed the social implications of Science. The Maths department had introduced some curriculum materials which raised issues concerning world inequality through the use of a computer data bank. Another significant development was the introduction of the Black Studies unit into the fourth year ACS, a course taught by a local group of Afro/Caribbean people.

Many of these developments in multicultural and anti-racist education were in fact similar to the model I proposed in my introductory chapter. In curriculum terms especially, the teachers at Milltown High had moved towards the model of education for non-racism that I outlined. It must be said, however, that the school's programme of social and political education was rather ad hoc with little co-ordination of objectives or curriculum content between different departments. This was perhaps a product of the dominance of subject sub-cultures in the school, the lack of any overall curriculum planning group, and the disruptive events in the school's recent history. Moreover, in pedagogical terms, although several teachers, especially in the English and Integrated Curriculum departments, were committed to the more discussion-based, collaborative, and egalitarian teaching styles that I advocated, they found it difficult to adopt such approaches, largely because of the problems of classroom control posed by the attitudes and behaviour of many students.

On the whole I concluded that ethnic minority students enjoyed equal opportunities with their white peers at Milltown High. Whilst racial attitudes are clearly a very difficult area to investigate, and it is possible that teachers concealed their 'real' views from me, in my formal and informal discussions with them and my observation around the school I found very few examples of racist attitudes amongst the teachers. In fact teachers were generally positive in their attitudes to student ethnicity. The students confirmed this view. Hardly any of those I interviewed thought there was racism amongst the school staff. Only one rather infamous ex-teacher was the butt of student complaints. Unlike the schools which Wright (1986) studied there was very little animosity between teachers and students along racial lines. Similarly relationships between students of different racial and ethnic groups were fairly harmonious. Thus the racial attitudes of teachers and students did not provide the basis for any inferior treatment of ethnic minority groups.

Moreover in my general classroom observations and in the case study I conducted of a third year class I did not find that ethnic minority students occupied lower status positions in classroom social structures, and I found little evidence of differential treatment of students on racial or ethnic lines. The school had abandoned the practice of dividing students into ability bands and introduced mixed-ability grouping to the end of the third year, followed by a mixed system of subject setting and mixed-ability grouping. This meant that racial discrimination was less likely to occur in the school's system of formal differentiation simply because there were fewer potentially discriminatory decisions to be made and students were not formally assessed before they had the opportunity to display their potential. Where students were divided into sets I found no evidence that allocation decisions were influenced by racist views.

There was a tendency for Afro/Caribbean boys to be less likely to be placed in the top sets than would have been anticipated given their numbers in the school. This may have been because Afro/Caribbean boys on average in this particular year had less ability. Another possible reason is that teachers used student behaviour as well as ability in making their assessments of a student's suitability for a top set place. Afro/Caribbean boys in the year group I studied were somewhat more likely than white students to behave in ways which brought them into conflict with teachers. They were thus more likely to be seen by the teachers as behavioural problems and thus less likely to secure a top set place. This might be regarded as unfair if we believe that a student's behaviour is an irrelevant consideration in judging their potential to utilize the opportunity of a top set place. My view is that this is not the case, that student motivation, as indicated by their behaviour, is an important factor in making judgements of this nature. However, it was possible that because this system was adopted Afro/Caribbean boys tended to be slightly disadvantaged by the formal system of differentiation at Milltown High, if we accept that the lower status groups received inferior treatment and allocation to such groups tends to reduce student motivation. I found that the reverse was true of Afro/Caribbean girls. They were slightly more likely to be allocated to high status groups and thus were perhaps advantaged by the process of formal differentiation.

There did not appear to be any other practices which disadvantaged ethnic minority students within the school. The assessment and evaluation procedures that I saw did not appear to be 'culturally biased' in the way I defined this term. There were clear policies on dealing with incidents of racial abuse and violence in the school, and few of the students I interviewed complained of racial harassment or intimidation. Many of the teachers were knowledgeable of and sensitive toward minority group cultures and teachers did not display the sort of cultural incompetence described by Driver (1979) in their interaction with minority group students. The school's disciplinary regulations seemed generally fair and relevant. They were related to universalistic behavioural expectations, but the cultural norms of minority group students were not unnecessarily regarded as deviant. For example, the use of 'patios' by Afro/Caribbean students was not frowned upon by teachers and rules about dress were flexible. In fact most teachers adopted a sensitive and open-minded approach to the expression of students' background cultures. The greater 'expressivity' of Afro/Caribbean youth culture did seem on a few occasions more likely to bring Afro/Caribbean students into conflict with teachers, but it is difficult to know how much such conflict derived specifically from ethnicity and how much from general youth culture. I did not come across any curriculum material which denigrated minority groups during my field work. Most teachers attempted to ensure that materials they used figured ethnic minority characters, although this was not always possible because such materials were not always available.

Thus the teachers had succeeded in eliminating or avoiding practices within the school that were racist or which indirectly disadvantaged students from particular racial or ethnic groups. So far as I could ascertain this was also the case in the appointment of staff. Whilst the staffing structure at Milltown High was still ethnically unbalanced[1] David Benyon took great care to ensure appointments and promotion procedures were fair and had appointed several ethnic minority teachers. He was, however, restricted in many appointments he made during the time I was in the school by an LEA policy, negotiated with the teacher unions, to appoint teachers from within the LEA. In a time of falling school rolls, financial constraint, and teacher surplus this was intended to utilize existing staff efficiently and avoid the need for redundancy, but as a result access to jobs tended to be restricted to existing, predominantly white, staff.

The question of providing additional resources for students from educationally disadvantaged racial or ethnic groups is a complex and sensitive issue as I explained in my introductory chapter. It involves deciding which groups are disadvantaged, in what way, and what form of positive provision is appropriate, questions which have rarely been adequately addressed in the area of race and ethnicity. Not surprisingly the staff at Milltown High had no clear policy on this issue. The school itself was favourably treated, in comparison to many other schools, by the LEA in terms of staff. This was mainly the result of a LEA decision to staff small secondary schools at the level they felt was required to maintain comprehensive curriculum provision, which was part of a wider policy of making a small additional provision to schools in the more socially and economically disadvantaged parts of the city.[2] This meant that the school was entitled to a minimum of forty teachers to cover all main subject areas and thus had a relatively low teacher: student ratio. The school was also allocated three extra teachers from funds under Section 11 of the 1966 Local Government Act to meet 'the needs of Commonwealth immigrants' and their descendants.

Within the school itself there was no system of assessing which students were educationally disadvantaged by virtue of their home background or of making compensatory provision specifically for such students. The school did make some positive provision, through its 'Learning Support Department', for those students with 'special educational needs'. This included students with specific physical handicaps (such as partial hearing), those whose academic progress was significantly behind the norm for their age, and those who were considered to be emotionally immature or 'disturbed'. Such students were identified by ordinary class teachers and tutors and referred to the two teachers in the Learning Support Department for additional help. These teachers aimed to bring the student's academic or emotional attainment up to an acceptable minimum level, although these levels were never clearly defined. The students who received this positive provision may have included some who were educationally disadvantaged by virtue of their home background, but it may also have included some genetically less talented from relatively privileged backgrounds. A certain level of underperformance, for whatever reason, rather than educational disadvantage (in the sense I have used the term) was the criterion used for allocating additional educational resources.

What of the school's 'Section 11 teachers'? I have explained that shortly before I began my field work the Home Office required LEAs to identify their Section 11 teachers, specify more clearly the work these teachers were doing, and tie it more closely to 'the needs of Commonwealth Immigrants'. Before this Milltown High, along with many others in the LEA, had used their Section 11 provision merely to add three teachers to the school staff. In the absence of a large number of students of Asian origin in need of first stage ESL tuition, the school had adopted a policy of utilizing this extra staffing for the benefit of *all* students in the school. The more favourable teacher:student ratio which resulted was seen as a way of indirectly providing for the needs of minority students, but it was also seen as an additional provision for all students in the school many of whom suffered educational disadvantages deriving from their class rather than racial or ethnic background.

As my field work ended the three Section 11 teachers at Milltown High had spent only a term in their new roles. Much of their time had been spent in discussion with other teachers and members of the local ethnic minority communities attempting to clarify their role and establishing the 'needs' of minority students. This was a difficult and sometimes confusing task. Many of the staff felt that ethnic minority students did not suffer educational disadvantages over and above their white peers and wanted the teachers to provide them with more general assistance in the classroom, especially when they were faced with 'difficult' teaching groups. Discussions with local minority people had been brief and often inconclusive. The Section 11 teachers themselves were committed, as were most teachers in the school, to working with students on a non-racial/ethnic basis and found it difficult to justify spending their time exclusively with ethnic minority students. They had gone some way in examining the disadvantages that might specifically be faced by Afro/Caribbean students as a result of background dialects, but this was still at an exploratory stage. Thus the Section 11 teachers found themselves in a difficult situation faced with different, sometimes conflicting expectations of their role.

A number of teachers in the English and Integrated Curriculum departments were aware of the potential language difficulties faced by some Afro/Caribbean students, but in the hurly-burly of classroom life

177

they felt it was difficult to identify which students, the exact nature of their problems, and the appropriate methods and resources required to rectify them. Moreover, they also felt that many of the white students suffered educational disadvantages and did not therefore feel that they could devote much extra time to dealing specifically with Afro/Caribbean students. A small amount of additional provision was directed towards the language needs of Afro/Caribbean students in the form of the Caribbean English Project, but this was very much a small-scale pilot project.

Thus Milltown High made only limited positive provision for students educationally disadvantaged by virtue of their racial or ethnic background. This is perhaps understandable given the difficult and sensitive nature of some of the issues involved in assessing disadvantage and in making such provision.

In my penultimate chapter I argued that it was important to consider the whole question of equal opportunities in a broader context than a single school. Milltown High was a small neighbourhood comprehensive school in the inner city. It was part of a wider local educational system in which economic, social, and cultural resources played a large part in determining the educational routes of students from different social backgrounds. Many of the students who attended Milltown High faced extreme social and educational problems as a result of the disadvantage and discrimination experienced by their parents. The sub-cultures which developed, partly in response to such disadvantages, and which were reflected and partly reproduced in the school, meant that a substantial proportion of the student intake at Milltown High was hostile to or ambivalent towards schooling. Faced with the problems such students presented in the classroom teachers were forced to adapt in order to 'survive' and this had implications for the educational experiences they made available to students. Thus I would maintain that minority students at Milltown High were disadvantaged not by racist teachers or by practices within the school which indirectly restricted their chances of success, but by the structure and organization of the wider educational system which permits those with greater economic and cultural resources to place their children on more favourable routes in the educational race. Even when equal opportunities are ensured within a single school, wider inequalities in the educational system will continue to place some students at a disadvantage.

Theoretical issues

The theoretical concerns of this study were with the broad question of the role of schools in the reproduction of some of the basic social characteristics of British society. I was interested in the extent to which within-school processes influence the chances of educational success of students from different ethnic or racial groups and thus the part they play in reproducing ethnic/racial inequality. I was also interested in examining an aspect of Marxist theory of education which suggests that the curriculum of working-class schools encourages amongst students attitudes and values which are supportive of capitalist organizations.

On the first question four main ideas have been advanced which suggest that within-school processes are likely to disadvantage especially Afro/Caribbean children and are an important factor in explaining their relative underachievement. First, there is the theory that teachers tend to have negative views and low expectations of Afro/Caribbean students, that such students therefore receive inferior treatment in schools, that their educational self-esteem and motivation are reduced, and that they consequently underachieve. Second, there is the associated theory that the curriculum of schools neglects or denigrates the culture of Afro/Caribbean students who, as a result, suffer lowered self-esteem and academic motivation, become hostile to their teachers, and underachieve. Third, is the idea suggested by Driver (1979) that minority students are at a disadvantage in schools because teachers lack the cultural competence to deal confidently and adequately with them. Finally, there is the view that the definitions of ability and worth that are routinely used by teachers are based on the cultural forms of dominant groups. According to this view working-class and ethnic minority students will find it difficult to perform successfully because evaluation criteria are culturally biased and they lack the appropriate 'cultural capital'.

What light does the data I have collected shed on these theories? My study gives little empirical support for the first two. As I have already explained I found very little evidence of negative teacher attitudes towards Afro/Caribbean students or of low academic expectations specifically of them. I also found no evidence of differential treatment of students on ethnic or racial lines either in classrooms or in wider school processes. In fact students of both main ethnic groups were, on the whole, treated equitably and fairly. Whilst I did not systematically examine student self-esteem, on the basis of the data I collected it seemed highly unlikely that the self-esteem or the academic motivation of Afro/Caribbean students specifically was lowered by the treatment they received from their teachers. Moreover, the curriculum of Milltown High School included substantial and positive reference to aspects of the history and culture of Afro/Caribbean people and therefore was unlikely to contribute to any lowering of self-esteem or alienation.

The sort of interaction patterns that Driver (1979) discovered were also not apparent at Milltown High. Teachers' relationships with their

Afro/Caribbean students were not marred by cultural confusion and uncertainty. Teachers did not misunderstand and misinterpret the behaviour of Afro/Caribbean students, nor did they feel threatened and react inconsistently to the expression of specifically Afro/Caribbean cultural forms.

I think there were two main reasons for this. First, as the majority of Afro/Caribbean students in the school had been born and brought up in Britain, distinctivley Caribbean aspects of their behaviour were less marked. The use of strong Caribbean creoles, for example, was much less common. In fact in this part of Milltown there had been considerable mixing of youth cultural forms. Aspects of Afro/Caribbean culture had merged with white working-class and popular media-based culture to form distinctively new youth cultures, often based on mixed-race groups (cf. Hewitt 1986). In this sense the behaviour of Afro/Caribbean young people was less culturally strange to their teachers. A second reason is that the teachers had discussed and developed policies on multicultural and anti-racist education which encouraged them to become more familiar with ethnic minority cultures. Many of the teachers had also spent a considerable proportion of their teaching careers in urban multi-ethnic schools. They had thus had far more opportunity than the teachers studied by Driver, for example, to become knowledgeable of and competent in dealing with Afro/Caribbean culture. Thus the confusion and uncertainty felt by many teachers in the early 1970s when dealing with Afro/Caribbean young people, who were sometimes fairly recent migrants, was not in evidence at Milltown High.

This conclusion gives some support to the application in the educational arena of views put forward by writers such as Glass (1960) and Patterson (1965). They argued that the cultural strangeness of recent immigrants, combined with the suspicion and cultural ignorance of the indigenous white population, explained many of the problems faced by New Commonwealth immigrants in the 1950s and early 1960s. They predicted that the immigrant population would, over time, adapt to British social norms and mores, and the host population would slowly come to understand and accept their cultural differences. They anticipated a process of mutual adjustment, a gradual integration of ethnic minority people into mainstream British society, and the eventual disappearance of hostility and discrimination.

On a societal level this model was clearly grossly optimistic. It underestimated the extent of discrimination and the desire of ethnic minorities to retain their distinctive cultures, and it failed to consider the significance of structural divisions in the society which immigrants entered. However, in an educational context these ideas have some explanatory potential. If the relationships that I observed between white teachers and Afro/Caribbean students can be validly compared with those described by Driver in the early 1970s, then there had been a process of mutual adjustment, an anglicization (for want of a better word) of Afro/Caribbean youth culture, and an increase in the cultural competence of white teachers. This appeared to reduce cultural confusion and uncertainty and helped to create more harmonious teacher/student relationships and equitable treatment.

It must be said, however, that Milltown High, because of its situation in a long-established multicultural area and its engagement with the issue of multicultural and anti-racist education, was probably a school in which this process was most likely to happen. For the same reasons it was a school where one might least have expected to find evidence to support the four theories discussed above. Clearly we need more research on multi-ethnic schools in order to establish if, when, and under what circumstances the processes outlined in these theories occur.

It might be suggested that my study lends some support to the fourth theory. Many students in the school clearly did not live up to their teachers' conception of the 'ideal student' (Becker 1952b), something which is largely based on the culturally dominant definitions of mainstream, white, middle-class society, and found it difficult to display the appropriate 'cultural capital' to be seen as successful by their teachers. Moreover, although this generally applied equally to both main ethnic groups and Afro/Caribbean students were not, on the whole, evaluated less highly than their white peers, the behaviour of older Afro/Caribbean boys tended to be regarded less favourably. In a sense their youth cultural norms conformed less closely to the teachers' conceptions of the 'ideal' and as a result they seemed somewhat more likely to be allocated to lower status groups in the school's system of differentiation. Thus it could be argued that teachers' cultural conceptions of the 'ideal student' placed many students, and especially Afro/Caribbean boys, at Milltown High at a disadvantage. In a sense this is true, but the problem with this argument, and indeed with the theory on which it is based, is that it implies that teachers' conceptions of student worth are somehow at fault and that if only they changed their culturally biased definitions then the problem of underachievement would vanish. This is to fall rather foolishly into the trap of cultural relativism in which no knowledge or quality is or should be any more valued than any other. As several writers have pointed out (see, for example, Lawton 1977) this argument is naive and dangerous. The evaluative criteria used by teachers will (and should) inevitably be based on the qualities and knowledge which are valued in the wider society, and, whilst every effort should be made to ensure that such qualities and knowledge are necessary, relevant, and not unduly narrow, in an industrial society certain values and therefore certain conceptions of worth will predominate. It is worth noting that teachers at Milltown High had to some extent broadened their conceptions of worth to include certain cultural characteristics of minority groups.

My study does, however, support an alternative explanation of the tendency for Afro/Caribbean youngsters to underachieve. At Milltown High School they did not in fact underachieve in comparison with their white peers. But they attended a school where achievement levels and norms were generally low for all students. Moreover, many students were hostile or at best ambivalent to their schooling and as a result teachers were frequently forced to orientate their efforts to control and survival rather than to the academic progress of the students. The fact that Afro/Caribbean students are more likely to attend inner-city schools like Milltown High is likely to amplify the existing cultural and economic disadvantages of home background that many such students face. My study suggests that Afro/Caribbean students are more likely to be disadvantaged by differences between schools than differential treatment within them. It is important to note that many white working-class students are likely to be equally disadvantaged by attending such schools. Thus perhaps class disadvantages in the educational system are, or have become, more significant than racial or ethnic ones.

The final theoretical question that I raised was whether the curriculum of Milltown High encouraged amongst its students values and attitudes supportive of contemporary social organization. I did not find this to be the case in the areas of the formal curriculum I observed. In fact here students appeared more likely to be exposed to views which were critical of existing social arrangements. Moreover, a number of the teachers in the school were committed to the development of a hidden curriculum with less emphasis on conformity, obedience, and autocratic teacher/student relationships, and greater emphasis on active student participation, more egalitarian social relationships, and critical thinking. However, in practice such a hidden curriculum was difficult to realize and, faced with student disruption and potential classroom disorder, teachers were forced to adopt more traditional autocratic roles and orientate their teaching towards control. Further, in the school as a whole, despite often friendly and informal relationships between teachers and students, the two groups were still divided by marked differences of status and power. Thus I think the school's hidden curriculum still tended to encourage conformist attitudes. Whether it actually had this effect on students is, of course, another matter.

Policy implications

I have already outlined my views on multicultural and anti-racist education at some length. I now want to briefly consider some of the more specific policy implications of this piece of research.

It seems to me that one major problem of policies in multicultural and anti-racist education is that they are too often couched in rather vague, rhetorical terms and do not specify clearly what is to be done in practice. Even at Milltown High, a school committed to multicultural and anti-racist education, there was confusion and uncertainty about what the LEA and school policies actually required teachers to do. Policy implementation will surely be enhanced if, after full discussion between teachers, LEA representatives, and school governors, policy statements specify more clearly the implications of multicultural and anti-racist education for curriculum, pedagogy, and school organization. It is also important that policies and their implementation are regularly reviewed and systematically evaluated so that the effectiveness of any changes can be assessed and knowledge of good practice accumulated. For a number of reasons this had not been done at Milltown High and as a result teachers were unaware of how school policy was being implemented by others and what it had achieved.

Teachers had no means of assessing whether they had succeeded in providing equal opportunities for their students. It has been suggested that one way of doing this would be to apply what is termed ethnic monitoring, a practice which is increasingly being used by employers committed to equal opportunities. Marland (1986), for example, has put forward the idea that ethnic monitoring could be used to examine the academic progress of students from different ethnic backgrounds, their attendance rates, the proportions of such students in different ability groups, options or extra-curricular activities, and the proportions receiving different disciplinary treatments. He argues that such a scheme could be used to identify potential inequities and to establish more clearly the specific needs of students from particular ethnic groups.

However, whilst I feel that sometimes ethnic monitoring can provide useful information it has a number of problems. First, there are practical problems in establishing meaningful ethnic or racial categories and an acceptable and workable system of recording students' ethnic/racial backgrounds. Then there are complex questions about the ownership of and access to the data which is produced and how it will be used (see Runnymeade Trust and the Radical Statistics Group 1980). If schools are to introduce ethnic monitoring then they will clearly have to engage in lengthy consultation with parents and representatives of various ethnic/racial groups in order to resolve such issues. But, in my view, the most problematic question is what ethnic monitoring tells us, if anything, about school processes. If we find, for example, that Afro/Caribbean students have lower achievement levels than white children in a school in some particular field, does this tell us that there are processes operating within the school which disadvantage those students? I think the answer is that it does not. Students may have entered the school at different levels and differential achievement may be the result of a wide range of factors, many of which are external to the school. If we found, as a result of ethnic monitoring, that Afro/ Caribbean students were disproportionately represented in low streams, bands, or sets would this be an indication of school processes disadvantaging such students? In one sense it might, but we would have to show that allocation to low status groups disadvantaged such students because they subsequently received inferior treatment and/or their motivation was reduced. Ethnic monitoring would not tell us this was the case. If it was the case then it would be an injustice whether there was an ethnic imbalance or not as any students allocated to such groups would be disadvantaged. If we found that it was not the case then an ethnic imbalace might be perfectly fair. It could quite simply be the result of meritocratic allocation procedures and the differential achievement of particular racial or ethnic groups in a school rather than the result of any unfair discrimination. Ethnic monitoring in fact tells us little about allocation procedures.

Thus ethnic monitoring gives us little information about whether there are processes within the school which disadvantage ethnic minority students. Unfortunately ethnic monitoring tends to encourage the idea that all is well in a school if students are found in ethnically representative proportions in a particular group or achievement level. This may not necessarily be the case. There may equally well be injustices in a school with ethnically representative groups and achievement levels as in a school with ethnically unrepresentative groups and achievement levels.

Perhaps a more effective strategy to assess whether equal opportunities have been achieved within a school would be the regular and systematic examination of actual school practices, following thorough discussions in which potentially disadvantageous practices were clearly defined and their indicators identified (my introductory chapter could serve as a guide here). Teachers could examine their own and their colleagues' attitudes to ethnic and racial differences, their classroom practice, and the processes of assessment and decision-making in which they are routinely involved. Here perhaps the development of collective or co-operative forms of mutual observation and appraisal are most appropriate. Small groups of teachers could work together, perhaps with the assistance of an independent researcher/consultant, to examine their own practice (see Foster and Troyna 1988 for a possible model). Training in racism awareness may be of assistance here as long as such training is orientated to identifying the ways in which specific school practices *may* disadvantage students from particular ethnic or racial groups, rather than to engendering a sort of collective messianic guilt which is of little practical help.

I think a case can also be made for the postponement of formal differentiation in order to enhance equality of opportunity. In a school like the banded Beachside Comprehensive described by Ball (1981), where students were allocated to ability bands before they entered the school, and where those groups were then treated differently, there was obviously inequality of opportunity which, moreover, was unequal on class lines. If equal opportunities is our aim then clearly this sort of system is undesirable. The postponement of formal differentiation, and having a flexible system when it is introduced, must reduce inequalities deriving from the premature (and therefore potentially inaccurate) assessment and categorization of students.

It is also important that LEAs, as part of their implementation of policy, consider the question of equal opportunities in their service as a whole rather than just within individual schools. While it is difficult to say conclusively that this is the case, my study suggests that the 'ethos' of schools like Milltown High may not be as advantageous to their students as might (and should) be the case. Thus students attending such schools, who are often disproportionately from ethnic minority groups, are likely to be disadvantaged.

This leads me to question the supposed merits of small, inner city neighbourhood comprehensive schools. It is argued that such schools provide a personalized, less anonymous environment within easy travelling distance for their students, that they can build up strong links with their feeder primary schools so that curriculum continuity is ensured, that they can act as a valuable community resource and become a focus of community life, that parents can enjoy easy access to the school, and that teachers can get to know parents more closely and work with them more constructively. Some of these benefits are important and may be realized in such schools, but several are more myth than reality. As studies of other schools have shown it is quite possible to break down larger schools into more personalized units (see, for example, Watts 1977), and at secondary school level the majority of students are able and willing to travel a few miles to school. Strong links with primary schools are important, but in practice it is extremely difficult to co-ordinate the curricula of several different institutions. Often a secondary school can become a community focus, but there are generally many other institutions that can, and are perhaps better able to fulfil this neighbourhood role. This was certainly the case in the area that Milltown High served. I would also maintain that a secondary school does not need to be on the door step to develop constructive links with parents.

Thus the actual benefits of a neighbourhood comprehensive school in the inner city may be less than we think. The big disadvantage of such schools is, of course, the very fact that they are not 'comprehensive' at all and in present circumstances they are likely to become less so. Recent government legislation has given parents increased power to select a secondary school for their children and as we have seen in Milltown the more aware parents have chosen to use these powers, and the spaces created in the system by falling rolls, to ensure their child a place in a 'better' school. As a result an educational 'apartheid' appears to be developing in which those with money or the cultural resources to manipulate the system ensure that their children go to certain schools, whilst the children of those without these resources (who are likely to be disproportionately working class and from ethnic minorities) fill up the remaining ones. Schools like Milltown High are left to cope with falling numbers and an increasing concentration of students with severe educational problems who are ambivalent or hostile towards their schooling. The result is declining staff morale and a schooling in which teachers are forced to direct their energies to control rather than learning.

The implication of all this is that LEA discussions about the types of secondary school they provide and the location of these schools should consider critically the priority which they give to small neighbourhood schools. It may well be that larger schools located in areas between the inner cities and the more suburban areas and serving both may be more effective in ensuring equal provision for all groups within the LEA. Such schools might be more likely to avoid the sorts of developments that I have described, would create greater opportunities for the social mixing to which the comprehensive school principle aspires, and would provide a broader base to the idea of 'the community school'.

I have argued that the principle of equal opportunities involves positive provision in favour of those students who are educationally disadvantaged as a result of the inadequate material and cultural resources of their home background. However, as I have explained, enormous problems are raised here because of the difficulty of defining and assessing educational disadvantage, especially where this relates to ethnicity and race, and devising acceptable and effective compensatory provision. Much more research needs to be done on this issue to identify more clearly the educational disadvantages and needs of particular individuals and groups.

In the meantime there is a strong case to be made for the extension of schemes to provide additional resources to schools in economic and socially disadvantaged areas which can be identified using methods similar to those developed for the Educational Priority Area schemes, whilst recognizing that indicators of educational disadvantage will inevitably be imprecise and such schemes may fail to provide additional resources for all those who are disadvantaged (see J.Barnes 1975). There is also a case for continued additional provision for those students whose first language is not English and for adopting a fairly broad definition of this term. The paramount aim here should be to maximize student competence in mainstream, 'standard' English, whilst respecting and where possible building on the 'language a student brings to school'. The work that some of the English teachers at Milltown High were doing in co-operation with the local Caribbean English Project seemed an interesting model. They aimed to explore different types of oral and written language use, encouraging students to be confident in using a variety of language forms, whilst at the same time improving their competence in 'standard' English. But again there is a need for greater clarification of students' 'second stage' language needs and how they can be most effectively met.

Another possibility is to allocate additional resources to schools where significant numbers of students are failing to reach specified minimum levels of attainment and to students within schools who fail to reach such levels. This, of course, is the policy already adopted in many schools (Milltown High included) which operate 'remedial' or 'learning support' schemes. The aim is to bring all students to a basic minimum level of attainment. This idea is based not on the view that everyone should receive equal total educational provision (as in the principle of equal opportunities), but on the view that it is unjust to allow some, no matter what their innate ability, to fail to achieve the basic minimum educational standards needed in our society. The idea is that additional educational resources should be provided in schools not just to those who are disadvantaged by virtue of home background, but to those students who fail, for whatever reason, to achieve certain minimum standards. Of course such underachievement may be the result of disadvantage, but it may also be the result of poor innate ability. This idea seems eminently reasonable and just, and it may well be that, in the absence of accurate ways of assessing educational disadvantage, such schemes may be a more practical means of directing positive provision. As educational disadvantage and poor attainment are strongly linked they may also be one way of directing additional resources in favour of disadvantaged students.

I do not have a great deal extra to say here on the implications of my study for education for non-racism. There is a need, especially at school level, to establish more clearly the aims, objectives, content, and pedagogy of multicultural and anti-racist education and its place within a broader programme of social and political education and the curriculum as a whole. As this type of work will come into several different subject areas it is also important that schools adopt a co-ordinated approach which avoids unnecessary duplication and inconsistency. This is sometimes difficult as secondary schools tend to be dominated by subject departments often working in isolation. There is perhaps a need in schools for a curriculum co-ordinating group led by a senior teacher to take an overview. Such a group could also play an important part in assessing the effectiveness of multicultural and anti-racist education and in accumulating ideas and experiences of good practice. It could provide a focus for teachers wishing to research and develop their own practice on the lines suggested by Lawrence Stenhouse (1975). It remains to be seen to what extent teachers can work along these lines within the framework of the new national curriculum.

Such a curriculum group and teachers involved in social and political education need also to develop a code of practice on the content and pedagogy of social and political education, not least to ensure that they are able to respond confidently to accusations that they are seeking political 'indoctrination' rather than education. Whilst it will be difficult to establish an agreement of what is meant by 'balance' and 'bias' in this area, teachers must consider and make decisions on these issues (see Jones 1986 and Stradling *et al.* 1984 for sensible suggestions). As I explained in my introductory chapter the teachers' role should be to ensure that students have the opportunity to examine a variety of perspectives on social and political issues. This need not necessarily require them to always present a balance of views on particular issues in the classroom. Their aim should be what Stradling *et al.* (1984) termed 'balanced learning' rather than balanced presentation. This means they must begin with an assessment of the existing biases of their students and attempt to increase their awareness of alternative arguments and opinions. However, this does not mean that they are justified in presenting only their own viewpoints. To do this would be to abuse their privileged position, to curtail rather than foster the free exchange of ideas which is so important in a democratic society, and to reduce rather than enhance students' opportunities to make their own judgements and decisions. A code of practice in this area should also attempt to specify the limits of views and political opinion which can be accepted and presented as legitimate in the classroom and also the sorts of teaching strategies that might be used in social and political education.

Further research

This case study is part of a programme of research which has attempted to address the question of how the educational system has responded to the presence of ethnic minorities in British society. I have described the way in which one secondary school has responded in terms of policy and practice. There are many other schools and teachers who are attempting to come to grips with the implications of ethnic diversity. One important avenue for further research is to document their efforts and to try to assess their effectiveness so that we can build up a knowledge of 'good' practice in this area. It is important also to examine the dilemmas facing teachers who attempt to implement multicultural and anti-racist policy, the constraints that impinge upon them, and how these are tackled, so that we can learn from their experiences. There is clearly a need for more collaborative work between researchers and teachers who are attempting to review and change their practice. Few teachers have the time or expertise to systematically evaluate any changes that they make in curriculum, pedagogy, or wider school practice. Here research workers can surely fulfil a positive role in helping to clarify the aims of proposed changes, observe their implementation, and assess their effects. In short, in the development of what Stenhouse (1975) calls 'research based teaching'.

We also need more research on the progress and experiences of minority students in the education system. We still have remarkably little information on the way ethnic minority students are affected by within-school processes. How are such students perceived by their teachers? Are the views of some teachers as negative and racist as many commentators would have us believe? They were not at Milltown High School, but perhaps this school is unusual. We simply do not know. Moreover, if we do find that some teachers subscribe to such views, we need to know how or if they transfer into action in the classroom or in other areas of school practice. Are minority students treated differently from their white peers and, if so, in what ways? Do minority students perceive differential treatment or negative teacher attitudes? Do they affect students' identity and motivation? There seems to be considerable scope for distortion here. In other words it is not simply a matter of students taking on unquestioningly the views of their teachers. The process of identity formation is far more complex than this. We need to examine the influence of the student's parents, siblings, and peers, and the effect of social class and gender as well as ethnicity. What we have at the moment is much commonsense and sometimes simplistic theorizing and very little empirical work. If we are to move towards a more accurate picture of the real social processes that occur in schools then we need far more empirical research in schools and classrooms.

Moreover, we do not just need research into the way ethnic minority students fare within schools, we need to investigate wider educational systems and the progress of minority students through them. Is it the case, for example, that minority students are disproportionately allocated to less 'effective' schools where their opportunities of achieving educational success is limited?[3] If so, why does this occur and what actions can be taken to prevent this happening?

The lack of research and consequent lack of knowledge about what happens to ethnic minority students in the education system means unfortunately that debate in this area remains at the level of assertion and counter-assertion. The Rampton Report (Committee of Inquiry 1981) was rightly criticized for basing many of its conclusions on very scanty evidence, and yet the Swann Report (Committee of Inquiry 1985) published four years later included little more of substance.

We also need to know more about how ethnic minority teachers fare in the system. We need to assess the effectiveness of programmes that aim to encourage minority people to become teachers. And we need information about their experiences and careers, and how they cope within a system which is at present in contraction.

We also still know remarkably little about the views and perceptions of different ethnic minority people of their childrens' education, or indeed of their own education, since many minority adults have now been educated in Britain. Are, for example, the high educational aspirations characteristic of many immigrants also a feature of their childrens' attitudes towards the education of their children, or does this second generation take on attitudes more similar to the indigenous working class? We also know very little about the perspectives of ethnic minority students (especially those of Asian origin) on their schooling. How do they see their teachers, their peers of the same and different ethnic groups, the school curriculum, multicultural and anti-racist education; what sub-cultural forms do they create in school life?

We need information on these questions for two main reasons. First, in order to inform policy and practice in this area. It is extremely difficult to formulate sensible, specific, and clearly directed policy if we have little idea of what is actually happening in schools or wider educational systems. It is a nonsense, for example, to have policies specifically orientated to eliminating racist attitudes amongst teachers if in fact the vast majority of teachers do not subscribe to such attitudes. To suggest that all teachers must attend compulsory racism awareness training so that they can be led to change their attitudes seems pointless and only serves to alienate and provoke hostility. The second reason for conducting this type of research is a more social scientific one. Sociologists have still made only limited progress in understanding the ways in which modern societies reproduce themselves and maintain their established structures. Race and ethnicity have clearly become very significant features of these societies. If we are to understand how they continue to remain so then we need to understand the role of the educational system in this process of reproduction. Research in this area can help to shed light on these more theoretical issues.

Notes

Chapter 1 Introduction: research questions and theoretical issues

1 The term 'race', of course, generally refers to a group of people who have the same or similar physical characteristics, whereas 'ethnic group' refers to those sharing a similar culture and cultural identity. In Britain the main (but of course not all) ethnic minority groups, who are migrants from what is often termed the 'New Commonwealth' and their descendants, are frequently distinguished by their racial characteristics and thus the terms race and ethnicity are often used interchangeably.

2 This dilemma parallels that which emerged during the EPA programme (Halsey 1972) over the idea of community education. On the one hand some advocated a form of education in which the curriculum and values of the school reflected the life and world of the local community. Others argued this was merely a form of 'ghetto' education which further deprived the working-class child of the opportunity of social mobility.

3 The concept of stereotyping has often been used to describe such perceptions. As Milner (1983) points out this concept is often used differently. Sometimes it refers to any generalization about a social group, in which case it may be an accurate description of the group. More often, however, it is used to refer to incorrect and exaggerated generalizations (in the latter instances, perhaps having some basis in fact). It is, of course, very difficult to determine the extent to which a generalization is exaggerated, but what we can say is that the universal application of such generalizations to members of a particular racial or ethnic group is invalid. And clearly negative differential treatment based on such generalizations would be racist and therefore unjust.

4 Clearly as students are also in the position to make decisions about their actions *vis-à-vis* other students and teachers then they too could be racist. For example, if other students are ignored, abused, or harassed because they are members of a particular racial or ethnic group which is thought to be inferior.

5 Examples from the area of employment are the practices of some companies in recruiting from the relations of current, predominantly white employees or from schools in designated, usually white areas (see Lee and Wrench 1983). In the area of housing, an example is the lengthy residence

191

requirement for council housing (Rex and Morre 1967) and more currently the use of the notion of 'respectability', indicated by conventional family patterns and practices, which is sometimes used to allocate council housing (Henderson and Karn 1987).

6 Inaccurate assessment and evaluation could, of course, disadvantage any student. It seems likely, however, given the greater cultural gap that often exists between ethnic minority students and their teachers, that misjudgements are more likely with these students.

7 Racial inequality in education has increasingly been explained by reference to the concept of 'institutionalized racism' (see, for example, Institute of Race Relations 1980; Mullard 1984; Saunders 1982; Shallice 1984; Brandt 1986). However, as several authors have pointed out (Williams 1985; Troyna and Williams 1986; Rex 1986a) this concept is rather ambiguous and, even more than the concept of racism itself, has had a number of different meanings. Troyna and Williams (1986) explain that it was originally used by American radicals Stokely Carmichael and Charles Hamilton in 1967 to draw attention to the perpetuation of racial inequalities through a complex web of 'interconnecting relationships of several institutional areas'. They argue that the concept has become oversimplified and its use frequently confuses the mechanisms by which racial inequality is reproduced. It fails to distinguish between those practices which are clearly racist in intent and effect, those which are not intentionally racist but which serve to produce racial inequality, and those aspects of inequality which derive from the class situation of ethnic minority groups.

8 This is not, of course, to imply that ethnic minority languages are linguistically inferior.

9 Such ideas might also be introduced in the primary school.

10 This concern led to the establishment of a Committee of Inquiry in 1979.

11 Sociologists adopting a functionalist perspective (for example Durkheim 1961) also see socialization as one of the main functions of schools, but they tend to view the process more benignly as the transmission of common norms and values and the consequent maintenance of a social system based on value consensus.

12 However, such a deterministic view has been challenged. More recent Marxist approaches suggest that the process of social reproduction is less neat. The education system, and other parts of the institutional superstructure of capitalist society, is seen as a relatively autonomous 'site of struggle' with the potential for the production of forms of consciousness which could challenge capitalism.

Chapter 2 The social context and social structure of Milltown High School

1 The LEA moved to a comprehensive secondary system at the same time.

2 The school did not as a matter of policy collect information on student ethnic backgrounds, but in complying with new Home Office requirements for Section 11 teachers the deputy head in charge of pastoral care, with the help of heads of year/school, allocated students to one of three ethnic groups. In order to confirm this data I checked with form tutors and heads of

192

year/school. It was apparent from their comments and my own observations that several students were of mixed Afro/Caribbean/white origin. I decided that for the purpose of my analysis I would classify them as Afro/Caribbean. This, I realize, may not always be appropriate, but from talking to many of the students it seemed that most (but not all) regarded themselves as Afro/Caribbean, and I would maintain that for the most part they would be treated as such by white society and by any teachers who responded to students on this basis.

3 Milltown LEA had over recent years managed to maintain its relatively high level of expenditure on schools and local services, but in late 1987 it was 'rate capped' and began to suffer severe financial restrictions.

4 The head came under very little pressure from parents in this respect.

5 The governing body at Milltown High School included the head, governors nominated by the LEA (mainly local concillors and education officers), representatives of linked primary schools, elected parent governors, elected staff (including ancillary staff) governors and co-opted governors (mainly people who had an interest in or connection with the school). During my field work the governors decided to seek to increase the number of co-opted governors from ethnic minorities, and succeeded in appointing a local community worker, thus increasing the Afro/Caribbean representation to three (one Afro/Caribbean parent and two co-opted governors).

Chapter 3 The development of LEA and school policies on multicultural and anti-racist education

1 This subsequently resulted in a new multi-faith RE syllabus which was circulated to all schools and parents early in 1986.

2 However, the activities of this group were severely restricted by the teachers' industrial action which began shortly after it was established.

3 Prior to secondary school re-organization in 1982 the City Council Education Committee acted as secondary school governors in Milltown.

Chapter 4 The headteacher, the school, and multicultural and anti-racist education

1 The scheme began in September 1986 and involved all fourth year students for part of their week and a small group of fifth years.

2 In this sense the school changed him rather than him changing the school.

3 David Benyon explained that my interviews often gave him the opportunity to clarify his ideas.

4 I did not observe appointments procedures and this account is therefore based on what David Benyon and other staff involved told me happened.

Chapter 5 Teacher response to school and LEA policies on multicultural and anti-racist education

1 Music has not been mentioned as I was unable to interview the Music teacher as she was on extended sick leave during this stage of the research.

Chapter 6 Multicultural and anti-racist education in practice – the English department

1   This was not a written policy, and, whilst it was consensus amongst the core English teachers, some of the other teachers who came into the department appeared uncertain what their approach should be.
2   My classroom observation included time in two academic years – 1985–6 and 1986–7
3   Class reading was also an effective control strategy serving to concentrate student attention on the text.

Chapter 7 Multicultural and anti-racist education in practice – the Humanities department

1   In September 1986 this system was replaced by the new GCSE Integrated Humanities course for the fourth year students.
2   See Hammersley (1974) for a detailed description of this style.
3   Stephen Barker himself called these actions 'pre-emptive strikes'.
4   In a discussion following my lesson observation, Stephen Barker explained that he had always been very much aware of my presence as an observer in the classroom and had therefore been more concerned than he normally would be with social order in the classroom. This reactivity is partly a product of the overwhelming importance of maintaining classroom control in teachers' occupational culture (see Denscombe 1985), which of course has implications for teachers' feelings of competence and self-worth (see chapter 9). It is important to emphasize that this form of reactivity influences many descriptions of classroom life.

Chapter 8 Racism, social differentiation, and equal opportunities at Milltown High School

1   Hewitt (1986) makes a similar point in his description of youth culture in a multi-racial area.
2   Mixed-ability grouping is still relatively rare. An HMI survey in 1979 of 365 secondary schools found that only thirty-four schools had mixed-ability grouping up to the third year and some of these made special arrangements to withdraw students with 'serious learning difficulties' (DES 1979).
3   During the meeting it was decided that this group would be referred to not as the 'top' group, but as the 'Lang/Lit' group.
4   My analysis was based on the group who entered their fourth year in September 1985
5   This draws attention to the fact that interviews are social situations and thus what is revealed in such situations will depend on the subject's perceptions of that situation. It also raises the issue of whether it is possible to deduce a subject's 'real' perceptions from what they say in interviews (see Hammersley and Atkinson 1983), or indeed what is meant by 'real'.

Chapter 9 The inner city school and the problem of teacher 'survival'

1   Approximately two-thirds of the staff left and had to be replaced.
2   The teachers at schools like Milltown High tended to be more militant in their interpretation of the industrial action than did their colleagues in more

suburban schools. Strikes and disruption were therefore more common in such schools.

3 Those staff who were not members of large subject departments, but were perhaps the only teacher teaching their particular subject, and there were increasing numbers of them as the school contracted, suffered in this respect.

4 In the autumn term of 1985 teachers at Poundswick High School, Manchester, refused to teach a group of students who were returned to the school following suspension. The teachers involved were then suspended by the LEA and the rest of the school staff went on strike in response. The dispute closed the school for much of the 1985-6 academic year (see the columns of the *Times Educational Supplement* for that year).

5 Only two students, an Asian boy and an Afro/Caribbean boy, achieved five or more O/CSE grade 1 passes in 1986.

Chapter 10 Conclusion

1 Of the twenty-five cleaning staff sixteen were of Afro/Caribbean origin, whereas of the forty-four teaching staff in September 1986 three were of Afro/Caribbean origin and one was of Pakistani origin.

2 The LEA provided an additional member of staff and extra nursery class places in some primary schools where the proportion of children receiving free school meals was above a certain level.

3 Mortimore *et al.* (1988) found there was a tendency for this to happen in the Inner London primary schools they studied.

Bibliography

Althusser, L. (1971) 'Ideology and ideological state apparatuses', in B.R. Cosin (ed.) (1972) *Education: Structure and Society*, Harmondsworth: Penguin.

Anthony, M. (1973) *Green Days by the River*, London: Heinemann.

Ball, S.J. (1981) *Beachside Comprehensive: A Case Study of Secondary Schooling*, Cambridge: Cambridge University Press.

Ball, S.J. (1983) 'A subject of privilege: English and the school curriculum 1906–35', in M. Hammersley and A. Hargreaves (eds) *Curriculum Practice: Some Sociological Case Studies*, Lewes: Falmer Press.

Ball, S.J. and Lacey, C. (1980) 'Subject disciplines as the opportunity for group action: a measured critique of sub-cultures', in P. Woods (ed.) *Teacher Strategies*, London: Croom Helm.

Barnes, D. (1976) *From Communication to Curriculum*, Harmondsworth: Penguin.

Barnes, J. (ed.) (1975) *Educational Priority*, Vol.3, London: HMSO.

Becker, H.S. (1952a) 'The career of the Chicago public schoolteacher', American Journal of Sociology, 57: 470–7.

Becker, H.S. (1952b) 'Social-class variations in the teacher-pupil relationships', in B.R. Cosin *et al.* (eds) (1977) *School and Society*, London: Routledge & Kegan Paul.

Becker, H.S. (1964) 'Personal change in adult life', *Sociometry* 27, 1: 40–53.

Bernstein, B. (1970) 'Education cannot compensate for society', *New Society*, 26 February: 344–7

Bernstein, B. (1971a) *Class, Codes and Control*, Vol.1, London: Routledge & Kegan Paul.

Bernstein, B. (1971b) 'On the classification and framing of educational knowledge', in M.F.D. Young (ed.) *Knowledge and Control: New Directions for the Sociology of Education*, London: Collier-Macmillan.

Beynon, J. (1985) Initial Encounters in the Secondary School, Lewes: Falmer Press.

Boudon, R. (1974) *Education, Opportunity, and Social Inequality*, New York: Wiley.

Bourdieu, P. (1973) 'Cultural reproduction and social reproduction', in R.K. Brown (ed.) *Knowledge, Education and Cultural Change*, London: Tavistock.

Bourdieu, P. (1974) 'The school as a conservative force: scholastic and cultural inequalities', in J.Eggleston (ed.) Contemporary Research in the Sociology of Education, London: Methuen.

Bowles, S. and Gintis, H. (1976) *Schooling in Capitalist America*, London: Routledge & Kegan Paul.

Brandt, G.L. (1986) *The Realisation of Anti-Racist Teaching*, Lewes: Falmer Press.

Brophy, J.E. and Good, T.L. (1970) 'Teacher-child dyadic interactions: a new method of classroom observation', *Journal of School Psychology*, 8, 2: 131–8.

Brophy, J.E. and Good, T.L. (1974) *Teacher-Student Relationships: Causes and Consequences*, New York: Holt, Rinehart & Winston.

Brophy, J.E. and Good, T.L. (1984) *Looking in Classrooms*, New York: Harper & Row.

Brown, C. (1984) *Black and White in Britain: Third PSI Survey*, London: Heinemann.

Bullivant, B. (1981) *The Pluralist Dilemma in Education*, Sydney: George Allen & Unwin.

Burgess, R.G. (1983) *Experiencing Comprehensive Education*, London: Methuen.

Burgess, R.G. (1984) *In the Field: An Introduction to Field Research*, London: George Allen & Unwin.

Carby, H.V. (1982) 'Schooling in Babylon', in Centre for Contemporary Cultural Studies *The Empire Strikes Back: Race & Racism in '70s Britain*, London: Hutchinson.

Carrington, B. (1983) 'Sport as a side-track: an analysis of West Indian involvement in extra curricular sport', in L. Barton and S. Walker (eds) *Race, Class and Education*, London: Croom Helm.

Carrington, B. and Wood, E. (1983) 'Body talk', *Multiracial Education* 11, 2: 29–38.

Cashmore, E. and Troyna, B. (eds) (1982) *Black Youth in Crisis*, London: George Allen & Unwin.

Coard, B. (1971) *How the West Indian Child is Made E.S.N. in the British School System*, London: New Beacon Books.

Cole, M. (1984) 'Teaching till 2000: teachers' consciousness in times of crisis', in L. Barton and S. Walker (eds) *Social Crisis and Educational Research*, London: Croom Helm.

Coleman, J.S. (1973) 'Equality of opportunity and equality of results', *Harvard Educational Review* 43, 1: 134.

Coleman, J.S. (1974) 'Inequality, sociology and moral philosophy', *American Journal of Sociology* 80, 3: 739–64.

Coleman, J.S. *et al.* (1969) *Equality of Educational Opportunity*, Cambridge, Mass.: Harvard University Press.

Commission for Racial Equality (1988) *Learning in Terror: A Survey of Racial Harassment in Schools and Colleges*, London: CRE.

Committee of Inquiry into the Education of Children from Ethnic Minority Groups (Rampton Committee) (1981) *West Indian Children in Our Schools* (Interim Report) (Cmnd 8723) London: HMSO.

Committee of Inquiry into the Education of Children from Ethnic Minority

Groups (Swann Committee) (1985) *Education For All* (Cmnd 9453) London: HMSO.

Cox, C.B. and Boyson, R. (eds) (1975) *Black Paper*, London: Dent.

Crisp, T. (1975) *Different Worlds*, Walton-on-Thames: Thomas Nelson.

Cross, M. and Smith, D.I. (1987) (eds) *Black Youth Futures*, Leicester: National Youth Bureau.

Davie, R., Butler, M., and Goldstein, H. (1972) *From Birth to Seven*, London: Longman.

Davis, K. and Moore, W.E. (1945) 'Some principles of stratification', *American Sociological Review* 10: 242–9.

Denscombe, M. (1980) 'Keeping 'em quiet: the significance of noise for the practical activity of teaching', in P. Woods (ed.) *Teacher Strategies*, London: Croom Helm.

Denscombe, M. (1985) *Classroom Control: A Sociological Perspective*, London: George Allen & Unwin.

Department of Education and Science (1975) *A Language for Life: Report of the Committee of Inquiry Chaired by Sir Allan Bullock (The Bullock Report)*, London: HMSO.

Department of Education and Science (1979) *Aspects of Secondary Education in England: A Survey by HM Inspectors of Schools*, London: HMSO.

Department of Education and Science (1986) *A Survey of the Lower Attaining Pupils Programme: The First Two Years, A Report by HMI*, London: HMSO.

Dhondy, F. (1974) 'The black explosion in schools', *Race Today*, February.

Douglas, J.W.B. (1964) *The Home and the School*, London: Panther.

Driver, G. (1979) 'Classroom stress and school achievement: West Indian adolescents and their teachers', in V.S. Khan (ed.) *Minority Families in Britain: Support and Stress*, London: Macmillan.

Driver, G. (1980) *Beyond Underachievement*, London: Commission for Racial Equality.

Durkheim, E. (1961) *Moral Education*, Glencoe: The Free Press.

Edwards, V.K. (1979) *The West Indian Language Issue in British Schools*, London: Routledge & Kegan Paul.

Edwards, V.K. (1981) *Language in Multicultural Classrooms*, London: Batsford.

Figueroa, M. E. (1984) 'Race relations and cultural differences: some ideas on a racial frame of reference', in G.K.Verma and C.Bagley (eds) *Race Relations and Cultural Differences: Educational and Intercultural Perspectives*, London: Croom Helm.

Fisher, S. and Hicks, D. (1985) *World Studies 8–13: A Teacher's Handbook*, Edinburgh: Oliver and Boyd.

Foster, P. (1985) *The Transmission of Values in Social Education Curricula*, Unpublished M.Sc. Dissertation, Open University.

Foster, P. (1989) *Policy and Practice in Multicultural and Anti-Racist Education: A Case Study of a Multi-Ethnic Comprehensive School*, Ph.D Thesis, Open University.

Foster, P. and Troyna, B. (1988) 'Conceptual, ethical and practical dilemmas of collaborative research: reflections on a case study', *Educational Review*, 40, 3: 289–300.

Furlong, V. (1976) 'Interaction sets in the classroom', in M. Hammersley and P. Woods (eds) *The Process of Schooling*, London: Routledge & Kegan Paul.

Furlong, V. (1977) 'Annany goes to school: a case study of pupil's knowledge of their teachers', in P. Woods and M. Hammersley (eds) *School Experience*, London: Croom Helm.

Furlong, V. (1984) 'Black resistance in the liberal comprehensive', in S. Delamont (ed.) *Readings on Interaction in the Classroom*, London: Methuen.

Furlong, V.J. (1985) *The Deviant Pupil: Sociological Perspectives*, Milton Keynes: Open University Press.

Glass, R. (1960) *Newcomers*, London: George Allen & Unwin.

Gleeson, D. and Whitty, G. (1976) *Developments in Social Studies Teaching*, London: Open Books.

Grace, G. (1978) *Teachers, Ideology and Control*, London: Routledge & Kegan Paul.

Green, S.J.D. (1988) 'Is equality of opportunity a false ideal for society?', *British Journal of Sociology* 39, 1: 1–27.

Guy, R. (1982) *The Friends*, London: Macmillan.

Hall, S. (1980) 'Teaching race', *Multiracial Education* 9, 1: 3–13.

Hall, S. and Jefferson, T. (1976) (eds) *Resistance Through Rituals*, London: Hutchinson.

Halsey, A.H. (1972) 'Political ends and educational means', in A.H.Halsey (ed.) *Education Priority*, Vol.1, London: HMSO.

Halsey, A.H. (1978) *Change in British Society*, Oxford: Oxford University Press.

Halsey, A.H., Heath, A.F., and Ridge, J.M. (1980) *Origins and Destinations*, Oxford: Clarendon Press.

Hammersley, M. (1974) 'The organisation of pupil participation', *Sociological Review* 22, 3: 355–68.

Hammersley, M. (1977) 'School learning: the cultural resources required by pupils to answer a teacher's question', in P. Woods and M. Hammersley (eds) *School Experience*, London: Croom Helm.

Hammersley, M. (1980) 'A peculiar world? Teaching and learning in an inner city school', Unpublished Ph.d Thesis, University of Manchester.

Hammersley, M. (1984) 'Staffroom news', in A. Hargreaves and P. Woods (eds) *Classrooms and Staffrooms*, Milton Keynes: Open University Press.

Hammersley, M. (1985) 'From ethnography to theory: a programme and paradigm in the sociology of education', *Sociology* 19, 2: 244–59.

Hammersley, M. and Atkinson, P. (1983) *Ethnography: Principles in Practice*, London: Tavistock Publications.

Hammersley, M. and Scarth, J. (1986) 'The impact of examinations on secondary school teaching', Unpublished Research Report, School of Education, The Open University.

Hargreaves, A. (1979) 'Strategies, decisions and control: interaction in a middle school classroom', in J. Eggleston (ed.) *Teacher Decision Making in the Classroom*, London: Routledge & Kegan Paul.

Hargreaves, A. (1986) *Two Cultures of Schooling: The Case of Middle Schools*, Lewes: Falmer Press.

Hargreaves, D.H. (1967) *Social Relations in a Secondary School*, London: Routledge & Kegan Paul.

Hargreaves, D.H. (1975) *Interpersonal Relations and Education*, London: Routledge & Kegan Paul.

Hargreaves, D.H. (1982) *The Challenge for the Comprehensive School: Culture, Curriculum and Community*, London: Routledge & Kegan Paul.

Hargreaves, D.H. (1983) 'The teaching of art and the art of teaching: towards an alternative view of aesthetic learning', in M. Hammersley and A. Hargreaves (eds) *Curriculum Practice: Some Sociological Case Studies*, Lewes: Falmer Press.

Hargreaves, D.H., Hester, S.K., and Mellor, F.J. (1975) *Deviance in Classrooms*, London: Routledge & Kegan Paul.

Heath, A. (1987) 'Class in the classroom', *New Society*, 17 July.

Henderson, J. and Karn, V. (1987) *Race, Class and State Housing*, Aldershot: Gower.

Hewitt, R. (1986) *White Talk: Black Talk*, Cambridge: Cambridge University Press.

Hicks, D.W. (1980) *Images of the World: An Introduction to Bias in Teaching Materials*, Institute of Education, University of London.

Hicks, D.W. (1981) *Minorities – A Teacher's Resource Book for the Multi-ethnic Curriculum*, London: Heinemann.

Hunter, C. (1979) 'The politics of participation, with specific reference to teacher-pupil relationships', in P. Woods (ed.) *Teacher Strategies*, London: Croom Helm.

Institute of Race Relations (1980) 'Anti-racist not multiracial education: IRR statement to the Rampton Committee on Education', *Race and Class* 22, 1: 81–3.

Jackson, B. and Marsden, D. (1962) *Education and the Working Class*, Harmondsworth: Penguin.

Jeffcoate, R. (1984a) 'Ideologies and multicultural education' in M. Craft (ed.) *Education and Cultural Pluralism*, Lewes: Falmer Press.

Jeffcoate, R. (1984b) *Ethnic Minorities and Education*, London: Harper & Row.

Joint Matriculation Board (1983) *General Certificate of Education, Integrated Humanities Syllabus*, Manchester: JMB.

Jones B. (1986) 'Bias in the classroom: some suggested guidelines', *Teaching Politics* 15, 3: 387–403.

Kemp, J. (1981) *Gowie Corby Plays Chicken*, Harmondsworth: Penguin.

Klien, G. (1985) *Reading into Racism*, London: Routledge & Kegan Paul.

Lacey, C. (1966) 'Some sociological concomitants of academic streaming in a grammar school', British Journal of Sociology 17, 3: 245-62.

Lacey, C. (1970) *Hightown Grammar: The School as a Social System*, Manchester: Manchester University Press.

Lacey, C. (1974) 'Destreaming in a "pressured" academic environment', in J. Eggleston (ed.) *Contemporary Research in the Sociology of Education*, London: Methuen

Lawton, D. (1977) *Education and Social Justice*, London: Sage Publications.

Lee, G. and Wrench, J. (1983) *Skill Seekers: Black Youth, Apprenticeships, and Disadvantage*, Leicester: National Youth Bureau.

Lee, H. (1960) *To Kill a Mockin' Bird*, London: Heinemann.

Lester, J. (1977) *The Basketball Game*, Harmondsworth: Penguin.

Lloyd-Thomas, D.A.(1977) 'Competitive equality of opportunity', *Mind* 86, 343: 388–404.

McCall, G.J., Simmons, J.L. (1969) *Issues in Participant Observation*, Reading: Addison-Wesley.

McDonald, I. (1969) *The Hummingbird Tree*, London: Heinemann.

McRobbie, A. (1978) 'Working class girls and the culture of femininity', in Women's Studies Group, Centre for Contemporary Cultural Studies, *Women Take Issue: Aspects of Women's Subordination*, London: Hutchinson.

Man: A Course of Study (1968) *Talks to Teachers*, Cambridge, Mass.: Education Development Centre.

Marland, M. (1986) 'From headcount to action: the analysis of the progress of ethnic minority pupils in schools', *Multicultural Teaching* 5, 1: 4–11.

Marshall, J.V. (1963) *Walkabout*, Harmondsworth: Penguin.

Merton, R.K. (1949) *Social Theory and Social Structure*, New York: Free Press.

Miller, W. B. (1958) 'Lower class culture as a generating milieu of gang delinquency', in M.E. Wolfgang, L. Savitz, and N. Johnson (eds) (1962) *The Sociology of Crime and Delinquency*, New York: Wiley.

Milner, D. (1983) *Children and Race: Ten Years On*, London: Ward Lock Educational.

Mortimore, P., Sammons, P., Stoll, L., Lewis, D., and Ecob, R. (1988) *School Matters: The Junior Years*, Wells: Open Books.

Mullard, C. (1984) *Anti-Racist Education: The Three O's*, Cardiff: National Association for Multi-Racial Education.

Nash, R. (1973) *Classrooms Observed: The Teacher's Perception and the Pupil's Performance*, London: Routledge & Kegan Paul.

Nash, R. (1976) 'Pupils' expectations of their teachers', in M. Stubbs and S. Delamont (eds) *Exploration in Classroom Observation*, London: Wiley.

Needle, J. (1979) *My Mate Shofiq*, London: Fontana.

Open University (1977) E202 Schooling and Society, Block 3 *Knowledge, Ideology and the Curriculum*, Unit 16, Culture, Class, and the Curriculum, Milton Keynes: Open University Press.

Parekh, B. (1986) 'The concept of multicultural education', in S. Modgil, G.K. Verma, K. Mallick, and C. Modgil (eds) *Multicultural Education: The Interminable Debate*, Lewes: Falmer Press.

Patterson, S. (1965) *Dark Strangers*, Harmondsworth: Penguin.

Plowden Report (1967) *Children and their Primary Schools, Vols 1 and 2*, Central Advisory Council for Education (England), London: HMSO.

Pollard, A. (1980) 'Teacher interests and changing situations of survival threat in primary school classrooms', in P. Woods (ed.) *Teacher Strategies*, London: Croom Helm.

Pryce, K. (1979) *Endless Pressure*, Harmondsworth: Penguin.

Ranger, C. (1988) *Ethnic Minority School Teachers*, London: Commission for Racial Equality.

Reed, A. (1984) *The World Now*, London: Bell & Hyman.

Rex, J. (1986a) *Race and Ethnicity*, Milton Keynes: Open University Press.

Rex, J. (1986b) 'Equality of opportunity and the ethnic minority child in British schools', in S. Modgil, G.K. Verma, K. Mallick, and C. Modgil (eds) *Multicultural Education: the Interminable Debate*, Lewes: Falmer Press.

Rex, J. and Moore, R. (1967) *Race, Community and Conflict*, London: Routledge & Kegan Paul.

Rex, J. and Tomlinson, S. (1979) *Colonial Immigrants in a British City*, London: Routledge & Kegan Paul.

Rex, J., Troyna, B., and Naguib, M, (1983) 'The development of multicultural education policy in four local education authority areas', Report submitted to the Swann Committee by SSRC Research Unit on Ethnic Relations.

Richmond, J. (1979) 'Dialect in the classroom', reprinted in A.James and R.Jeffcoate (eds) (1982) *The School in the Multicultural Society*, London: Harper & Row.

Richter, H.P. (1978) *Friedrich*, London: Heinemann.

Riseborough, G. (1985) 'Pupils, teachers' careers and schooling: an empirical study', in S.J.Ball and I.F.Goodson (eds) *Teachers' Lives and Careers*, Lewes: Falmer Press.

Rist, R.C. (1973) *The Urban School: A Factory for Failure*, Cambridge, Mass.: MIT Press.

Roberts, K., Noble, M., and Duggau, J. (1983) Young, black and out of work, in B. Troyna and D.I. Smith (eds) *Racism and the Labour Market*, Leicester: National Youth Bureau.

Rosenthal, R. and Jacobson, L. (1968) *Pygmalion in the Classroom*, New York: Holt, Rinehart & Winston.

Runnymede Trust and the Radical Statistics Race Group (1980) *Britain's Black Population*, London: Heinemann.

Rutter, M., Maughan, B., Mortimore, P., and Ouston, J. (1979) *Fifteen Thousand Hours: Secondary Schools and their Effects on Children*, London: Open Books.

Saunders, M. (1982) 'Education for a new community', *New Community* 10, 1: 64-71.

Scarth, J. (1983) 'Teachers' school-based experiences of examining', in M. Hammersley and A. Hargreaves (eds) *Curriculum Practice: Some Sociological Case Studies*, Lewes, Falmer Press.

Schaar, J.H. (1971) 'Equality of opportunity and beyond', in A. De Crespigny and A. Wertheiner (eds) *Contemporary Political Theory*, London: Nelson.

Schools Council (1970) *The Humanities Project: An Introduction*, London: Heinemann.

Shallice, J. (1984) 'Racism and education', in All London Teachers Against Racism and Fascism *Challenging Racism*, London: ALTARF.

Sharp, R. and Green, A. (1975) *Education and Social Control: A Study in Progressive Primary Education*, London: Routledge & Kegan Paul.

Silver, H. (ed.) (1973) *Equal Opportunity in Education: A Reader in Social Class and Educational Opportunity*, London: Methuen.

Smith, D. (1977) *Racial Disadvantage in Britain: The PEP Report*, Harmondsworth: Penguin.

Smith, R. (1983) *Rainbows of the Gutter*, London: Bodley Head.

Smucker, B. (1978) *Underground to Canada*, Harmondsworth: Penguin.

Stebbins, R. (1975) *Teachers and Meaning*, New York: Brill.

Stebbins, R. (1977) 'The meaning of academic performance: how teachers define a classroom situation', in P. Woods and M. Hammersley (eds) *School Experience*, London: Croom Helm.

Stebbins, R. (1980) 'The use of humour in teaching', in P. Woods (ed.) *Teacher Strategies*, London: Croom Helm.

Stenhouse, L. (1975) *An Introduction to Curriculum Research and Development*, London: Heinemann.

St. John-Brooks, C. (1983) 'English: a curriculum for personal development', in M. Hammersley and A. Hargreaves (eds) *Curriculum Practice: Some Sociological Case Studies*, Lewes: Falmer Press.

Stone, M. (1981) *The Education of the Black Child: the Myth of Multiracial Education*, London: Fontana.

Stradling, R., Noctor, M., and Baines, B. (1984) *Teaching Controversial Issues*, London: Edward Arnold.

Sugarman, B. (1970) 'Social class, values, and behaviour in schools', in M. Craft (ed.) *Family, Class and Education*, London: Longman.

Tawney, R.H. (1931) *Equality*, London: Unwin Books.

Tomlinson, S. (1983) *Ethnic Minorities in British Schools*, London: Heinemann.

Tomlinson, S. (1986) 'Ethnicity and educational attainment', in S. Modgil, G.K. Verma, K. Mallick, and C. Modgil (eds) *Multicultural Education: The Interminable Debate*, Lewes: Falmer Press.

Troyna, B. (1984) '"Policy Entrepreneurs" and the development of multi-ethnic education policies: a reconstruction', *Educational Management and Administration* 12, 3: 203–12.

Troyna, B. (1985) 'The great divide: policies and practices in multicultural education', *British Journal of Sociology of Education* 6, 2: 209–24.

Troyna, B. and Ball, W. (1983) 'Multicultural education policies: are they worth the paper they're written on?' *Times Educational Supplement*, 9 December: 20.

Troyna, B. and Ball, W. (1985) *Views from the Chalk Face: School Responses to an LEA's Policy on Multicultural Education*, Policy Papers in Ethnic Relations No. 1., Centre for Research in Ethnic Relations, University of Warwick.

Troyna, B. and Williams J. (1986) *Racism, Education and the State*, London: Croom Helm.

Trudgill, P. (1975) *Accent, Dialect and the School*, London: Edward Arnold.

Turner, A. (1985) *North-South Lifestyles – Case Studies from the South*, London: Longman.

Turner, J. (1983) 'Integrated Humanities and the public examination system', Unpublished M.Ed. Thesis, University of Leicester.

Waller, W. (1932) *The Sociology of Teaching*, New York: Wiley.

Ward, R. (1979) 'Where race didn't divide: some reflections on slum clearance in Moss Side', in R. Miles and A. Phizacklea (eds) *Racism and Political Action in Britain*, London: Routledge & Kegan Paul.

Watts, J. (1977) (ed.) *The Countesthorpe Experience*, London: George Allen & Unwin.

Wedge, P. and Essen, J. (1982) *Children in Adversity*, London: Pan.

Wedge, P. and Prosser, H. (1973) *Born to Fail?*, London: Arrow Books.

Weis, L. (1985) *Between Two Worlds: Black Students in an Urban Community College*, London: Routledge & Kegan Paul.

Werthman, C. (1963) 'Delinquents in schools: a test for the legitimacy of authority', *Berkeley Journal of Sociology* 8, 1: 36–60.

Whitty, G. (1985) *Sociology and School Knowledge: Curriculum Theory, Research and Politics*, London: Methuen.

Williams, J. (1985) 'Redefining institutional racism', *Ethnic and Racial Studies* 8, 3: 323–48

Willis, P. (1977) *Learning to Labour*, Aldershot: Gower.

Woods, P. (1979) *The Divided School*, London: Routledge & Kegan Paul.

Woods, P. (1981) 'Strategies, commitment and identity: making and breaking the teacher role', in L .Barton and S. Walker (eds) *Schools, Teachers and Teaching*, Lewes: Falmer Press.

Woods, P. (1986) *Inside Schools: Ethnography in Educational Research*, London: Routledge & Kegan Paul.

Wright, C. (1986) 'School Processes: An Ethnographic Study', in J. Eggleston, D. Dunn, and M. Anjali *Education for Some: The Educational and Vocational Experiences of 15-18 year old Members of Minority Ethnic Groups*, Stoke-on-Trent: Trentham Books.

Young, K. and Connelly, N. (1981) *Policy and Practice in the Multi-Racial City*, London: Policy Studies Institute.

Young, M. (1958) *The Rise of the Meritocracy*, Harmondsworth: Penguin.

Young, M.F.D. (1971) *Knowledge and Control: New Directions for the Sociology of Education*, London: Collier-Macmillan.

Index